# Fiha-Ma-Fiha

**(*Table Talk of Maulana Rumi*)**

*Translated by*
**Dr. Bankey Behari**

*Edited by*
**Chhaganlal Lala**

**B.R. PUBLISHING CORPORATION**
[A Division of BRPC (India) Ltd.]
Delhi-110052

*celebrating silver jubilee*

*Distributed by:*
**D.K. Publishers Distributors (P) Ltd.**
1, Ansari Road, Darya Ganj
New Delhi-110002
Phones: 3261465, 3278368
Fax: 091-011-3264368


ISBN 81-7646-029-X



*Published by:*
**B.R. Publishing Corporation**
[A Division of BRPC (India) Ltd.]
A-6, Nimri Commercial Centre
Near Bharat Nagar, Ashok Vihar
Delhi-110052
Phone: 3259196, 3259648
E-Mail: brpcltd@del2.vsnl.net.in

*Laser Typeset at:*
Divya Computers
Meerut

**PRINTED IN INDIA**

**Dedicated to**

***Sri Mata Krsnaji,***
***The renowned saint of***
***Vrindaban***

# Introduction

Saints are verily the salt of the earth. The vicars of God dwellers of the spiritual world, come as messengers to our world to invite seekers and adepts to the land of eternal beatitude and immortality. In this alien land, they adopt the mortal coil and spread a lasting perfume which invigorates and enlivens many hearts seeking the lotus feet of the Lord. Although they leave the body after a brief sojourn here, their words defy the corrosion of time and shine in the citadel of eternity for ever and ever. Their names are written on the Divine Tablet, which can be read by those who are gifted with the intuitive perception as the result of austerities, penances, night vigils, fasts, obeisances, prayers and worship. Their message can be expressed in one word, LOVE. This love entails total withdrawal of vision from everything non-God.' "The Prophet Muhammad felt grieved when angel Jabriel left him in the middle and the Lord ordered him to proceed further to heaven. The Lord told him that it did not behove him to share his love with any one besides. Very great is the explosive force in this one word but the technique behind it is such that it defies the wit of the rhetoricians, because the intuitive experience that follows on its pursuit is beyond the grasp of intellect. The personal spontaneous revelation, the ecstatic fervour and emotion, the agony of the soul, the bleeding of the pining heart, and the warmth of the sighs are all the inevitable legacy of the malady of Love. The attributes of love are patent that it creates, nurtures and kills him who wooes it, to whatsoever clime or period he may belong. He must pass through the same route taken by Mansur and Sarmad and Attār. Yes the cross shall have to be kissed and the scaffold to be climbed to be called the immortal martyr of Love.

Saints are great lovers. Maulānā Jelāluddin Rumi (1207-1273) was a such one. A scholar, mystic, saint, theologian, and litterateur of eminence—these are a few of his well known epithets by which he has come down to us. Although at first, he was a great revolutionist against poetry, which he decried in strong words yet, he offered the world the greatest poetical work, a vade-mecum of Sufis, the Masnavi, in six stupendous volumes, styled and honoured as a veritable the Quran in Pehalvi. This earned for him the coveted title Sultane Ulluma. His greatest collection of odes is styled Diwane Shamsh Tabraiz. When Sadi was asked to choose the best poem in Persian literature, he chose one from this work of Rumi. As Masnavi 'is the exposition of experimental mysticism, not doctrinal mysticism (Whinfield)' and is like 'a mystic river calm and deep, meandering through many a rich and varied landscape to immeasurable ocean (Nicholson)' so 'the Diwān is a foaming torrent that leaps and plunges in ethereal solitude of the hill. There is no gainsaying the fact that these two works are supreme contribution to the world culture.

Jelāl-Uddin was the greatest exponent of Islām, great thinker, past master and marvellous expounder of Islāmic Mysticism. In piety, austerities and penances, he has carved out a permanent place in the niche of Time. Where can you find a person rolling on the thoroughfare in mystic ecstasy, oblivious of his dignified office of being the teacher of the Sultān of the time, founding the Maulvi sect and practically proclaiming its tenets by dancing with uplifted hands to the tune of the sound proceeding from the shop of Salah—Uddin Zarkob whilst he saw the immortal scene of which he sang at the time?

*Ekey ganj padid āamad azin dukāney zarkobi*
*Zehey surat zahey māni zahe khütey zahey khubi.*

(A hidden treasure revealed itself to my eyes in the shop of the goldsmith. Its form, its import, its grace and beauty was tantalising and bewitching.)

This self-loss and ecstasy that kicked all formal decorum of society made him a total surrender at the immortal door of love, which he wooed whilst observing the tenets of Islām, the five articles of faith and the five practices. He always leaned in his heart to the spiritual side of worship, which was revealed by his night-long vigils, by his eyes constantly flowing tears and his yellow face. Every pore of his body spoke, 'Here is the man, who practices what he professes.' The principles he followed and the path he showed, he speaks with fervour that penetrates into the heart and sends it soaring in high spiritual skies. His instructions uttered in ecstasy defy all comment. Let him speak for himself:

*Ishqast dar āsman paridan*
*Sad parda ba har nafs daridan*
*Awwal nafs as nafs Gusashtan*
*Aakhir qadam az qadam buridan*
*Nadida giraftar Yin Jahānrā*
*Mar didayey, khosh ra nadidan*

(Love urges thee to fly heavenwards, and to tear at every moment a hundred veils. The first step in it is to transcend oneself and merge into the Over-self. The last step is to travel without the feet to consider this world as evanescent and to rise above one's self). About the nature of his Namāz in which often he passed the whole night he says:

*Chu namāzay shām har kas baniahad*
*chirāgh wā khwaney*
*Manam wa khyaley bari gham wa*
*nauha wa ihughāney*
*Chey wazu ze ashkam sazam bud*
*ātish ey namazan*
*Dar masjid am basozad chu dar rasad*
*azaney*
*Ajbam namazey mastan tu bage*
*durast hast aan*
*Ki namanad wu zumaney na*
*shanasad wu makaney.*

(When the evening is arrived, tables are laid, candles are lit and the hour of prayers is reached, I offer my prayers with lamentation, sighs and agony to my Beloved and offer abulation with tears, and the mosque (within me) is set on fire (with Love). Of us, the mad ones, this is the way we offer prayers without regard to time and occasion). About his eyes remaining whole night filled with tears and therefore leaving no place for sleep, he says:

*Didey khün gasht khün nami khuspad*
*Win dilam az janun namin khuspad*

(The eyes flow tears of blood in agony of separation and bid good-bye to sleep for ever and ever.)

And about experience that follows, he says:

*Shabey yār hami gardad khashkhash majhur imshab*
*Mar handey dahan az khud ta tamey danan bini.*

(The beloved visits thee in midnight, intoxicate thyself not with opium tonight, taste no food so that the nectar of His lips may fall to thy lot).

His warning should ever be kept in sight:

*Ishqast wa ishqast ki baqist ta abud*
*Dil juz barin maneh ki bajuz mussaar nest*
*Ta key kinar giri mashüg murda ra*
*Jan ra bakinar gir ki wü ra kinar nest.*

(Love and lover alone survive till eternity, all besides is a copy or a shadow. Set thy heart on nothing else. How long wilt thou be embracing the dead beloved—the mortal of clay. Embrace the limitless soul vast in its sphere.)

This is the immortal sublime theme—Divine Love, the Quest of the Self, the annihilation of the self (nafs), the vagaries of the mystic path, turning your back to the world to face God, dislike of wealth and the association of the rich are some of the many subjects on which he speaks with candour. The vibrations caused on hearing the recital of his personal experience strike the chords in the heart of the genuine seeker of the Lord and draw unmitigated applause for the Maulānā.

Of his experience, he speaks in simple brief words:

"I was raw. I ripened. I was turned to ashes." To the intellectuals he said,

"I seek One. I know One. I see One. I call One."

He had realised God, Truth, and he said that all that was due to the Lord's grace that flowed at the intercession of his spiritual Teacher Shamsh Tabraiz, of whom he says,

"I am not a Maulvi, till I am not a slave to Shamsh." and again,

*Pirey man wa muridey man dardey man*
*wa dawāyey man*
*Rast baguftam yin sakhun shamshey*
*man wa khudāyey man.*

(He is my disciple. He is my Murshad (teacher) He is the agony of separation for the Lord in me. He is the nectarean balsam of Divine meeting with God. I tell you the truth which I reveal to you that He is the sun in my dark heart. Aye, he is my God.)

What cannot be achieved through this surrender to Murshid in the spiritual realm?

Shamsh was the king of the saints and saints were the cynosure of the eyes of Maulānā. For, does he not say?

"Fools laud and magnify the mosque,
While they strive to oppress holy men of heart,
But the former is mere form, the latter spirit and Truth,
The only true mosque is in the heart of the saints.
It is the place of worship of all, for God dwells there."

(A. Iqbal).

Glimpses of his free thought appear now and then in his poetry:

"I am neither Christian nor Moslem nor Jew nor Gabrel I am neither Indian nor from China nor Bulgarian. Duality I have cast aside. I seek the One." But this must not be denied that he was a Moslem to the core, as he says and argues with fervour in Fihā Mā Fihā. About his religion, he says, "I have my goal as Allāh. I recognise one leader Prophet Muhammad. I seek guidance from one book, the

Quran." Fihā Mā Fihā at places speaks of his belief in incarnation. He says, "Man has several stages of evolution from the mineral he evolves into the vegetable, from there to the animal kingdom and thence to man, from man he will go to the angelic state and proceed on till God is reached."

**Rumi's life may be divided into three periods**

(1) The first period is from 1207-1244 A. D. in which the intellect dominated and in which he had instructions from his father Burhun Uddin, a great scholar and mystic, who was steeped in the philosophy of Imām Ghazāli. For twenty four years, he had schooling at his hands and due to him, he also imbibed hostility against Greek philosophy which was attacked by Ghazāli to whom Qurhan Uddin owed fanatic allegiance. It had a permanent impression on Rumi.

During this period, when the Mangol invasions were the order of the day, he had to witness many harrowing scenes, incendiarism, slaughter, indiscriminate burning of properties, humiliation suffered by men and indignity by women. At the age of five, he left Baghdād with his father in 1213. In the itinerary, he met Farid Uddin Attār who embraced and blessed him and presented him with a copy of his Isrār Nāmā. Thence his father went to Mecca, thence to Laranda and Zurjan in Syria in 1225. At the age of eighteen, he was married to Gauhar Khatün and three sons were born to him, of whom Baha-Uddin-wald was the most influential son. After his father's death, at the instance of his father's disciple whom he revered as a teacher and who took him through many austerities and mystic practices, he went and studied in Halab Madrasa and then in Damascus his ability earned him the enviable place of his father and he was recognised as the foremost teacher.

From there he proceeded to Qunia. Here he married Khatun Qunivi and here his father died in 1231. After his deaths he had as many as 10,000 disciples and was known as Sultane Ulama. He revitalised decadent Moslem society, put interpretation of the Qurān and the Traditions on a scholastic basis, and like Ghazāli, he was a pioneer in the work.

(2) 1245-1261. In this period Love dominated in Rumi's life. He took to experimental mysticism, at the hands of Shamsh Tabraiz. Shamsh initiated him into the greatest mystical experience. He withdrew him into solitude, made him good-bye to all scholastic activities, and led him to found the Maulvi sect in which dancing and music were the special featurers which threw the adherents into ecstasy. The contact with Shamsh was of two and half years but it metamorphosed Rumi's life and the erstwhile intellectual became intuitive mystic. On the disappearance of Shamsh, Rumi found in Zarkob a confident whom he loved much. He too passed away.

(3) 1261-1273. In this period, Poetry and Mysticism ruled Rumi. For seven years he was given to producing the aforesaid immortal works of poetry. Here for a confident he found Husain Uddin Chalpi who survived him. He was so pleased with him that he nominated him as his spiritual successor.

The only prose work that is ascribed to Rumi and which contains his brilliant exposition of the tenets of Qurān and the Traditions, is Fihā-Mā-Fihā, the Persian work which contains besides the above matters, the instructions he gave to people coming to him for that purpose, as also the answers to various queries and the secrets of mystic way. They are answers mostly given to the Prime Minister Amir Parwana. It contains his elucidation of Mansur's statement 'I am Truth.' The commentary is very illuminating. He discusses the ephemeral nature of the world and its activities. He discusses the superiority of Islām over Christianity, and of the superiority of Muhammad over Christ. He discusses unlike Christianity and Zorastrianism, Monasticism is unknown in Islām. His emphasis on dance and music in SAMĀ is very helpful in waking up dormant spiritual secrets in man. His discussions extend to many important spiritual matters like the various aspects of Namāz. On prayers, he lays great emphasis. The reader will enjoy this work as it was discovered only in the beginning of this century by Prof. R. Nicholson in Turkey. On it he read before the R. A. S. a paper, a copy of which he sent to me when he looked into the first portion of this translation over thirtyfive years back. It could not be completed as I left the legal profession and took up the hermit's robe in 1940 and at the instance of Mātā Krishnāji of Vrindāban India and my friend Wilfred Lavigne of Canada, at this advanced age again I took it up and have completed it by Lord Rādhā Krishna's grace.

The book reveals many of the ultra human traits of Maulānā. His humility, his charity, his dislike for the wealth, name and fame of the world, and above all it gives in the end the Will or the last testament of Maulānā Jalal Uddin Rumi as follows:

> I make this testament "Fear God both externally and internally." I further advise you, "Sleep less, converse less, avoid sins, and conversation and ever go on renouncing your desires and continue to endure troubles offered to you by others. Always keep fasts and worship night long and seek the company of the good and respectable people and avoid association with the mean and ignorant people. O my brethren! remember this will of mine and never aspire for name, fame and wealth, but remain constantly praying that God may open your hearts."

Sri Mātā Krishnā Satsang,
VRINDĀBAN (India)
15-6-1971

**Bankey Behari**
Hermit of Vrindāban

## Jai Sri Radha Krishnaji

### In The Name of God, The Merciful and Compassionate

Thus runs the Tradition which the Prophet (on whom be the blessings and peace) said, "Such a man of learning who visits the rich is to be despised, and amongst the rich he who associates with the men of learning is deserving of praise. So amongst the rich, he who goes to the religious mendicant is respectable and the Dervish who visits the rich with expectation stands condemned." The Prophet has stated the Truth.

The people of the world interpret the above tradition in the following way. He who is learned should not call on the rich, lest he should become corrupt. However, this is not the correct meaning of this tradition. For, if a man of learning who seeks the company of the rich, putting on the cloak of piety and apparently behaving in a pious manner with a view to humour them, and out of fear of their displeasure and has acquired the knowledge of the Sciences in expectation of rich rewards being bestowed on him by them, and a high seat of honour conferred on him, then his righteousness is assumed and is with the definite motive to please the rich, and his learning is acquired due to the fear of the rich and with a view to please them. He pursues that course of conduct under the same impulse, with effort and not spontaneously and is sometimes carried away by the current of events, inspite of himself. That being so, it follows whether he goes to meet the rich or they call on him, he will be called the seeker and he who is visited will be an enlightened man (learned). The enlightened men think that they acquired knowledge from the beginning to the end not to please the rich but for the sake of their learning. Such a person pursues the right course, guided by the light of knowledge and controlled by it, and for him to act contrary to its directions will be as fatal as for the rich to attempt to live his life without water. He cannot live without the light of learning and cannot disobey its behests. Such a learned man has his knowledge as his guide which protects him from danger, warns him against error and is his guardian. The fear of the displeasure of the rich does not control his acts. The learned of his time will pursue the right course because of the fine example and he will serve as a guide to them who will look for his assistance, from their hearts even if they may not be formally introduced to him.

That being so, if such a man (learned) calls on the rich, although externally he is the seeker, but in fact, he has taken that journey in order to help the people who will be fortunate to meet him. This is because it is the rich who by such association shall gain, and the learned visitor is not to be benefited thereby, nor does he care for the rich. You can compare him to the sun, which showers light on everyone. It is its nature to bestow and be charitable. His charity converts the stones into emeralds, rubies, gems and pearls, and the minerals it changes into iron, gold, silver and copper and the trees are turned green and rich with fruits which it helps them to bear. It is deeply engrained in its nature to bestow and scatter plenty all round. Similar feelings find expression in the Arabian proverb, "We know only to give and we don't know how to take back." Therefore, I say it will be this class of learned people whom the people will seek and will deem their visit as an honour to them.

God has said, "Do not depend on your learning and on your strength and achievements, take repose only in Me and in Me alone, you will see the Strong One, the Learned One and the Creator, so that I might save you from seeking help from the kings and the nobles." As is said in the Tradition, "O Lord! We bow only to Thee and from Thee seek aid and assistance." I feel like giving a detailed exposition of this verse of the Quran although I feel this is not the occasion for it. But as it has possessed my heart, I cannot resist the temptation, so hear it. God says, "O Prophet! tell this to the prisoners of war that had the Lord seen any goodness in their hearts, He would have bestowed a yet greater gift than the one of which they have been deprived and would have forgiven them. He is the great Forgiver and the Compassionate One." This verse was revealed to the Prophet on the occasion when he had defeated the non-believers, had routed them and taken many in custody and they had been brought before him in fetters and amongst these in captivity, was the Prophet's own uncle, Abbās. In his captivity, the whole night Abbās shrieked and felt bitterly the torment and humiliation, little hoping to be rescued and was just biding the approach of death. When the Prophet saw him in that plight, he smiled. The prisoners of war interpreted the smile as a sneer at the humiliation and defeat of the uncle. Among themselves they began to point out, "Look here! this Prophet still suffers from human frailties and his profession that human element has left him (and divine element has dawned) is without foundation. Seeing us in fetters as prisoners, he takes pleasure in it and mocks at us in the manner of other human conquerors who rejoice after the defeat of the enemies." The Prophet read what passed in the hearts of the prisoners and said, "No, what you think is incorrect I do not rejoice in your trouble for having gained victory over you and because I see you humiliated. I smile because I see with my eyes wide awake that so many of the people whom I have brought out of the mother's womb, from the hell and evil families, have tied them in fetters and I am dragging them from this house of pain (world) in spite of themselves, into Lord's presence, into the garden of Eden, they weep and shriek at this act of divine benevolence and enquire the reason why they are being dragged from this house of suffering to the House of Peace and Plenty. At this incongruity I am inevitably made to smile. But this intuitive and spiritual insight had not fallen to your lot. You cannot, therefore, understand the import of my act and cannot see it for yourself. "I am surprised at these people who are halting and with difficulty are carried in bonds to the gate of Paradise."

Then, the Prophet proceeded, "God Himself says, 'Tell those prisoners about their conduct, in first gathering a large army with great pomp and show of strength of which they were very proud and in which their hearts were rejoicing that they would crush the Believers (Moslems) in no time and finally suppress them. They, however, forgot that there dwelt a still greater Power than themselves. It could even crush them and It is greater Being than their weak proud selves. It was for this reason that they failed in their deliberation and could not achieve what they were confident they would. And now although they are involved in pain and subjection, yet they are not prepared to give up their conceit. In spite of the consciousness of their helplessness which they see before them, they do not even now pray for forgiveness and do not yet realise that there is still a Greater Power than themselves." Take heed, therefore, that when, in future pomp, show and greatness fall to your lot, remember with all humility that there is One Greater than yourselves even. Before Him you are nothing and recognise His Omnipotence.

If you take my advice and work it, I promise you the fulfilment of your wishes, the success of your aspirations and you will not lose heart when you are surrounded by fear, because I can in my Omniscience and Omnipotence take you out of fear and protect you. Know that He who can make a white cow give birth to a black calf has power also to reverse the order and it has been truly said of that Reality, "He turns the night into day and transforms the day into night and it is by Him that the living is born from the dead and the dead of the living. Do not deny Him merely because at this time you happen to be prisoners of war and do not go away helpless from my presence so that I may render you help." There is not a shred of doubt in it that they who are infidels alone have lost faith in His mercy. God says, "If now you beware of your former faith, and both in time of hope and fear, you fix your attention on Me, and remember that in whatever state you may be, you are in My power and cannot get out of My possession, then I promise that I shall release you from this fear and shall return to you that which you have lost, or rather I shall bestow on you greater wealth than the one that you have lost. This means I shall forgive your transgression and shall usher you into the eternal region and bestow on you the wealth of this world and the next. Thereupon, Abbās sought forgiveness and said that he was sorry and would not do so as he did before. The Prophet then said, "This profession and promise that you have made to your Lord needs a witness before being acceptable to the Beneficient Lord."

It is easier to make a profession of love. But this profession must also offer proof and arguments in its support. Abbās, then inquired, "In the Name of the Lord, tell me what kind of proof you demand." Thereupon the Prophet replied, "Bestow on the army of the Moslems that portion of the wealth that you still own so that they may become still stronger. It is but meet for you to obey me, if you say you have been converted to Islām and have become a well-wisher of that Faith." Abbas said, "O Prophet of God! Tell me what is left with me, now, that they have deprived me of the last straw mat." The Prophet said, "You have not yet adopted the right Path, and have not yet given up your old ways. If you want it, I can disclose what further riches you still possess and where they are deposited and with whom and how buried." Abbās replied, "It is incorrect I have nothing left with me now." The Prophet reprimanding him said, "Is not so much amount deposited with your wife and buried in that wall and also you have made a will in favour of your wife that on your safe return will to be given back to you, and in case the unfortunate event happens, out of it a certain amount go to such and such a person and another sum will be sent on a particular count and the balance will be retained by her for herself?" Having heard this, the very moment, Abbās confessed and honestly believed in Islām with a true heart and said, "O Prophet! I had till now considered that you had attained to this eminence like the previous kings, Hamām, Shalād and others but now since you have disclosed my secret I am convinced that your eminence is rooted in Divinity and your greatness has a spiritual foundation." The Prophet said, "Now, you have honestly uttered the turth. The necklace of heresy that hung in your heart is shattered and I hear the sound of its breaking. I have also a spiritual ear that is hidden in my soul. With that ear I hear the sound of the breaking of the necklace of heresy, doubt and absence of faith in Unity. It is, now, perfectly true that you have become faithful and adopted the right Path."

Maulānā Rumi pointed out to Amir Parwānā that the object of expounding this verse of the Qurān was that he should make of faith a shield and cherish it to his heart's content. In the propagation of Islām, he should spend his riches, knowledge and resources. He added, "Since you have till now depended on your prowess and never taken notice of God and, therefore, have imagined that whatever is done by you is from God, therefore, the Lord has changed that intellect and resources that you employed into causes for your discomfiture and your efforts have proved a source of trouble to Islām, because you have entered into a confederacy and bestowed on them a corps of auxiliaries. You are, in effect, permitting them to destroy the Moslems in Syria and Egypt, and thus bring into ruin the land of the Moslems, although, as a fact, that very reason which was sought by you as a means for defeat of Islam has been made by Him an occasion for its preservation. These being the circumstances you should rivet your attention on God now so that no evil may befall you. Therefore, spend in charity so that the Lord may take you out of that pitiable condition in which you have fallen. Do not lose heart because the Lord took you out of the life of faith and adoration and cast you in error and sin, because all your reverence and faith was veiled with egoism and arrogance. Due to it, you fell into error. Granted that, now, you have become a sinner, you should not despair. Bitterly pray to Him. He has power in Him to convert your sins into prayers just as He has converted your prayers into sins. This He did by consciously making you feel the shame of your actions. He may create such conditions that once you may again be a source and instrument of propagation of Islām. Despair not because to lose faith in His mercy is fitting only to an infidel."

My object in expounding this saying was to impress on the Amir the necessity to spend more on charity and beg forgiveness of the Lord that he had fallen from a very high situation to the lower one and he should in this fallen state see that the acts of the Lord have a meaning and He is the great Contriver. From ugly things, He can bring out beautiful ones. This marvel is showed to dissuade a person from getting proud of his knowledge and achievements. Do you not see that despite the deep insight which the Prophet himself possessed, he was equally anxious to bestow on others? How bitterly did he not pray to God and entreat Him to show him the reality of things, through His mercy?. You display a thing which, in fact, is bad as good so also you display a thing which, in reality, is ugly as beautiful. Pray, reveal to us the things in their essence so that we do not get entangled in a snare and for ever stray away from the right path. Now your opinion may be right and nice but it cannot, in any case, be superior to that of the Lord. This has also been said by the Lord. Therefore, do not be too sure and confident of your opinion and do not depend on it. Be humble before the Lord. Fear Him at all moments. This was the object in view and with it I gave this detailed interpretation of that verse with heart so that at this time when you are sending out your armies, you should not place too much reliance on your opinion and on their strength and even though defeat may fall to your lot, in that helpless state also, you should not lose hope in Him nor refuse to fear Him. I have completed this discourse according to my desire and what was the purpose I have illustrated.

## CHAPTER 2

Somebody, once, remarked that the Maulānā was constantly discoursing. The Maulānā thereupon said, "I told that gentleman that it was my thought (discourse) that had brought him there. Did not this thought of his concerning me, not tell me what he was like and what he felt (like meeting me)." Is it, at all, possible that he should be driven to this place without any cause? The fact is that there is no occasion for surprise, if my discourse drives him to this place. A discourse is but the image of reality (within me) and may be described as its branch. If the image of something drives a thing to itself, it will also absorb the reality behind the image in due course. Discourses are mere pretexts. It is in men the similarity of essence and tendency that draws one to the other. The fact is that even if thousands of miracles and arguments and marvels could be urged and displayed by a Prophet or a saint to an aspirant, the latter will not be affected by them until both have from before similar tendencies within themselves. Just as in the absence of any element of similarity in their natures, a straw shall never be attracted to the magnet. That similarity of family (being of the same genus and having the same nature and attributes) is hidden between them and is not visible to the external eyes. A person is driven to that object whichever he imagines or thinks of. The thought of the garden will take him to the garden, that of the shop prompts him to the shop. But the point hidden behind these ideas is sometimes lost sight of by us. It is not observable but it happens at times that although it is the prompting of our heart that we visit a place, yet when we reach there, we regret having come there. A disillusionment comes. You had thought it would be a thing of joy whereto you were bound, but on reaching it, it turned out to be a source of pain. Those thoughts may be metaphorically represented as a big sheet of cloth and wrapped in it is a person. When this sheet will disappear between him and his self, and reality will display itself in its nakedness, believe me, then, it shall be the Day of judgement. The virtue of this day is that we forget our regards on reaching it. Believe that the reality that draws you to itself is the only genuine stuff and nothing besides it is real. This is the only reality—"The Day on which the secrets shall be examined (that is, shall be revealed)." On that occasion this shall be the state of reality as it has been portrayed by me to you. Stated honestly and with brevity, in reality there is only One Who attracts us to Himself, although externally He appears like so many. This will be better understood by an example. Do you not observe that a hungry person feels tempted to take a hundred things, fruits, different dishes, varied meats, dates, figs and the like. He sees in them different objects and asks for them. But all this craving for their variety has but one reality—hunger. This is proved by his refusal to ask for anything till his sole craving—hunger (the reality in the case) is satisfied, even on tasting only one dish. It follows that in all that variety, the reality was only one. "We have created them to appear so many with a desire to cause disturbance." One of the mischiefs is apparent in the belief of the people generally that whilst they consider themselves created in hundreds, they say the Prophet is one. This insight which sees the Prophet as a smaller number, a unit, whilst they consider themselves much larger in number—a hundred—is indeed a great mischief. What is considered as hundred and fifty has a numerical value, like so many lifeless bodies, unable to stir and move on the right path, intoxicated with material things, a huge concourse all lifeless and unstable like mercury.

Now, if you call these people as hundreds or thousands and the Prophet as one, it is alone he who can be styled, "the man," the others have so many useless numerical values. He is far above the *horde*, the valueless multitude. "When you number them, they appear as so many, but if you try to discover the essence in them, you will not find an atom of reality in the whole lot."

A certain king had bestowed on one person enough food to satisfy one hundred people. All the soldiers of the king were expressing their annoyance at the favouritism on the part of the king. The king was musing within himself, "Let them await the day when I shall tell them the reason of my preference." When the time of war came, and there was actual war, all other soldiers showed their back, but those favourite of the king continued to fight, and faced great dangers to the end against the enemies. Pointing to the soldiers, the king said that there was the reply to their query, why that favouritism on his part in that favourite soldier's attitude.

It is the function of a human being to develop his faculty of discrimination, leave all desires and pray for the bestowal of faith, because faith consists in recognition of the Friend. But if he wastes his life mixing with ignorant people, devoid of all discrimination, his faculty of discrimination will also lose strength. He will grow so weak that he will not be able to recognise the Friend. You have cared for this body and supported it, and it is devoid of all discrimination. This faculty is one which is hidden within a man and is one of his attributes. This is evident from the fact that although a mad man, too, has a body, hands and feet but there is no discriminative faculty in him. He puts his hands without discrimination in everything filthy and eats it up. If his external body had this faculty in him, he would not even go near the filth. It follows, therefore, that hidden within thee is that faculty of discrimination but alas! you are ignorant of it and do not discover it, whilst you waste your time in pampering this gross body on the pretext that if the body suffers how will the discriminative faculty, of which it is the home, grow to its full stature? But you must realise that the body is alive because of this discriminative faculty and this discriminative faculty is annexed to this body. There is no gainsaying the fact that the Supreme light does peep through the holes of the eyes and ears but if these holes are absent it will find another outlet, different windows. You can be described in terms of one who dares to show the lamp to the sun. Do you imagine that the sun is visible in the light that the lamp sheds? But you must know that if you had not brought the lamp with you, even then, the sun must have been visible to you. The sun does not need the aid of a lamp to manifest itself. "Despair not of the mercy of the Lord." "Verily, they who have lost faith in His mercy are heretics." "For what, after all, is faith like?." It is a resthouse that leads to divine protection, If you do not desire to pursue the Path, take your seat at the end of it, then. Do not grow hopeless that you have sinned. Follow truth and darkness shall disappear. The true Path is like the rod of Moses and untruth is like magic-tricks. When truth dawns, it swallows up untruth. If you have sinned, it is your doing and you have to suffer for it. Your sin cannot touch Him:

The bird sat on the mountain and flew away.

Tell me how did the mountain gain by its perching or lose by its flying away.

The association of king's is dangerous because you may lose your head some day, be it today or tomorrow, but it is to be feared because if a man attends the court of the king's (whose ego has grown up into a dragon), lays claim to their friendship and accepts their presents, he seldom can avoid losing his individuality and succumbing to theirs, endorsing whatsoever they say, adopting with his heart their opinions and thereafter, never acting in contravention to their wishes. Viewed from that standpoint their company is dangerous as it is injurious from the religious point of view. When with your heart you are anxious to support them at all times, your profession will always be opposed to your practice. As much you will try to humour them and move that way, to that extent the other side (God) shall turn His face away from you, and the more you will extend your affection to the people and things of the world, the more you will cause displeasure to the Beloved. "Whosoever supports a tyrant, is tyrannised over by God through the tyrant." So, the question is, towards whom you are proceeding? When you proceed towards God, He will see that He wins a victory over you and subdues you. The matter is one of regret that even if, fortunately, you reach the current, you feel satisfied with a handful of water from the sea from where others take away pearls and other valuable gifts. What, then, is the value to be attached to you whose possessions consist only of a handful of water (such a minor achievement)? This world is like foam and the water of the river is comparable to the knowledge of the Prophets. But where is the pearl, the great secret? The world is like so much dirt and straw in the foam. It looks pretty only because of the upheaval of the waters, because of the waves that rise now and then to the surface of the waters. "To the people of the world are displayed women, children, heaps of gold and silver, horses, animals and the corn growing in the fields. This is the world and such are its provisions."

So, when the world appears pretty, it does not mean that it is beautiful in reality but that its charms are shortlived and are derived from elsewhere. It is just like a play or a bad coin, plated with gold, It means that this world which is like the feam, or like a bad coin is valueless, We have plated it with gold and hence it is said of it, "It is shown beautiful to the people of the world."

Man is like a telescope to see truth. But it demands an astronomer who can use it. The shopkeeper and the vegetable dealer too possess this instrument but unfortunately, they cannot derive full advantage out of it. How can he know the motions of the planets, the movement of the stars and the effects that they produce on the destiny of the people and how do they affect human affairs? The telescope can be of use only to the astronomer and can benefit him alone. As it has been said, 'He who has known himself has known God.' Just as this fine telescope is a mirror of the affairs of the stars, so also is man, of whom it is said, "Verily I have made man great." He is the telescope in the hands of the Lord. When God, the Knower of his essence creates him, that telescope of human self begins to reflect and denote His divine excellence every moment and is not separated from Him. Great is His Omnipotence and Majesty and well do some of His servants disguise His attributes within themselves, the marvels of God-realisation by veils, from the eyes of the people and the people have not inward sight so as to see them. Whilst these human beings themselves in sheer modesty will not disclose those secrets, therefore, they lie hid in them as it has been said by an Arabic poet:

"Those women have put on regal dress, not to show
themselves off,
But to treasure their beauty and protect it by
charming veils."

## CHAPTER 3

Amir Parwānā said, "All day and night, my heart and soul is engaged in prayers but the duties and affairs of the world do not permit me to perform them faithfully." Maulānā said to him, "The worldly duties are also works of God for, whatever worldly duties are performed by you, are prompted with the motive to comfort the Moslems and to bring solace to them, and you spend all your wealth to please and satisfy them, with a view that other Moslems may also be engaged with you in prayers. This being your pious intent, all your acts are spiritual acts. God has naturally inclined you to the performance of such duties and you are much drawn to them. This is the proof and argument in favour of you that He is extremely kind to you and merely because you fail in one such work, you should not bemean it as cruelty from the side of the Lord, for it will then, mean that He wants such a servant of His may be unable to perform an act whereby he will attain to high station in His eyes. As some disagreeable and undesirable effects are produced, it is no proof of lack in His dispensation of mercy on you. For just as, bath is heated with fuel of straw and wood, all of which look so ugly, yet, it helps in producing such beneficial results, so apparently, these undesirable causes may produce effects that are productive of some good to the servant of the Lord. Just as, when the bath is warmed, its warmth comforts the people and has other beneficial results.

(The discourse was interrupted at this stage by the entrance of a huge concourse of friends. Maulana apologised and standing up said, 'If I am not respectful to you and do not inquire after your health, perhaps you should not feel offended, for, unfortunately, this is the current idea that prevails in regard to respect. The idea of respect always conforms to the idea of time and occasion, for example, at the time of prayers, it does not behove one respectfully to inquire about the health and relations. It is not permitted by the tenets of religion. Therefore, to be unmindful about the approach of relations during prayers is to be steeped in genuine prayers and is at the same time tantamount to the greatest affection shown to the relations for such relations are also, thereby, served and protected from the divine wrath and displeasure. This disinterestedness, then, becomes the highest attention because his act cannot be interrupted but prompted with a desire not to cause the wrath of God to descend upon them.'

The companions of the Maulānā asked him, "Is there any other easier way to attain to Him than through by prayer (Namāz)?" He answered, "If such a method, ever existed, it would also be called Namāz. But the prayers that you say are sheer skeleton, mere form of rituals, since, it has a beginning and an end. It is an inert object. Just see Namāz begins by raising hands and ends by a bow and obeisance. So, also the words signifying belief (martyrdom) are not those that are simply uttered by mouth, because they too, have a beginning and end. That thing which can be circumscribed by words and sound must of necessity have a beginning and a close, and it is but a formality and is mere skeleton. But spirit is beyond all expanse, limitless and incomparable. Such prayers are offered by the Prophets. Now, he who has propounded such forms of prayers, thus speaks of it, "There is one moment in my life when I am so close to the Lord that even the angels envy my nearness." It follows, therefore, that the soul of prayers is not its external form which we see but to forget oneself in His remembrance and get intoxicated in His thoughts. All these formalities disappear on that occasion and cannot exist, in so much so that even the angel Gabriel who has a spiritual (subtle) form cannot even come between.

An incident from the life of Maulānā Bahāuddin Wald is thus related. One day his disciples saw him completely oblivious of his surroundings whilst seated in remembrance of God. The hour of prayer arrived. Some of the disciples shouted "Master, the hour of prayer is reached." The Maulānā did not take heed to it as if he did not hear it. All the disciples rose to say their prayers except two of them, who remained in their seats opposite the teacher. Amongst the disciples who rose was one Khwajgi, who had an occult sight. He noticed that all the disciples who had stood up and were saying prayers had their faces turned away from Kābā and their backs were towards the Kābā. But the Maulānā and his two disciples seated opposite him were facing the Kābā as it is usual in the prayers. The reason for this was clear. The master at the moment was lost completely in God, was dead to his ego, and had merged himself in the Divine Light. As it has been pointed out, "Die before actual death overtakes you." Now, he had himself become the Divine Light. It is a fact that Divine Light is the spirit of Kābā. It would, therefore, be far praise-worthy if his personality itself were made Kābā. For, it is because of him that we style it Kābā.

Muhammad once got annoyed with one of the companions of the Bench. He questioned him why he did not appear before him when he was summoned. He replied that he was answering prayers. The Prophet said, "After all, it was 'I' who had summoned you." The gentleman stood calm and silent.

After reciting the story, the Maulānā continued, "It is well, if you remain helpless always and in every condition, and to such an extent that you may not be able to perform literally any act, just as you experience inability when you have not requisite means to perform it. As there is a higher Power that controls your powers also, so you are helpless in every state. It is mistake for you to imagine that you have two conditions—one of Omnipotence and the other of submission and helplessness. Keep your view fixed on that Reality that is All-powerful and consider yourself always helpless, without hands and feet, humble and unable to achieve anything. This is not only true of the frail human being, but it is also true of the crocodile, lion and the tiger as well. They all tremble before His Majesty. The earth and heavens are all under His control. He is the King of kings and His effulgence is unlike the light of the sun who keeps the things in their places. For, when He sheds His light, that is, when the Divinity is unveiled, neither the heaven nor the earth, nor the sun, nor the moon remains in itself, nor exists. He and He alone shines everywhere and nothing also remains. "All things will pass away. He alone will survive."

A certain king requested a dervish to remember him when he reaches the presence of the Almighty Lord. The dervish replied, "When I am ushered into the Divine Presence, alas! I do not even remember myself, all consciousness leaves me, how can you expect me to remember you, at that time? But when the Lord is pleased with somebody and accepts his services, He fulfils his wishes even without asking. He does it of his own accord without any expression of the wish by the servant.

A story runs thus: "A certain king had a slave who was extremely close to him and was his great favourite. Whenever that slave went to the king's palace, the people in want would present their applications to him to be laid before the king. He took them all and put them in a leather bag and with it went to the royal presence. When he reached the king, before his august personality, he so forgot himself that he swooned away. The king, therefore, searched his bag and pockets, found out the presents he had brought with him for Him and read the applications and wrote favourable orders on them and again placed them in his bag and pockets. The wishes of so many applicants were fulfilled without the favourite servant's even mentioning them to the king and the applicants got rewards more than they had applied for, and had expected. But the other slaves of the king whose senses always remained in tact before the king seldom dared to make any petition and if ever such petition was made, out of a hundred, only one such was granted and the rest were rejected."

## CHAPTER 4

Somebody told the Maulānā that he had forgotten something there. The Maulānā replied, "In this world there is only one thing that should not be forgotten, for, if you were to try to remember all things and were to utilise them and never forget them, there is no harm in forgetting that one thing. Suppose, a king were to send you on a particular errand to a certain village and you were to perform there many acts satisfactorily, but you did not perform the particular act for which you were specially commissioned, then, it would be taken you did no work. You must, therefore, know that man is born in this world for a definite purpose and that is the chief work he is to perform. If you do not perform it, your life is worthless. "When I (Lord) offered my trust to the mountains, they refused, so also the skies refused to shoulder the burden of creation (trust) and feared they would not be able to acquit themselves of the task. Man, however, shouldered it. Verily man made a great blunder. "Just notice that the very sky (heavens) which refused to take up the responsibility is now responsible for many virtuous acts which cause so much wonder. It turns the stones to emeralds and rubies, turns the hills into mines of gold and silver and gives newer life to plants and trees and turns everything into veritable paradise. From vegetation it produces seeds and these seeds in their turn produce fruits and other articles which provide us with garments and performs many other beneficial acts, too numerous to mention. So, also the mountains are responsible for many good products. They do all such acts, except the one which can be performed only by man and which has rightly given him the designation. "Verily, I have bestowed greatness on man, and it has never been said that I have conferred supremacy on heavens (sky) and the earth. It is for this reason that man performs those acts which the heavens, the earth and the mountains are unable to carry out. When man performs that act, ignorance and mistake leave him. If you say that you can not perform that particular act whilst you have been able to do many others, I shall say that you have failed to perform the act for which you are born and all that you have been able to do is so much labour wasted, for, man is not created for all such acts. Your action can be compared to your bringing a valuable sword made of Indian steel studded with diamonds straight from the king's treasury and trying to cut with it a dead animal into pieces. You are constantly saying that you make use of the sword and do not permit it to lie useless. Or, again, if you were to cook some radish in a vessel of gold, from a piece of which a hundred cooking vessels of copper could be purchased, or again if you were to hang the creeper of cucumber on a knife of gold studded with diamonds and you would have thought that you had usefully and well employed the knife, the people would ridicule at you for such act of yours. For that creeper could be hung on an iron nail or a wooden one not worth more than one-eighth of a pice. No purpose is served by hanging it on a knife worth hundreds of sovereigns."

God has put a very high price on man (you). He says, "Verily I have purchased the lives and possessions of the faithful paying paradise as the price." You are valuable as life itself. Alas! you do not know your worth. How precious you are! Do not sell yourself as cheap for you are worth very much. So, God says, "I have purchased your all-possessions, time, life-breaths. If you spend them on Me and bestow them on Me, I promise you entry into Paradise till eternity." In my eyes you are so valuable that if you dispose yourself off in return for hell, you will be exposing yourself to torment and heading towards perdition just as the man in the previous illustration hung the creeper of cucumber on the knife of gold studded with gems worth a hundred sovereigns. He erred. I shall expound again the real meaning. You simply pretend that you are performing good acts. You study logic, philosophy, law, medicine, astronomy etc. and are proud of them. Do you not see that you do so all to benefit yourself? The result of the study of law is to preserve your possessions, and protect yourself from aggression, so that nobody may deprive you of your garments and may not take away your life, and you may pass your days in comfort. The knowledge of astronomy is also acquired to the same effect, viz., to understand the motion of the stars and their effect on earth? Thereby this rise and fall of the prices in the market, for the good or evil effect of stars affects our life. So also this knowledge is acquired for your benefit. If you give a moment's thought, you will find that you are the essence (the objective of every one of those things. All these things will be like so many of your branches (mere causes). When your branches have so many details and these sciences are so very marvellous that, it is impossible to gain their depths, so limitless are they, then you can know what can be the depth of your essence (self). All are anxious to watch and understand the decay and growth, the bright and dark character of their branches, let them give a moment's thought to the rise and fall, the stability and flow of their own self (reality). They should watch what is the nature of a particular soul and enquire as to the good that ensues from it and the purpose it can serve. Besides the food that thou taketh, the sleep that thou enjoyeth, O man! for thee there is another food. And in the night you are with the Lord Who feeds you and supports you. You have neglected that food on your birth in the world and have engaged yourself in the food of this world. All night and day, you are engrossed caring for the body. This body of yours is a vehicle, merely a conveyance for yourself. This world is its fodder. The food of a horse is not fit for yourself (the rider). Within you (the rider) is extant everything, sleep, food, rest, joy, but you are alas! so much steeped in carnality, that you have stopped short at the care and anxiety for the food of the horse and have not taken your seat amongst the kings of eternity and immortal nobility. Although your heart is there, yet your body is so enveloped and overpowered that you have yielded to it and are entangled in it. Truly, your condition is similar to that of Majnun. Majnun proceeded rightly so long as he was in senses (conscious of his purpose) but the moment he was absorbed in the thoughts of beloved Leila, he lost all consciousness of the journey. The she-camel which he rode had her young one living in a village closeby from where Majnun had hired her. The moment Majnun became absorbed in his thoughts, she got an opportunity and instead of proceeding further retraced her steps towards her young one. The journey which Majnun had covered was retrieved. Thus three months were wasted and no advance was made. Majnun in sheer desperation shrieked that the camel had become the bane of his life. He got down from her and started his journey on foot. The following couplet is ascribed to him on that occasion:

> "My camel turned back, whilst my beloved dwelt in front,
>
> My camel and I are opposed to each other, and the beloved stands before me."

Maulānā Rumi said that Syed Burhān Uddin was discoursing when one of the audience apologetically said, "Sir! I heard a gentleman sing your praises." Burhān Uddin replied, "Let me also try to find out that man who praises me, for I would like to know the stage of his spiritual development as he professes to know the depth of my soul, for how else could he shower praises on me? But if he has known me only through the discourses I have delivered then, I dare say he does not know me, because all this conversation, these words and these sounds are transitory. If he has known me through the actions, he has also failed to appreciate me for these actions are, likewise, ephemeral. But if he has understood my essence or my individuality, I shall, surely, admit that he has known me, recognised me and he is entitled to praise me and I shall be benefited by that praise. Else, his state would be like that of the prince who was put under the best and most learned tutors of the time to study astronomy. After he had finished his course, the king, to test him, hiding something in his fist, asked him, "What does the fist contain?" The prince exerted his brain and then said, "It is a yellow round thing, hollow at the centre, and gave such a minute description that the king was surprised. Then, the king asked him to draw the conclusion from that description and name the thing. The boy replied that it must be a sieve. The king admonished him saying "You are clever in giving minutest details and signs but you have arrived at such a wrong conclusion. Did it not occur to you how a sieve can be contained in the fist of the hand?"

Such is the state of the learned men of today. They are given to too much hair-splitting, and idle criticism, Whatever appertains to their body, they know perfectly and are masters thereof. But they do not know that essential knowledge of the self that they should attain to. They say that such and such a thing is to be followed and such and such a thing is to be condemned, but they do not know in which category they themselves are, whether their self is to be praised or condemned, whether it is lawful or unlawful, whether it is pious or impious, and pure or impure. Like the prince mentioned above, they know that the object in the hand of the king is yellow, round and hollow at the centre, but these are all ephemeral attributes. The reality is not known. For, if it is thrown in the fire, all these forms will disappear and will be lost on the object being melted. The reality alone, which is indestructible will be left.

This knowledge, act, and ideal so much cherished in the world is like the form and signs of the above illustration. None of them can lead to the knowledge of reality, and some point to the reality which is latent and behind the forms and worldly knowledge. Their knowledge and description is just like giving correct signs but drawing incorrect conclusion like the prince saying that he has a sieve in it. They are not acquainted with reality, and do not know to what genus they belong and what sort of bird they are, a nightingale or other sweet tongued bird. If you ask me to imitate the sound of another bird, I shall not be able to do so. But one who has learnt to imitate the sound of other birds will easily do so. Such a man will not be a friend of the birds but their enemy or a hunter who utilises that knowledge in hunting and entrapping them by imitating their sound. If you ask that man to speak in another language, he cannot do so because it is not his language, only he has learnt it, and acquired so much proficiency in it that he can imitate it. So also the thief who has learnt the act of stealing, can steal other people's property and commit burglary in a house.

## CHAPTER 5

Amir Parwānā said to Maulānā, "It is the height of kindness on your part that you should yourself visit my house. I could never dream or even wish in my heart that you should take the trouble of coming yourself to my place. I am only fit to stand with folded hands in the row of your servants and await your commands. Really speaking, this is also a bold profession on my part. I am not even fit for it, and am surprised at this extreme favour that has fallen to my lot." Maulānā said, "This is because you are high spirited and have a great spiritual position. You are performing great deeds and in spite of such a high state, you still consider that you are performing nothing and are discontented with your achievements and feel that you should do much more. My heart is always with you, yet I sometimes like to see your face too, because the value of the face cannot belittled. It is not a question of more regard for your face, but because the face is connected with the spirit and is related to it. Just as no work is possible without the essence (the kernel) and the outer covering is necessary. If you sow a seed after removing its outer covering, it will never sprout out. But, if you bury it in the ground with the covering on it, it shall sprout out, and grow into a tree. So also the body is an indispensable thing and wonderful. Without it, no work is possible and no purpose is achieved. By God, the root of the inwardness is this body and before being acquainted with the inside and being enlightened, it is absolutely necessary to have a body. Look here, the people say bowing twice in prayers is far more valuable than the world and the all that is contained in it. But this is not true and apparent to everybody. This is realised by him who feels this life is a huge burden, the moment, he forgets to say prayers, and experiences the loss of a valuable object and feels extreme pain due to it."

A certain Dervish saw a king. The king inquired, "O man of piety! What is it you want?" The Dervish interrupting said, "It is not I but you are the man of piety." The king was surprised and said "I am a worldly man. Why do you say I am a pious man?" The Dervish said, You are mistaken. This world ,and the next and thy kingdom are all under my sway and I control the universe whilst you are content with a garment and a leaf of bread. Look wherever you may go, God is seen. He is an asset that is always coming in and going out and never knows the close and for all times continues to shower Himself. The lovers have sacrificed themselves to his face and do not seek any recompense for it. The remaining people are like so many brutes."

The Maulānā continued, "Although there are so many brutes, yet they are entitled to be rewarded. Although they are within the stable, yet they are beloveds of the master of the stable. If the stable-keeper so desires, he might remove them from the stables and put them in a better one.

Just as a person before being brought into this world was nothing. He was first brought into the stable of existence, then put into the category of mineral kingdom, thereafter into the vegetable kingdom, thereafter into the animal kingdom and from the animal kingdom, he evolved into a human being. From the human being, he will rise into the angelic state. In his evolution, he has passed through so many stages. This was all done to prove the existence of the Lord and make you accept that He has several such stables, every one superior to the other. "They grow steadily from stage to stage, yet it is not understandable, why they do not rest their faith in Him."

I stated these things so that you might believe in those stages of evolution that you would have to undergo in future. It has not been stated so that you may lose faith in them and say that the present is the only real state. A teacher displays his art that people may have faith in him and may accept and believe in other things that he has stated but has not demonstrated before them. So, when a king bestows his gifts on deserving subjects, it is with a view that they may have expectation of yet other things from him, and hope to get honour and reward at his hands. He does not bestow those rewards in order that they may thereafter silently sit without further hope, in perfect contentment, that they have got what they were to get, the king will bestow no more boons on them, and that which has been bestowed is enough. But if the king were to know that the person rewarded would argue like this within himself and would think in that strain, he would confer no more reward on him.

He who sees the result is a pious person. Unfortunately, the world sees only the externals (stables), their present state. There are others who neither see the externals nor the internals (results) but these knowers of God and His own people have fixed their attention on the First Cause and are acquainted with its foundation just as the owner of wheat knows the result that when they are sown, they will yield wheat, so his attention from the start is riveted upon the end (result). The same holds good in the case of sowers of other cereals. When he sees the beginning, he does not care for the end, as he knows at the start what will be the end. Such people are a few and far between, and those who see the end are available in moderate numbers but those who dwell on the externals (stables) are innumerable.

It is love that guides man, in whatever work he may be engaged. For, unless the pain (agony and desire) for that object or act is within him, he will never intend to do that work and without the desire and ache for that work, he will never be prompted to perform it sucessfully. The same rule applies whether it is the work of this world or the next (spiritual) world, whether it relates to Commerce, astronomy, learning or law or any other subject. So long as Mary did not feel the anguish of child birth, she did not draw close to the palm grove, but when the pain of child birth overtook her, that very instant she was under the palm tree. A poet has thus described the incident:

> "You shake the palm tree, the dates shall fall there from,
>
> And it is within His powers to let fall the dates without shaking the tree, but to every act He always assigns a reason.

He prompted Mary to go to the palm grove, the erstwhile dry tree turned green and gave fruits. The human body is comparable to Mary and within everyone of us there is a Christ carried by us. If we have the same anguish aroused in us, our Christ will also be born in us. If this pain does not capture us, in due course, our Christ will refuse to come out, will retrace his path and go back to the essence from where he had come. We shall be left without hope.

> The soul within is vegetating whilst the body is displaying colours,
>
> The Devil due to overeating is suffering from constipation and Jamshed goes without food.
>
> Now that thy healer is living in the world, undergo his treatment,
>
> Else, once departed to heaven, the occasion to get thyself treated as also thy medicine shall both be lost.

## CHAPTER 6

This discourse is meant for those who cannot otherwise follow, but he who can follow without explanation needs no discourse. The earth and the sky are all vocal and created out of words to him who has understanding. God said, "Be thou" and they came into existence. Therefore, he who can hear the feeble voice need not be disturbed by the noise.

An Arabian poet visited a king who was Turkish by birth unacquainted with the Persian literature, and Arabic. The poet composed an exquisite ode in his praise and attended the Court where all the nobles were in attendance. The king was seated on the throne and the nobles on their seats on the lower ground. The poet stood up and began to recite his composition. The king expressed his pleasure with a nod wherever the line was excellent and sat bewildered and awe-stricken at places exciting fear, and on occasions, feeling humility, he cast his looks down. All those in attendance were surprised that when their king did not know Arabic, how could he display such appropriate gestures, and thought perhaps he was acquainted with the Arabic language and had kept that secret from them all along. They feared that something evil might now befall them for the rash and disobedient acts that they had done. They, therefore, approached the favourite servant of the king and after offering him gifts of camels, horses and money, begged him to investigate and let them know the secret about the king, whether he knew Arabic or not. If he did not know, how could he appreciate the work of the poet and bestow applause on appropriate occasions? Did it come to him as a revelation or was it a miracle? The servant found an opportunity when the king was out on a hunting tour and was in a pleasant mood. He begged him to answer his query whether he knew Arabic or not. The king smiled and answered in the negative, but added, "Yet I could follow the poet, so I made appropriate gestures."

It follows, therefore, that the principal thing to understand is the essence. Couplets are mere branches, purpose is the root of it. If there was no purpose (meaning) behind the words, Couplets would be impossible. If you look to the real meaning, duality ceases to exist. It is visible only in the branches. The root is one. So also are the different ways of the teachers (different). The practices they teach, the methods they tell, the experiences they detail and the stages they point to are all different, but looking at the purpose behind them all, it is one, and that is, "Quest after God." When the wind blows hard, the carpets in the room are turned over, the floor is disturbed, dust spreads all over, waves rise in the waters and the branches and leaves in the tree begin to dance. So very different are all these manifestations, but looking at the essence, the cause is one the wind, which is one but is disturbing so many in different ways.

Amir Parwānā said, "Sir! We are unable to perform any duty." The Maulānā replied, "If a man thinks in this strain and endures such discomfiture and regrets his incapacity, verily, it is the sign in him of being the recipient of God's extreme kindness. So long as the reproach persists, take it to be the sign of friendship." (The friend alone can be angry.) Anger is not shown to strangers. It is reserved for friends. But there is variety in wrath even. For example, the nature of the wrath consequent on some undesirable act done by someone dear to you is, of course, of the nature of affection shown to him, or God-sent kindness and evidence of love. As the carpet is struck with sticks in order that it may be cleaned of the dust, the wise will not consider it as an expression of anger. When a child is so dealt with on account of an outward act, it is evidence of kindness towards him. So long as, you consider such strokes of Providence as evil, when you are dealt with in that strain by another brother of yours, this is the evidence that there is evil within you. This whole Universe is like a mirror in which you see yourself reflected every moment. "Every honest man is a mirror to another honest man." Take out the thorn of pain that is within you, for, you are, to a great extent, responsible for his act that causes you pain. They brought an elephant to a tank to allay his thirst. He was annoyed at seeing his face reflected (in the water), ran this way and that. He was feeling that he was disturbed by the presence of another elephant, but the truth of the matter was in that he was running at his own sight. All evil habits, tyranny, cruelty and pride are all present within you and you are not displeased with them at all. But when you see them in others, you are disturbed with them. You ought to know that you are flared up by yourself, and in fact, displeased with yourself. A man does not feel repulsion at the sight of his own sores. That very wounded hand he places in his meals and licks his own injured fingers and does not feel the least aversion. But, if he is presented with food touched be such a person, he hates that food and does not take it. His evil habits are like so many wounds at which, if they exist in himself, the man does not feel worried but if he finds them in another man, he is sadly disappointed and avoids him. If he also were to avoid you, that would be but meet. Then, why do you not tolerate him? That is what is meant by the tradition. "Every one with faith is a mirror of the other believer." The fact is, not that the heretic does not possess a mirror (heart) but that he is not consciouss of his heart.

In a state of great annoyance, a king was seated by the side of a canal. All his nobles and ministers stood in terror round him and were shuddering all the time. The face of the king was flared with wrath. The king had a buffoon who was extremely dear to him. The nobles offered a great prize to the buffoon if he could make the king laugh. The buffoon approached the king and tried many wiles but the moody king did not raise his eyes and was looking into the water of the canal. In the end, he asked. "Sir! what are you seeing in the water?" The king answered that he was seeing a fool (meaning the buffoon). The buffoon answered "So also, your majesty, I too am not blind to the sight (that is I also am seeing a buffoon)." The reality is that if you are pained at the sight you see in the water, that object too is not blind. It also sees that which is visible to you.

In His presence, the ego "I" has no place. If you call yourself "I", so does He call Himself "I" Either you die before Him or let Him die before you. Then only, duality will disappear. His death is not possible. "He is such a living One, Who shall never die. He is so Compassionate that if it were in His power, He would even die Himself and rend asunder the veil of duality that persists between you and Him. But since that is not possible, it is but meet that you should die in His presence so that He may shed His lustre on you and duality may be destroyed. Take an illustration. Tie two birds. They have now four wings but they cannot fly because, now, duality intervenes. But tie a dead bird with a living one, it flies, for, duality is gone. The sun is so merciful that it would die in the presence of the bat if it were possible. But that is not possible. So, he says to the bat, "I am giving light to the universe. I wish to give it to you also, so you should die because your death is possible so that I may confer my beneficence on you that you may be reborn as a Simurgh (bird's king) Of Mt. Caucasus, and you will be so near to me."

Of the men of the Lord, there was one who had this speciality that he died for his friend. The story goes that a person prayed to the Lord to favour his friend. The Lord, however, did not answer his prayers. The Divine voice said, "I do not like your friend," Even then this servant of the Lord did not desist from his prayers but continued his prayers and instead, began to pray most fervently on his account with all humility. He told the Lord that it was He Himself that had aroused love for his friend in him. Now it was impossible for him to relieve himself of it. At last, the Divine voice was heard, "If you seek fulfilment of your wish, sacrifice your life, make an offering of yourself, annihilate yourself and for ever be lost to the world and renounce it." "O Lord! this is acceptable to me" said the servant to the Lord and he stood by his words and laid his life for his friend. The wishes of the friend were soon fulfilled. When a servant of the Lord can sacrifice so much that his one life which can not be sacrificed by the whole humanity from the beginning of creation till the Day of judgement, was given up by him, will the Lord Who had aroused this love in him, not be kind enough to confer on him an equallty grand gift? It follows that since the death of the Lord is impossible, you should annihilate yourself (so that you may deserve His grace and blessings.)

## CHAPTER 7

A gentleman entered an assembly and sat on a seat higher than the one occupied by the saint seated there. The Maulānā, on hearing the incident, observed that the sage was not thereby affected by that act of irreverence. Whether he was seated on a higher seat or he occupied a lower one, he was unaffected. For, he was like a lamp. A lamp occupies a higher seat not that it gains thereby but with the object of benefiting others because from a higher place, the light reaches many people. It will remain a lamp in any condition you place it.

These reverend beings are more than lamps even as they are eternal suns. If they seek a higher seat, it is not with a view to aggrandisement. As many have not the proper insight, these saints want by adopting the worldly course to entangle the men of the world in the very net spread by them. (It means that they adopt the course of instruction which is held by the people of the world in high esteem). This is done in order that they may achieve the other higher Path and also attain to righteousness and spirituality.

It was this attitude of mind with which Muhammad conqured Meccā and other countries not for the purpose of extending his domain and ruling it but with the object of conferring enlightenment on those subjects and removing the veils from their eyes. Their hand is habituated to confer objects and not to take away from others. When such sages draw people to their faith they are prompted with a view to confer some good on them and not with a view to take away anything from them. If some one spreads a net to entangle the birds and having caught them, to sell them or eat them up, this is really very tricky of him. But if some king does the same thing to entangle some Irān's eagle which is so valuable and train it in order that it may perch on the royal wrist and occupy high place and become well-versed in etiquette and courtly manners and thus be raised in its status, then the act of the king in spreading the net is extremely commendable. Although to all appearance, this act of the king may be considered as deceitful, yet, in truth, this is an act of extreme benevolence and magnanimity like giving life to the dead or transforming the stone into ruby, or converting a drop of semen into a human being. It must be considered as something higher than what is expressed by these illustrations. Had that the eagle known the object for which it was caught, there would not have been the necessity of snaring it by throwing food to it, by itself it would have run to such a net and with its whole heart would have got itself entrapped in it and would have rushed to sit on the wrist of the king.

The people of the world only look at their words with external sight and they are accustomed to that conversation and feed on it. The heretics say that their hearts are covered with veils. This, however, is not so, rather the Lord has rebuked them for their disobedience. The heretics say that many such words are engraved in their hearts. God says, "That is incorrect. In fact their hearts are filled with heresy, doubts, duality and similar unbecoming thoughts, and above all with curses." God has reprimanded them for their heresy. "Would that they were devoid of such accursed thoughts, and that the noble thoughts might have accepted them. Alas! they are not even fit for that. God has placed seals on their hearts, eyes and ears, so that they may see another colour and a Joseph may appear a hideous wolf in their eyes. Their ears may hear a different tune, and they may construe a noble discourse as a desultory prattle. Their heart, too, is dyed in a different hue, because it has become a repository of unworthy thoughts and passions. Just as, in winter all becomes jumbled up due to cold and the hands and feet shiver." It means God has put seal on their hearts and ears and veils on their eyes. That being so, how can you expect wisdom in them? They lack the least perfume of it in them. Neither they, nor their relatives who direct them, have a little knowledge of reality in them.

The discourse of the Prophets is like a water-jug. Some people see the water in it and allay their thirst with it. There are others who simply see the empty jug. When the jug appears empty to them, why should they express gratitude to the Lord? On the other hand, he who sees the jug full, expresses his gratitude to the Lord. What, after all, is this body or man? It is the jug of above illustration, for has not God made man of clay and water. God says, "I kneaded the clay of man for forty days. Then I kept it tied for a long time. Satan, the despised One, came down from heaven and entered the body. He coursed through the veins, the blood and every part of the body of man. Surprised, the man exclaimed, "If the Satan whom I saw in heaven, is anyway available on the earth, he is here." He saluted the man and disappeared.

## CHAPTER 8

The son of Aitabak called on the Maulānā. The Maulānā told him that his father always remembered God and had extreme faith in Him and this was apparent at every stage of his conversation. The Maulānā continued that the heretics used to say that they would marry their daughters to the Tārtārs so that there would be one religion thereafter and this new religion—Islam—would be lost to the world. Aitabak asked, "But was ever any time in the history of the world that there was one religion and no more? There always were so many religions and amongst their adherents constantly crusades were going on. How is it, then, possible to change the course and fuse all religions into one?" Then, Aitabak nipped the mischief in the bud. Maulānā commented, "One religion is possible only in the next world. This is because in this world every man is swayed by different desires and pursues different hopes, of which he seeks fulfilment. It is, therefore, impossible to have unity in this world. But on the Day of judgement when all will be arrayed on the same plane, their ears and eyes will all be fused into one."

Within man, there are stored innumerable things, there is bird and the mouse. If the bird raises the cage, the mouse pulls it down. And man is a storehouse of millions of such animals within him. But, when they reach that place in the (next world), the mouse will leave its propensities and the bird will bid adieu to its habits. All will be melted and fused into a whole, because their objective is higher and not lower. When the principal meaning is disclosed, it (the cage) is neither lifted up nor lowered down. Take an illustration. Somebody has lost something. He searches for it in the right and in the left and behind himself. Once he has discovered it, there is no need left for him to look sideways or scan the sky or dig deep into the earth. On the day of Judgment, the sight, the tongue and the faculty of thought will become one whole. You can illustrate it thus: Suppose, there are ten partners in a firm and they own a garden. All of them will have one anxiety, will express in one strain and will act in one and the same way. This is because they have one object in view. It can be inferred that on the Day of Judgment when every one will have to deal with only one object—God, all will become one. All will unify. It means that in the world every person is engaged in his own affairs. Affection of some body is centred in his wife and of the other in his children. Another person loves his wealth, the fourth one is engaged in his business and the fifth one in exploring fresh avenues of knowledge, but everybody feels that whatever work he is engaged in constitutes his happiness and this is God's mercy. When he reaches the goal and does not get happiness that he dreamt of, he retraces his steps in utter helplessness and thinks himself, after a moment's pause, that it is worth while because he discovers eternal happiness in ephemeral pursuits. He feels that he has not pursued his search properly and indefatigably. He feels that his failure is due to lack of zeal and determines to repeat his quest with greater effort the next time. This second failure crosses him and then, he makes a third attempt also and so on till that moment is reached when that effulgence dawns on him and he sees it before his eyes and then alone he feels that the former course that he was pursuing was not the right path. There are Lord's servants who have seen all these things through their inward sight even before the Day of Judgment. The commander of the faithful (Moslems) said, "Even if the veil is removed, I shall have no greater faith than what I have now." It means that when the body falls (dies), our faith will not suffer or grow.

This point can be illustrated in the following way. Suppose, there are many people sitting in prayers in a house. In the night, their faces are in various directions. But by the dawn they are all set right. However, he whose face is already turned towards Kābā needs not change the direction of his face for it is already in that direction in which the faces of all devotees are turned. These devotees have turned their faces away from the world and even in the night, they face the Kābā because in their eyes even today is the Day of Judgment. For them, every day is such. This is an endless subject, only that much which one has the capacity to follow is related. "There is nothing of which we have not treasures but you take only that much that is enough for your requirements. Wisdom is like the rain. Although in its storehouse there is plenty but wisdom consists in showering only that much that is necessary for the purpose of the earth. In the winter, in the summer, in the rains and in the spring, it rains heavily or it drizzles and that much of the rain that is enough for the purpose of the earth falls although at the source, from where the rain comes, there is no scarcity rather there is plenty of water. Just as, the grocer sells you sugar in small packets. It does not mean that he has a little stock. Likewise, the chemist who gives medicines wrapped up in a piece of paper has much greater stock. They have immeasurable stock of sugar and medicine, all of which cannot be contained in a paper or in a packet. Someone sarcastically remarked to the Prophet, "Why was the Quran revealed by degrees, a verse at a time and not the whole at once.?" He replied, "Ignorant ones! You do not know that if the whole were revealed at one time to me, I would be consumed and not a trace of me might be left." This is because he who is wise can follow by a hint, or many things through one thing. A line of the book reveals to him the contents of the whole. This can be illustrated thus. In an assembly, many persons are hearing a story. One amongst the audience knows the whole story, although he has come in the middle but from a certain description, he catches up the whole trend and in his body are seen the whole set of emotions caused on them who have heard the whole story and are in attendance from the start. But those who have never heard the whole story previously and have come in the middle, follow only that much of the story that they have heard. Likewise, you go to a grocer for sugar. He looks at your face and finds out how much money you have brought, then, although he has large quantity of sugar in his stock, he gives you only that much for which you pay. In the spiritual path, faith and courage are the current coins. You will hear that much of the discourse as you have courage and faith in you. When you come to purchase sugar, your bag will be examined, how much it will contain and according to its capacity the sugar will be doled out to you. But if you come with camels and large bags on them to purchase sugar, the seller will send for weighmen for he knows that you will not be satisfied with a maund or two. So, there are men whose thirst cannot be quenched with the water of a thousand rivers whilst a few drams satisfy another. If on one person is bestowed more than his capacity, he will burst. This is true not only with internal virtues like philosophy and wisdom, it holds good in the case of everything. There are numerous mines of silver and gold. But a man gets according to his capacity. If he gets more, he will not be able to endure the heat and will turn mad. Have you not seen that Majnun and Ferhad in love for their beloveds of flesh and blood (human beings) wandered in the forests and over mountains aimlessly? This was because their passions exceeded their capacity to bear them. They turned mad. Look at Pharoah. He got more wealth and treasures than he could dream of. He lost his head and began to measure shoulders with God and His Omnipotence. God says "There is not one thing of which I have not got huge treasures, whether it is good or evil, but I always confer on every person according to his capacity."

Yes, here is a person who has faith, but does not understand the meaning of it. Just as a child likes a leaf but does not actually know in what he believes. So also, a tree is dried up for lack of water but it does not understand thirst. The existence of man can be compared to a flag. First, that flag (man) is put up, then the Lord introduces in him from whichever direction He desires, understanding, anger, unpleasantness, charity, fear, hope and numerable qualities and states. Armies are assembled underneath this flag. From a distance, to the people only the flag is visible but if a man draws closer to it, he witnesses many people there. This nearness or distance is not measured in terms of space. It means that to the ignorant person only the body is visible whilst the enlightened one sees the many secrets it hides, and qualities and virtues it possesses.

A certain person came to Maulānā. Maulānā inquired of him where he had been as he wanted to see him. He replied that a certain thing happened which kept him back. The Maulānā said, "I too knew that the thing would happen. I wish it may not recur. That happening which causes separation may not happen again. Verily, all things emanate from Him. But when you attribute them to Him, they are allright but when you assign them to yourself, they lose their value. What the Dervishes say is correct, namely, looked at from the standpoint, that they emanate from the Lord, they are good and well but looked at from our standpoint namely, that we are their creators, they become wrong. Evil deeds, theft, impiety, prayerlessness, heresy on one side and faith, piety and prayers on the other side if looked at from the standpoint that they emanate from the Lord, they are good but if they are looked at from our standpoint, they are both good or bad according to our actions. The actions that we perform namely, theft, heresy and evil are bad and to believe in the unity of God, to pray and to be charitable are all good things. Just as, the king, in his kindgom has dungeons, scaffold, pain and misery as also wealth, power, flags, bands, army and so many other things. Looked at from the point of view of the king, they are commendable possessions, just as the award of these valuable objects is his excellence, so also hanging the criminal and imprisoning the ruffian in dungeon are also his excellent acts and possessions. So, if these things are judged from the point of view of the ruler, they deserve applause, but if they are judged from the standpoint of the common people, the rewards and scaffolds are not equally praiseworthy.

## CHAPTER 9

Somebody asked Maulānā what was superior to prayers. He answered that the spirit behind the skeleton of prayers was more praiseworthy than its outer form. The essence was to be appreciated more than the form. The second answer is that faith is higher than prayers. This is because prayers are ordained five times a day but faith is insisted upon every moment. Default in prayers is many times excused for sufficient reasons and lack of punctuality is not heavily dealt with. But faith does not permit such lapses. The second excellence of faith on prayers is that it is constantly to be kept on, not for a moment can its absence be pardoned, nor any delay or unpunctuality is connived at. To retain faith and not to pray is profitable but prayer in the absence of faith is something useless. Just as, the mode of prayers in the various religions is different, but the form of faith in all of them is the same. Neither its form, nor its states, nor its purpose, changes from one to the other. Besides it, there are other distinctions which reveal themselves according to the attainment of the individuals. God says "I have treasures of everything with Me, but I distribute them according to the attainments of the individuals. Before the kneader of the flour, the person who hears the discourse is like the flour that is kneaded. The discourse is like the water that is put in the flour. Only that amount of water which is sufficient for well kneading is put in it.

> My eyes do not turn to any one else, what am I to
> do? If you have to make any complaint of Him make
> it to yourself for you are the light of the eye.

What I mean when I say that my eyes do not turn to anybody else is that they do not seek any other besides yourself. So, I am helpless, for you are light of these eyes and this is because you understand your nature although you have not yet annihilated your ego, else, you would be a million times better.

A story is often told that there was a very lean, and humble person who appeared in the people like an humble little bird. So meek was he that even the meekest person regarded him humbler than he and prayed to the Lord that he was not so low as he. Since he had seen him, he had ceased to complain to the Lord about his ugliness. Yet, in spite of this, the gentleman was very arrogant and used to utter before the Prime Minister the words that were very unbecoming, harsh and utterly vain. This caused the vazier great annoyance, yet he controlled himself and did not display his displeasure. Once, he could not restrain his wrath and cried out, "Ye people! This mean fellow was picked up by me, brought up in affluence at my expense and today the result of the boon, I conferred on him, is that he calls me names and behaves in a such petulant manner. The mean fellow, immediately, stood up and remonstrated and addressing those assembled there said, "Ye people, ye nobles and ministers! the Vazier has stated truth. I have attained this eminence at the cost of his father and grandfather. It is the reason that I have acquired this arrogance and petulant manner today. Had I been nurtured in different surroundings, had eaten the food of another person and had enjoyed another persons hospitality, I am sure, I would have been more handsome, better behaved, stronger and abler. The Vazier prides that he picked me up from the street. In utter helplessness, I am today. Would to the Lord that I had been mere earth and then some one else had picked me up, then I am sure, I would not have been formed so ugly as to be the laughing stock of the people."

The soul of Lord's servant, who is brought up by the Lord's beloved, attains to the full stature. But the soul of him who has for his teacher a cunning and deceitful person, who is brought up by him and who performs his spiritual practice under him, is for ever displeased with him like the poor, weak and dejected person of the above illustration. They who do not believe, have the Devil for their teacher who takes them out of light and ushers them into darkness.

In man's temperament, at the time of creation, all knowledge was kneaded in his essence in his self. It is for this reason that the soul displays, at times, these secret qualities, just as clear water manifests all that lies in its bottom and above it on its surface. The quality of the water (namely, reflecting the bottom and the surface), the Lord has placed in its nature. This virtue He has put in it without any effort or education on its part. But just as, the moment, water mixes with some colour or dirt, it loses its virtue of clarity and that essence (reflective power) leaves it and it forgets it. The Lord has, therefore, sent the prophets and the teachers. They are like that great ocean of clear water that if any little quantity of that dirt or coloured water falls in it, it loses its colour and dirt and becomes like the clear and pure water of the ocean. He, then, remembers wisdom that he had forgotten. When he sees himself clearly, he is reminded that in eternity he was similarly clear and neat. He understands that the colour and dirt were merely a temporary phase. He is reminded of his condition previous to the time he took upon himself the dirt and colour temporarily. He says, "It is the same food that we had received before." The Prophets and the godly men are like the reminders who tell us of things we have forgotten and disclose to us our previous condition. It is not true that they introduce something new in our nature. Now, that dirty water which believes that it is part of the great ocean and its property, loses itself in that ocean. On the other hand, that which does not recognise the ocean and considers itself of a genus different and of a separate family continues in its dirty condition and colour and tries to avoid the waters of the ocean, with the result that such a one ever recedes from the ocean from day to day and therefore, it has been said, "The soul which held Him dear was merged in Him but that which disliked Him always continued to remain away from Him and was separated from Him." So God has said, "Verily, a prophet who was of your stock came to you." It means that the little water and the river are of the same family and are of the same nature and essence. The fact that the little water does not see its similarity with the water in the ocean is due to no cause in the water itself but the reason is to be found in the dirty companionship it has formed here. It is the evil friend's reflection that is reflected in the water and in delusion, it cannot understand that and so, it avoids the water of the ocean. Similarly, he who eats clay does not know whether he does it out of his natural desire or because of some malady from which he suffers.

You must know that whatever tradition or verse is cited in support of an argument is like the evidence of a witness and it is capable of different interpretations (like witnesses who are of different classes and are deposing to suit the occasions) just as there may be the same two witnesses who attest to a trust deed and may also be attesting witnesses to a marriage declaration. In both the cases, they depose in a manner which is useful to the issue before them. Their faces are the same but their internal intentions are different. "May God bestow the joy like the colour of blood and fragrance like that of musk."

## CHAPTER 10

I said to him, "God felt like meeting you." He was also praying to God, "May thou meet me!" Maulānā said, "It will be difficult to see God when the wish to meet Him is present there because this very wish will be like veil on the face of God. He will not be able to see God unveiled at the time." This explains that many desires for the things of the world and its possessions viz. palaces, knowledge and affection of relations, parents, brothers and sisters, are created by the Lord to serve as so many veils between man and God. They do not permit him to see God. When he will leave the world, he will witness the Lord unveiled as these veils will be absent. Then, he will find that what he is seeking is the One Reality and all his difficulties will be solved then. He will get an answer to all those queries that are confronting him and all the secrets will be revealed. God will not answer every one of those questions individually but as if by a flash, the answer to all his questions will be given in a moment and all his difficulties will be removed, as in the winter every one is wrapped with clothes due to the cold and is seated by a warm oven or in a heated cave and as the various plants due to the poisonous effect of winter's cold are bereft of fruits and leaves and hide all their possessions within their body with a view to avoid injury at the hands of cold but when the spring comes, by its manifestation, it answers the queries relating to growth and decay and they are solved in a moment. All the causes that were responsible for suppression sprout forth and unveil themselves. The leaves appear once again and they now understand the reason for the previous disappearance.

God has created these veils with the object that man may be able to gaze at Him, for, if He appears in His nakedness and glory, these eyes of a man have not the power to stand that effulgence and bear with His glory without something intervening. These veils are in our interest and beneficial to us so that we may rap benefit by gazing at His glory. Take the case of our sun, we derive benefit from its light. With its light, we walk in the streets and can discriminate between evil and good and receive warmth at its hands. The trees and orchards bloom due to its warmth, the bitter and unripe fruits turn sweet and are ripened. Mines of rubies, emeralds, gold and silver are created by the heat of the sun. But these benefits do not come out directly, but indirectly through various means. If the sun were to come too close to us, none of these profitable effects would be produced, instead the whole world and the objects contained in it would be consumed to ashes. On the mountains, it sheds its lustre and thereby acting from behind the veil transforms the flowers, greenery and plants into a blooming bride. But when it bursts in its virginity and nakedness, it burns it to ashes and turns it to pieces. When the Lord of Moses manifested Himself in His fulness, the mountain was shattered to bits."

Someone said, "But, it is the very sun which shines also in winter." The Maulānā said, "I had intended to illustrate a point and not to investigate into the reality of the sun. But when you reach His presence, there is no need for an illustration, remark, hint or example or a circuitous argument. To be like a thing is one thing and to illustrate it is another. All the things of that place cannot be understood with the help of the intellect but seldom does the intellect give up its attempt or we shall not call it intellect. Intellect is that which is busy all the day and night anxiously striving to get God and is restless to attain Him. This is so in spite of the fact that God cannot be understood by the intellect and He is, as a matter of fact, beyond the comprehension of it and is also incapable of being circumscribed by it. Intellect is like the moth and the Beloved Lord is like the flame. Do you not see that the moth hovers restlessly, all the time about the flame and ultimately, burns itself in it? Although the moth experiences the pangs of burning, yet it does not run away from the flame. Although another insect externally may look like the moth and may hover round the flame, yet it will not sacrifice itself on the flame. So we shall not call it a moth nor shall we call flame, on which the moth did not offer itself. It follows that we shall not style him a man who gives up striving a flame effort and sits content, and if he pretends that he has understood truth, I would say, it is not truth that he has comprehended. Therefore, we shall call him a man who is constantly striving and restlessly hovering round the flame i.e. God, and that is truth which consumes man, and takes him out of the ambit of all knowledge and beyond the circle of intellect.

## CHAPTER 11

Amir Parwānā said that formerly when Maulānā Burhan Uddin appeared before him, he used to apologise that he did not want to appear before him as he was experiencing different states, in some of which he was discoursing, in others he was wooed to silence, sometimes, he was paying attention to his disciples and instructing them by casting cooling glances at them, whilst on other occasions, he was sitting alone in solitude and at times, he was seated in meditation and was passing through the valley of amazement. That was the reason why Amir was requested not to meet him and without any purpose take the trouble to see him, lest he should approach him at a time when due deference might not be shown to him, and he might not have the leisure to instruct him and converse with him. Therefore, the Maulānā added that it was but right for him that when he had leisure, he would call on his friends and give them the requisite instructions and confer benefit on them thereby. Thereupon, Amir Parwānā said that he replied to the Maulānā Burhān Uddin that the object of his coming to Maulānā was not to seek his instructions or hold converse with him but to gain by the visit to him and have the benefit and honour of sitting amongst his servants and if he did not converse with him when he called on him, that too had its beneficial effect on him. For, then, he would learn that he should not keep good Moslems (who called on him) waiting when they came to see him but call them at once, because waiting is a very trying and terrible experience. The Maulānā gave him a foretaste of its bitterness and instructed him not to behave in that fashion with others.

The Maulānā remarked, "That was not the object in keeping him waiting. His object was sheer kindness." People often say that the Lord says, "When you weep bitterly, I can at the moment, fulfil your wishes, but your plaints are so sweet to Me that they give Me pleasure to hear them." It is for this reason that a period intervenes between the prayers and their fulfilment, so that one may weep still more bitterly and complain harder, because that appeals to the Lord intensely. This can be illustrated thus: Suppose there are two mendicants who go to the door of a certain gentleman. One of them is dear to the master of the house and the other is disliked by him. The master of the house asks the servant to give the alms immediately to the person he dislikes so that he may depart atonce and worry him no more with his unpleasant appearance. He asks the servant to keep the other he likes, waiting on the pretext that the food will take sometime to be ready. This is because he is fascinated by his appearance. The Lord says, "That is the reason why I desire heartily that my friends may be kept longer by my side that I may enjoy their company to my heart's content and they may also profit by my company according to their desire."

The reason is that when these friends meet one another closely here so that on the Day of Judgment their friendship will be further cemented and they will recognise one another as having lived together in this world, their remembrance will lead to an earlier meeting. Man does not forget the friends too soon. In this world, do you not find that he to whom you are devoted or love you him as a dear friend of yours and who is like a Joseph unto your eyes lowers himself before you the moment, he does an evil act. Your eyes have no place for him and he is forsaken by you. He is no more a Joseph to you, but is transformed into a wolf, although in appearance, he is as before but now, you detest him. A single passing act of his lowered him in your eyes and you have severed him from you. Now, on the Day of Judgment when every one will be reborn and this nature will be converted into another, how will it be possible for you to recognise him there until you have fully understood and recognised him here. The net result of the discourse is that you should understand your friends fully and forgive them their shortcomings which are short-lived and reach the bottom of their nature and comprehend them fully. For this exchange of greetings is not real self of men. This is mere externality.

A certain person said that he knew a man fully well and could give his credentials correctly. The other gentleman inquired, "Then, please give them." He replied, "The said person is my tenant and owns two bullocks," and gave other minute details of him. Similar is the kind of knowledge which the people generally have about others, and describe them as above, namely, that they have two bullocks and so on. But this is a mistake and is not the correct description of the person, nor his chief mark and is a useless description that leads nowhere. I, therefore, ask you to be unmindful of the virtues and shortcomings of a man, try to probe deeper into his nature and try to seek and understand his ingrained virtues which are the real man.

I am extremely surprised when people ask me "Why do the Prophet and sages fall in love with God and why do they adore Him when He possesses no settled abode, nor any particular form, nor He can be classed under any category? They say, "How is love possible with such a Beloved? How can one gain comfort and strength from Him? How can man be affected by Him although the people meditate on Him day and night and that is their principal vocation?" But just ask of the questioner, "Do you love your friend, to seek any assistance from him? You enjoy the assistance, comfort, pain and pleasure only through his kindness. All these influences have no set place of their own, or any abode. They cannot be seen by the eyes nor experienced. But the man is always affected by these experiences internally and is assisted by these effects. Are you not surprised at the thought how one is happy and enjoys in the eternal home and profits by it?"

A philosopher did not believe. Once, he fell and found all assistance useless. He called a physician who believed in the existence of God. The latter asked his patient what he wanted. The patient answered, 'health'. The God fearing physician, then, inquired if he could just describe the form of health in order that he might search for it and get it for him. The ailing philosopher said, "Health has no form nor any definite colour nor expression. I cannot, therefore, understand how you can trace it." The physician, then, said, 'Tell me what is it that you call health?' The patient said that he knew that much that when he was healthy, he felt strong, put on flesh and change in complexion and looked fresh. The physician said that was not the answer to his question. He asked what the nature of health was and how it could be recognised. The patient replied that he did not know as health had no form and no features. The physician said, "If you are converted to Islām (faith) and desist from your early heresy and faithlessness, I promise I shall bring health to you and you shall recover completely."

People, once, asked the Prophet, "Assuming that the attributes of God are proved and established, is it possible for the people to derive benefit through those divine qualities?" The Prophet replied, "Look at the sky, it is by its external form that it is deriving benefit from that great Reality. Do you not observe that the revolution of the planets, the seasons and the changes in weather and proper distribution of rainfall at definite periods and in specified amount are all dependent on His plan? After all, what does this lifeless cloud know where, when and how much to rain at a place? You also notice that whichever seed is accepted by the ground sprouts out and gives a tenfold return. After all, there must be some power which sees to all this. Try to see and know Him. And take assistance of that understanding and revelation as you employ in matters relating to the body of a man. So also, by the spiritual body's aid seek to understand the divine realities.

When the Prophet got beside himself, intoxicated with God-consciousness, he used to say, "God says this," Although the words came were from his lips, yet, in reality, he had ceased to intervene between himself and God. The real speaker was God Himself. When he realised himself, he found that he was ignorant of all that he had said before. But, when he annihilated his ego, through such instrumentality of tongue, such words came out. He realised on that occasion that he was not then, what he was before (ignorant). This is the possession of God. Just so when he was in that state, he described things and events from the lives of the Prophets and sages and of a period thousands of years gone by and he also foretold what would happen till the Day of Judgment, in heaven, on the earth, in the void and in the universe. True, they are ephemeral but he does not say that in their entirety. They are accidentally brought into existence for else, can that which is ephemeral make us acquainted with that which is eternal and lasting? This means that it is not that he himself spoke but it is God speaking through him "It is true that he does not speak of his own accord but whatever he speaks is something revealed."

God is beyond all descriptions and forms. That which relates to Him cannot be confined in words and sounds. But, it is up to Him, if He so desires, to manifest Himself through any language, at any time, and through any sound. The case is similar to the various animal forms of stone constructed at various caravans *sarāis* (inns) and roadsides indicating sources of water through which water trickles out. All the wise men know that it is not the stone images that are the sources of water that flows through them but that it has its source also somewhere. If you want to know a man, engage him in conversation and you will know him. An exception may arise when applying this rule in the case of a person who is acquainted from before that the object of conversing with him is to gauge his depth, and then he will be cautious in his conversation and keep silent or carefully express himself sparingly. The case is similar to that of a child who told his mother that in darkness a shadow like that of a demon was visible to him in the night in the jungle. He was frightened of it. The mother advised him not to get frightened but once, attack it courageously when it appeared, and then, he would realise that it was not reality but a shadow. The child replied, "Dear mother, if the dark one has also been advised by his mother as you have advised me, what shall I do." It, therefore, follows that if someone is warned already that he should not converse lest his secret should be revealed, how is it possible for me to know him?" Maulānā replied, Try to keep silent before such a person and give up yourself completely to him biding time when he should speak himself. Even then, if he continues to be silent, it is possible that some words may unconsciously blurt out from yourself whereby some idea may cross your mind or a meaning may flash to you and thereby, you may come to know something about him. The reason is that this blurting out on your part is due to his reflection which he has cast on you and which has found a seat in your inner consciousness which has been aroused in you.

The great teacher Sarārāzi whilst seated with his disciples, once, ordered one of them to fetch a roasted piece of meat for a disciple seated among them. The others inquired how he could know that the particular disciple wanted a piece of roasted meat. The teacher replied, "It is now thirty years that all desires in me are dead and none are left now. I have cleaned myself of all desires and have become clear of all scratches and impressions like a mirror. In my heart, arose the desire for meat so, I concluded it must be the desire of the one seated before me. The reason is clear that if an impression appears in the mirror, it follows that before it there must be somebody who is responsible for the impression.

To achieve fulfilment of certain of his desires, a sage was undergoing a fast and penance of forty days. He was advised by somebody that he could not attain his goal by the penance and that he should give it up and search a sage whose glance will lead to the fulfilment of his goal. The penitent inquired where he would find such a sage. The man replied, "In the yonder mosque." The man asked, "But in the large concourse of people in the mosque, how shall I be able to spot out the sage I seek for?" He was told to go in the mosque and the sage would himself come to him and cast his glance at him, and he would be able to recognise this from the fact that on such occurrence, the jug of water would drop from his hand and he would fall senseless on the ground. Thereby, he should know that the sage had cast his glance. The man did as he was directed and as he entered the concourse of the people in the mosque, he experienced a queer sensation in his body. He shrieked, the jar fell from his hand and was broken, whilst he fell senseless on the ground. When every body had left the mosque, he recovered his senses and found himself alone there. He did not see the Dervish but his purpose was achieved.

"Some of the devotees are such as do not desire to reveal themselves to the people out of modesty and grandeur. But on those who are real seekers, they confer their blessings and lead them to their goal. Such Dervish-kings are far and few in number."

I asked the Maulānā, "Do such people come near you?" The Maulānā said, "Coming near has lost all significance for me. Years have gone by since "coming near" has left me. If, at all, they visit me it is really to meet my that idea on which they have fixed their faith. People told Christ that they would come to his abode. Christ replied, "But where is my house in this world or when was it there?"

There is a story current about Christ that once he was passing through a forest when it began to rain heavily and he entered a cave where dwelt a fox. When, for a moment, the rain stopped, to Christ came the message of God, "Come out of the abode of fox, for fear of you the young ones of the fox are not entering the cave." Christ shrieked and said, "O God! Even the fox has a den but alack! the son of Mary has no place of shelter to protect against the inclemency of weather."

Maulānā, thereupon, commented, "Although a fox could pride in such an abode, yet he could not vie with a Beloved Who could even cast him out of it. Fortunate art thou that such a One, Who can turn thee out exists for thee. What does it matter, then, that you have no home? For, with this mercy conferred on you namely, of turning you out, the crown of mercy has been placed on you and you have been accepted as a dear one, His own. That he turns you out is something more valuable than thousands of kingdoms, happy other worlds and the highest of heavens.

Therefore, Amir should not mind if he called and I did not come out to meet him immediately. He should consider that, after all, what was the purpose of his coming. Did he mean to rise himself in his estimation or did he want to honour me? If he had come to honour me, the longer the stay, the greater the honour he bestowed on me. If, on the other hand, he desired to rise himself in his estimation by meeting me, then also, the longer he waited, and the more he experienced the pain of waiting for me, the greater was the benefit that fell to his lot and the greater were the blessings conferred on him. It, naturally, follows that whatsoever may be the outlook from which he sees a thing, his purpose is achieved two-fold. He should, therefore, feel delighted.

## CHAPTER 12

The people often say that similar hearts meet together and feel for one another. This, too, has a meaning, only that they have not understood the full import of it. For, if the heart itself is the witness, it does not need arguments to support it.

The Junior Amir said, "This is true, if the heart feels, the further evidence is not necessary. But the fact is that the functions of the heart, the ears and the eyes are different and every one must have something to one's liking to satisfy one's taste."

The Maulānā replied, "If the heart is in meditation, luckily all these get engaged in it likewise and the tongue becomes useless. Just see that although Laila had not the gift of divine beauty in her, her body was formed of gross material, water, clay, and her charms were merely human and gross, yet that gross passion was so strong that it intoxicated Majnun so much that he ceased to crave with these human eyes to have look at Laila and he did not desire with these external ears to hear her voice," He said, "In my both eyes, there is thy picture formed by imagination and I am repeating with my tongue thy name and my heart is filled with remembrance of thee, tell me, then, O beloved, how can thou get away from me?"

Even affection for the physical beings could grow so much in intensity that the love might so torture that the lover could turn his mind from everything and see the beloved ever near him. All his senses might be so steeped in his beloved that his ears, nose, limbs and such like craved for no other tasty thing. This craving on the part of one of these senses was the proof of the unsatisfied desire in comparison to the other limbs. Only this sense had just a sip at the cup of bitter passion, and that was not enough to intoxicate him completely, so if another limb of his desires, it craves for larger quantity. Every sense must have its individual enjoyment. Esoterically looked at in their essence, all are a whole. It is only exoterically that you find them (senses) distinct.

When one of the limbs gets intoxicated, all others are absorbed in it. So long as a fly is in the air, its wings, its head, its body and its limbs are all moving, but the moment, it is immersed in honey, all its parts cease to move and flutter and reach a unified state. This is the state of absorption. When personality (ego) of the seeker (drowning person) does not intervene and all capacity for effort finally leaves him, all actions and sensibility depart from him. Only he remains drowned in the water. If, then, any act is manifested by him, it will not be attributed to him but will be assigned to the water itself.

But, so long as, he throws his hands and feet in the water and displays various gestures, we shall not call him a drowned person. If he shrieks or sighs in agony, he cannot be said to have attained the state of absorption.

Mansur-Al-Hallāj meant to convey the same idea when he cried out "I am Truth." People, however, took it to be a bold assertion and a heretical profession on his part. I am, however, inclined to think that a bolder profession is to say, "I am the servant." "I am Truth" is the height of expression of humility, for, to call oneself a slave is to recognise two entities of existence, one that of the Master, God and the other that of the slave, namely, his own self. But, he who says, "I am Truth" recognises only one existence of God, for, he must mean to convey that he has ceased to exist, only God exists. There is no other existence but of His. His own self is for ever destroyed or better merged in the Divine Self. This is the height of humility. People, however, do not appreciate it.

He who supplicates before the Lord, puts his self between himself and the Lord although his prayers are to God, yet, while he sees God, he sees himself too. He cannot, then, be said to be absorbed in Him. He, in whom there is no motion or action left or whatever action is visible, it is the motion of the water alone, can be called drowned.

A lion pursued a stag. The stag ran. There were two entities of existence, one of the lion and the other of the stag. But, when the lion caught him and pressed him under his claws, the stag fell senseless before him at that time, only the individuality of the lion was left and that of the stag was annihilated.

Immersion (in God consciousness) is a sort of fear, as one feels for the lion or the tiger or the ruffian, only its nature is different and it is but meet that the servant should fear the master. This is, in order that the people may know that fear also issues from Him, just as comfort, peace, joy, food, drink and sleep are all from Him and are His gifts First, God manifested Himself in a state which He witnessed in His wakeful state, later on, He manifested in the state of the lion or tiger or fire and this in such a way that the devotee understands that this appearance of the lion or the tiger or the fire is not the genuine appearance but that the reality is making its appearance in a disguise of a pictorial form. Later on, He manifests Himself in all His glory and beauty in His natural form and displays before him such gardens with buds, fine canals, beautiful damsels, various delicacies, beautiful dresses, white shining horses and many cities. On looking at them, he is convinced that it is the Lord Who is displaying Himself. Those various things are all from Him. He understands that all these-joy, fear, and hope are from Him and these he witnesses with his inner sight. It follows, therefore, that this fear of his is not like that fear which is caused by the people because this is vividly painted and requires no argument, God having displayed it in His fulness.

The philosopher also knows these things, but he appreciates them intellectually, and those intellectual arguments are fleeting. That enjoyment which is the result of arguments is not lasting. As long as, you are arguing, a man is happy hearing them and feels elated and puffed up. A man follows by pursuing arguments that there is a builder of a house. He cannot be blind. He can do whatever he likes. He is present, not absent, is living and not dead and he existed before this house came into existence. All this he will follow from the arguments and arguments are shortlived and are soon forgotten. But when the saints practise austerities, they realise the Builder and witness Him with the eyes of faith. They dine with Him and hold discussions with Him. The Builder, then, will never be absent from their eyes. So also, as God is permeating a man's self, if a man sins, thereby he is not contaminated. If he commits a crime, then, too, he cannot be described as criminal, because he is immersed in water of God consciousness.

A certain king ordered every one of his servants to hold a cup of gold in his hand as he was soon expecting a guest. His favourite servant was also commanded likewise. But, when the king appeared, the favourite servant was so bewitched by the sight of the king, so intoxicated, that he got beside himself. In that state of selflessness, the cup fell from his hands and it was broken to pieces. When the other servants saw this action on the part of the favourite, they thought that they should also act likewise and purposely threw away their cups. The king was much displeased with this and asked them the reason of this behaviour. They replied that they followed the favourite servant in this. The king remonstrated, "Ye fools! that act was not done by him," It was I who was responsible for it. To all external appearance, all the servants erred but the action of the favourite servant was pure service (devotion) and much higher than that of all other servants because that servant was particularised and all other servants were subordinate to him. This was because the first servant was the king whilst the other servants were the king's servants in view of the observation (of the king) referred to above. That particular slave was the king while the gown of service that he had donned was mere sham. He was steeped in the glory of the king. Says God, "If you had not existed, O Muhammad, I would not have created heaven." This, too, is the statement like unto "I am Truth."

The above expression means that God created heaven for Himself. Although it is in a different form, this is like the statement, "I am Truth."

Although the words of the saints are expressed in a hundred different languages, they are the same. Although apparently, they appear as different, Truth is one and the path to it is also one. How can you, then, expect that their words would be different? Although the words may look as distinct, really the meaning is the same. There is difference only in externals, but internally (esoterically) they are the same. Take an illustration, suppose the king orders that a tent may be pitched up. One of the servants twists the threads of the rope, one makes the poles, another is preparing the tarpaulin and the other is sewing it. Some one is tearing the cloth in proper lengths. Apparently every one is seen to be acting differently, being occupied in different occupations, but really they have all one purpose in view and are collected to complete one business. Just so, if you look at the affairs of the world also and examine them carefully, you will find that all of them are carrying on the commands of God whether he is an evil-doer or a good man disobedient or faithful, Satan or an angel, all are engaged in praying to God. None is exempt from the obeisance to his Lord. Suppose, the king were to examine his slaves for various reasons to find out who amongst them was sincere and who was not, who stood by his words and who did not, so that the sincere and the hypocrite may be distinguished. For this self-examination, it is necessary to have somebody who would arouse passion so that the faith of the slave may be tested. If no such incitement is present, how will it be possible to realise his sincerity? He who is responsible for this incitement is also doing it at His command, for, he is also carrying out the order of the king. He ordered the wind to separate the restive objects from the restless ones, and remove the insects from the trees and the fruits so that the object may be left pure and alone after the removal of the insects.

A king ordered a pretty slave of his to dress herself gorgeously and appear before his servants that he might be able to test their virtue. The action of the maid apparently appears to be a sinful act but, in fact, she is obeying her master, the king. When Lord's devotees see with their divine sight, they notice that everyone, be he good or evil, pious or impious in this world is praying. "And is there anything which is not engaged in singing the praises of the Lord?" It follows, therefore, for those people this world is the Day of Judgment. For the Day of Judgment connotes that on that day, all shall be engaged in praying to the Lord and in no other work. These devotees are seeing this interpretation here in this world, and at this moment. They say, "Even if the veils are removed, our faith shall remain constant and not increase any way."

In words ordinarily, we describe the knower of God as a man of learning. God is, therefore, described as the Learned One but we cannot call Him the knower of God. The knower is he who did not know before but knowledge has dawned on him now. But this cannot be said of God. In ordinary discourse, however, the status given to the learned is lower than the one accorded to the knower of God. This is because the knower is he who transcending the ambit of argument has known the thing. He has witnessed knowledge with his open eyes and has understood it thoroughly. In common parlance, the knower is thus described.

People say that a single learned person is better than a hundred persons of piety. How is it possible for this learned person to be superior to hundred pious persons? After all, this person follows the course of piety because of his learning. Without learning, piety is impossible. What is, after all, piety? It is to leave this world and to devote oneself to God and turn one's attention to that end. This, therefore, requires, as a preliminary condition, realisation of the ephemeral nature of the world, its ugliness and the glory of the next (spiritual) life and its immortality and to understand the value of austerities in spiritual life and its piety and the meaning of prayers. All this is learning and without knowledge of it, piety is impossible so, the pious is both pious and a man of learning. The people have not understood the meaning of the expression that the learned man is superior to hundred pious men. This is a different knowledge beyond his former knowledge and piety which has been bestowed on him by his God and this new knowledge is the fruit of the former knowledge and the piety that he had acquired. Such a man of learning is, of course, superior to hundred pious men. Take an illustration. A man planted a tree which bore fruit. Then, this tree which has borne fruit is superior to those hundred trees that have not done so far. It is also possible that those trees may never bear fruit. The path that leads to Meccā is fraught with difficulties. The pilgrim who has reached Meccā is, of course, superior to those pilgrims who are still on the way. For, who knows if they will reach Meccā (the Reality) or not? So one reality is superior to hundred doubts."

The Junior Amir said, "At least, the sojourner is hopeful that he will reach the destination." Maulānā remarked, "There is great distinction between the expectant and one who has realised as there is great distinction between one who fears and one who is fearless. To what purpose is all this distinction, for, every one, here knows, that what I state is to the effect that one stage of success is to be distinguished from the other. The highest place accorded to Prophet Muhammad is due to the greater degree of peace attained by him in comparison to the other prophets, for, it is due to the knowledge of every body that, the other prophets too, enjoyed peace but of a lower degree, although all of them dwelt above the degree of worldly fear for there are degrees of peace and grades in it. God says, "Among those Prophets I have assigned grades to them, one higher than the other," In this world of fear, it is possible to describe those grades, however, it is not possible to describe and give hints regarding the grades of peace in this world for they have no signs in this world. When we look into this world of fear, we notice that various people make varied sacrifices offering in the name of the Lord. Some offer their bodies, others their wealth and some their lives, one gives alms, the other fasts, and the third one says his prayers and amongst the persons who pray are those who do so five times a day and yet others who do it a hundred times a day. We witness their acts and so can also see their grades which are mentioned and enumerated. They can be described too. You can, likewise, conceive of the route from Kaiseria to Qouiniya whose stages you can describe. The first stage is Qima, the second Cobrakh, and thereafter Sultan etc. But the journey from Antalia to Egypt is by water and there is no description possible of the intervening stations. They are known only to the mariners. Those living on the land cannot understand them and so, it is not possible for them to describe those stages."

The Junior Amir remarked, A discourse, too, profits. If all may not be able to understand, at least, some will be able to understand, and some will be able to get certain hints and ideas. Suppose, a person keeps awake for the whole of the dark night, waiting for the morning so that he may start on the journey of the dawn. Although he is unacquainted with the conditions of the journey, yet every moment, he is approaching near the dawn. Or take the case of a man accompanying a caravan. He does not know in the dark night, overcast with clouds, the distance he has covered and the stage he has reached, but with the appearance of the day, the result of the journey dawns on him and the benefit following it appears, for, after all, he has reached a particular stage. He who for a flash of the wink remembers God, is benefited by it and his act is not without purpose. God says, "He who does a grain of good to others shall be rewarded."

But when the heart is blind and veiled, he does not know how far he has advanced. At the close of his life, it is revealed to him that this world is the preparation ground, the field for the next. God says, "Whatsoever is sown here, shall be reaped in the next world."

Jesus Christ was given to laughing too much. St. John was accustomed to weeping too much. The latter once told the former that he (Christ) was so fearless and ignorant about his faults that he should be constantly smiling. Christ said that he (John) was very unmindful of the hidden mercy that he should always be in tears. A saint was present whilst this discourse was going on. He prayed to the Lord to reveal to him the relative superiority of the rival prophets. Came the reply, "I am near him who thinks of Me in terms of goodness." This means that God is present where His servant believes Him to be. God continues, "To every servant of Mine, I am revealed in a different form as he has a specific idea of Me. I am as he thinks Me to be. I am slave to the idea where dwells the Truth whilst I am distressed with the place where Truth is absent. My servants cleanse their thoughts for, therein I dwell and it is My abode. Now, examine whereby you get greater consolation whether by shedding tears or in smiles, in fasting or in prayers, in solitude or in which of these methods is your condition better and you progress further. Adopt, then, the course that is beneficial. Make thy heart the guide care not for other instructors who try to guide you. Your heart is your preceptor. Place the suggestions of other preceptors before your heart and adopt those that are acceptable to thee. Just as when a physician approaches, a patient questions the doctor within. For, one of his doctors resides within his heart and it is he (his temperament) that accepts or rejects the medicine administered to him by the outer doctor. For this reason, the physician outside questions this doctor who is within him as to the effects produced on him consequent upon his taking the medicine, whether relief follows or the ailment is aggravated. He will answer the physician (outside) as the doctor within him directs him. The physician outside will also accept the commands of the doctor within him.

So, the real doctor is the one who dwells within thee (and it is thy temperament). When this doctor within thee grows weak, the effect of all external application is just reversed and the information that it supplies is not trustworthy. It will, then, say that the sugar it takes tastes bitter and the vinegar is sweet. Then, a necessity arises for seeking the help of the doctor outside to heal the temperament (doctor) within so that it may record correctly and resume its original function. Thereafter, this internal doctor resumes to function properly, once again as before.

So, man has also internal nature. When it is weak, whatever it expresses is incorrect and just the converse of what happens. The doctors of the spiritual ailment are prophets and saints who assist that inward temperament so that it may be set right and may function spiritually in the right manner and his heart and religious tendencies may gain strength. Therefore, it has been said, "O God, reveal unto me things in their reality that I may witness them in their nakedness."

Man is a great thing. Within him everything is written. The veils and darkness do not, however, permit him to read the knowledge that is written within him. The duties and desires of the world are like so many veils. Although man dwells in such deep darkness, yet he is able to read some of the inscriptions within him and he is acquainted with them. Consider, then, if those curtains and darkness are wholly removed, how much more will he not be enlightened? How much will he not be instrumental in giving birth to various arts and sciences, for, these various professions, namely, those of tailor, mason, carpenter, farmer, goldsmith, astronomer, doctor and the like, too numerous to detail, have all been born out of men and not produced from stones and pebbles? The popular belief that man was first instructed by a crow (in burying its dead) too started in the desire issuing from the man himself, the reflection whereof fell in the heart of the bird and prompted him to act thus. The animal is also a part of man and how can the part, then, instruct the whole? Do you not observe that when a person attempts to write with his left hand and takes up the pen, though he has a strong heart, yet his hand shivers, but when the heart orders the hand to write, it does so immediately and with confidence?

The Amir said that the Maulānā was always saying something very high. Maulānā replied that he who was fitted for high things was always receiving them and never did they (discourses) stop coming to him. If in the winter season, the leaves and fruits did not make their appearance, it should not be taken to follow that they were sitting silent. On the other hand, they were constantly working.

Maulānā continued, "The winter season is the season for making collections, the summer is meant to spend that income. All do not direct their attention to this income. Take the case of some one who holds a great feast. All the persons who are invited look to the feast, none to the income which he has collected by bits. The real thing is that income. It is by the income that the expenses go on. I am always discoursing with him who is known to me whether he is before me or away from me, or he is gone to the war front or is indulging in childish feaks. I am always with him and merged in him. In the state of silence, in the field of war and in his petty quibbles, I am with him, as though I am talking to him and seated by him. Do not consider this fist as fist. It contains an invaluable article in it. If you are not convinced, come and examine it for yourself the valuable object that it contains. Look to the other people who describe, in detail, difficult and intricate problems in prose and in verse. At this time, the attention of the Amir is directed to me and he is with me not that I am discoursing on learned subjects for that kind of discussions are taking place everywhere at all times and there is no scarcity of them. But the Amir meets me because he likes me and leans towards me and the discourse he enjoys here is of a different nature than the one given elsewhere. The Amir finds something different here from the ones he comes across elsewhere and the light he finds here is distinct.

It is current that the king once ordered Majnun to present himself before him and reproved him for his madness and shamelessness in having forsaken his home and having ruined himself completely. He asked, "What is Leila, after all, worth? What are her attributes?" The king, thereupon, offered to bestow on him the most beautiful girl. The moment Majnun was presented to the king in the hall of audience, a bevy of beautiful girls was brought before him. Majnun, however, stood crestfallen deeply engrossed in himself. The king ordered him to raise his head and look at the girls that stood before him. In case, he disobeyed the king's order, his head would be severed off. Manjun, however, replied, "Love of Leila stands with a sword over my head ready to chop it off, if I dare raise my head." So absorbed was he in his devotion for Leila that all anxiety for anybody else had left him. To cast his glance elsewhere was like courting death at the hands of the overhanging sword. He was so absorbed in the love of Leila that the thought of everybody else had left him. To look at anyone else was like the stroke of the sword on his neck, although there is no gainsaying the fact that the other girls, too, had beautiful faces, beautiful necks, beautiful noses and beautiful eyes, yet it is difficult to describe what was it that was responsible for his sticking to Leila alone.

## CHAPTER 13

The Maulānā said that he was extremely keen to meet the Amir, but as he knew that the latter was constantly engaged in humanitarian work, he did not feel like disturbing him or sending for him. The Amir replied that it was incumbent upon him to call on him, then that no fear was left that he would be disturbing him. He would be going to him himself. The Maulānā said that there was no difference whether he (Amir) called on him or he (Maulānā) went to him. It was all the same thing. He (Amir) needed not take the trouble for he (Maulānā) knew that in those days he (Amir) was the only man who was engaged in that work. He (Maulānā) was, therefore, inclined towards him. The Maulānā said, "We were just discoursing that of two persons one was childless and the other had children. Apparently we see that we take the children and deliver them to the one who is childless but by that act of ours, we cannot say that the one without children becomes one with progeny. Just as, a Dervish who was acquainted with the path reprimanded a novice on some mistake committed by him, with a view to save the latter from future mishap; apparently every body would sympathise with the novice, but the truth of the matter was that the striker (dervish) was the oppressed and he who was struck was the oppressor, for the striker was acquainted with the mystery of the path and was steeped in divinity. Whatever he did, in reality, was done by God and we could never accuse that Almighty of oppression. So also, Muhammad used to kill the people in war and although, he did it all, yet we should never call him the oppressor but always the oppressed. Or take another illustration. An enlightened westerner resides in the West. An Easterner comes to visit him. Then, in fact, the real visitant is the westerner and he who has come from the East is no pilgrim. The reason is that the whole world is like a big house and if a person gets up and goes from one corner of the house to the other, he still continues to be in the house and cannot be said to be a sojourner but the westerner who is the enlightened one and who has come from outside the house is the pilgrim. They say the beginning of Islām was in poverty, "It has, however, not been said that the birth of the easterner was in poverty."

When the prophet gained victory, he was oppressed as if defeated because in either case, he was serving Truth. He who is the servant of truth, is the oppressed one. The heart of the prophet melted when he saw the prisoners of war in chains. God sent His revelation to him, "Tell those who are in chains and tied in huge cords that if they turn believers, I will excuse them and their property shall be returned to them and they shall gain freedom and over and above that I shall forgive them and give them twice their share in eternal life." This meant that they would have two treasures, one that which they had lost in the war would be returned to them and the other they would have in eternal life. The Amir, next, enquired, "When the servant of the Lord does an act, does grace that follows such an action result, from the goodness of the act itself or is it a gift from the Lord? The Maulānā replied, "It is a gift from the Lord." Although, grace is also from the Lord, yet God in His kindness assigns both these acts to His servant, and says, "It is your doing. This is the fruit of that whatever you did." When He is so kind, it follows that he who will genuinely crave for Him shall find, Him but without a prophet that is not possible. Just as men, the Jews were devoted to Moses and obeyed him. Moses dried the sea for them and a way was made for them on it. Thus, they easily crossed the water and were safely taken to the other bank. But when they opposed Moses, they had to suffer and remain entangled in a forest for full forty years. God said that for forty years, they were roaming about aimlessly in the jungles. The aim of the leader on such occasions was to convert the opponents so that they might tread on the right path. Take an instance.

Suppose there are some soldiers who implicitly obey and follow the mandate of the Amir. He also takes care of them, equips them well and spends money to improve their lot. But, if they are not obedient, how can it be possible for the Amir to spend time to improve their condition?

In the body of man, the intellect (mind) is the leader, all other parts of the body are subordinate to it (are its subjects). As long as, the subjects behave well, the work goes on smoothly, but the instant, the body disobeys, everything goes wrong. Just watch a drunkard, the moment, he has gone tipsy, his tongue, his feet, his hands that were his subjects at one time become riotous. When he recovers from the effect of the drink, he repents and is sorry for the behaviour of the previous day. Therefore, it follows that the village constitution works so long as there is a headman whom the villagers obey. Just so the mind is careful about the body as long as it finds its orders are obeyed. It will only think of a walk if it is sure that the feet will obey his orders or else it will never think of it. Just as, in man mind is the controller, so also in this world all existence with its accomplishments and possessions including the mind and intellect are like the body (in the illustration) of which the prophet is the mind (controller). If these people who are like the body before the prophet who is like the mind, do not obey him, they will suffer and will have to repent in their lives. If, now, they become obedient to the prophet, the obedience must be of such a degree that they will also be like him. They should not be disturbed in such obedience by the prompting of their mind lest the mind should be unaware of the meaning of the secret. It follows that they should, therefore, follow him implicitly with closed eyes. Just as, if a child is sent to the tailor, he must remain obedient to the tailor (teacher) whilst he is an apprentice. If the tailor asks him to make a shirt ready, he should do so and if he is asked to sew a trouser, he must do it. That is, if he has to gain proficiency in the art, he should give up his own way of thinking and follow the one dictated by the teacher. If he does so, I feel, God shall have mercy on him and shall improve his lot. His mercy is greater than a million efforts on our part. "The night of prayer is superior to a hundred months. 'Amongst attractions one such is superior to that attraction caused by the fruit of prayers in this life and the next.' Both these statements are to the same effect, namely, when God is kind, His kindness leads to a million efforts and is responsible for them and is rather superior to them. Effort is quite a useful thing but is valueless before His kindness."

The Amir inquired, "Maulānā! Is it not that mercy of God also gives fresh strength to our efforts?" The Maulānā replied, "It is so, when mercy dawns, fresh strength follows. Did Christ make any effort when he said in the cradle," I am the servant of the Lord and the book is revealed to me. "Jahovah was in the womb when he described the attributes of the Lord. Amir Parwānā said that the prophet attained to this eminence without any effort on his part, God Himself said, "What do you inquire about the prophet whose heart has been opened to receive Islām?"

His grace is the first requisite!. When He wakes up from his dreamy state, this is His kindness for else, how can you account for the absence of this virtue amongst the Prophet's companions who lived close to him. A spark emanates. The beginning is merely small but when you put certain cotton over it, you desire the spark to develop and the necessary good consequence follows. Man, in the beginning at birth, is very weak and tiny. As it has been said, "Man is born weak." Just as, a flint strikes on an iron piece and the spark is caught by some cotton; the spark at the outset is very feeble but when that spark is tended, it develops into a conflagration and can light the whole world. As it has been said, "Of course, you are of an enviable kind."

The Amir told the Maulānā that God was very friendly to him. Maulānā replied, "Neither my conversation nor my presence before Him can lay claim to His august friendship. I do express whatever I feel like expressing out and as His grace dawns, the little talk proves to be of great benefit and it shall be permanently fixed in your heart and shall benefit you considerably. However, if it is not His wish, a million discourses will be of no beneficial effect. All will be lost and forgotten.

Just as, the spark of fire that falls on the cloth burns it, it can light it into a conflagration if it is the will of God. If, however, it is not His will, hundred sparks may fall on that cloth, they will all be extinguished and will produce no effect. "In the universe, it is all God's army." These discourses, too, are included in that army. If it is His will, they will conquer the fort of the heart and will take possession of it. If, however it is His command to His army to go, the thousand soldiers will go but if He orders them to stand by, they will do so. Whilst if He orders man to conquer, he will go and do so. He commanded a mosquito to overpower king Namrood, it did so and killed him. So it has been said, "Before the enlightened one, a pie, a sovereign, a cat and a lion are all the same." If God bestows His kindness, a pie may produce a greater benefit than a thousand sovereigns and if His grace does not dawn, a thousand sovereigns can not be as useful as a pie. Exactly so, if He commands a cat to overpower a man, the cat will do so and kill the man as Namrood was killed by a mosquito. If He so ordains, the lion will become the conveyance for the mendicant and the lion will tremble at His command. It, sometimes, does happen that the mendicant does ride a lion. Fire was turned to a flower garden. This was because God had not permitted that the fire should burn it. The conclusion is that when these people (Prophets) learnt that everything is from Him, everything before them was the same without any distinction and gradation. I hope, God willing, you will also give thought to what I have just said as that is beneficial. Suppose, a hundred thieves attack a house, but if the thief inside is not their friend, who will open the door to let them off? So also, you may give a hundred discourses but unless there is somebody within who testifies to their veracity and soundness, all is useless. As when some tree is dry and its root has rotted, you may flow a hundred rivers, it shall not be benefited. First, there must exist some life (dampness) in the tree itself before the water outside can help it.

> If a million things of effulgence were witnessed by
> a person, They are of no avail, if they are not
> connected with the root (eternity).

If the whole world be full of light, the blind eye
(being not rooted in light) cannot witness it.

The reality is distinct from the ego (self) nafs. Ego is distinct from the soul. Do you not notice how the self (ego) wanders in different places assuming different forms when you are sleeping? But, the soul remains undisturbed all the time in the body. The Commander of the faithful, Hazrat Ali said, "He who understood his self, understood Self (God). You must have noticed that self (ego) is not the Soul (Self). Assuming for the sake of argument, that by self (ego) the human Self within is meant, even this, too, is not an ordinary achievement, for the simple reason that if we dilate upon the other Self (Soul), even then man will ordinarily understand this very self, because he does not know that other Self....

Man has been defined as a rational being (animal). It follows that a man is a combination of two beings (traits). What is visible (apparent) in him in this world (outside) is the manifestation of his animality viz., his desires, wants, but his real trait (the thing within) craves for knowledge, philosophy and vision of God. The animality of man runs after the world, away from God, but his humanity turns its face away from the world. It follows that within you is the heretic as also the faithful. That is, within the body two individualities are ever fighting. The Irānians call them Yazdan (the originator of good) and Aherman (the originator of evil). No one knows who will dominate in him at any time and claim him as his own.

There is no gainsaying the fact that this world is like the autumnal season and the inorganic substances are called inanimate because they are solid and congealed. All these minerals, the stones, the mountains, and the clothes ye put on are all inorganic. If this world does not resemble the autumn, why are all objects in it dry and solid? Ordinaily, if you look, you will find that this world is a mere idea. It is not so apparent and unveiled, but it is so felt and experienced by its effects, from its winter and its deserted stages. Like the autumn season in this world, all objects are inorganic and soldified ones. This autumn is experienced through intellect. Apparently, it is not so felt. When that divine breeze blows, it will melt the very mountains, the whole earth will get covered with water, as in the summer heat of the month of June, the snow on the hills melts. So also, the solidified things will melt. Similarly, When the sun rises on the Day of Judgment, all things will melt away. The Lord shall shield you with many Kalmas (words of God), the armies, so that they shall protect you against all enemies and shall subjugate them. By enemies, I mean your internal enemies, and as compared to them, your external enemies do not count at all. Do you not see that thousands of heretics are under the control of a single heretic king, and that one king is subject to one idea? It follows that the only one thing that matters is an idea. Now ponder when a single evil idea can befool and subjugate thousands of men, what must be the detrimental effect where hundreds of evil thoughts accumulate and sway at one place, how many persons will they not subdue and how many learned men will they not overpower? We notice with our own eyes that an uncountable number of people are subjugated by a single person and controlled by him and that person himself is under the control of a single evil thought. Now, consider the excellence that will follow if instead, a pure, serene and divine thought controls and rules the sovereign controlling millions. It follows that what determines is an idea, and all forms are subordinate to it, and futile like the arms held in hand which is congealed and inanimate. So, he, who rivets his attention on form is also like congealed inert matter unaware of the essence, or of the essential meaning. Such a person, if he may be even a hundred years old, is no better than a minor child.

We have to return from the smaller towards the greater crusade. It means to fight the ego is the greater crusade. Up till now we have been fighting with the forms and the visible enemies, but now we are fighting with the big armies of ideas in order that the pious ideas may conquer the evil thoughts and exterminate them from the kingdom of the body. This is the reason why this crusade is the greater crusade. And this way is real war indeed. At this time, we have to concentrate on the ideas, although no part of the body is working without their aid and sanction, just as, the director of intellect without any visible instrument is revolving the sky. Such revolution needs no directory words or command by words or sound.

You are the reality and this world and the next are mere phantoms (fading forms). If you seek reality through forms, you will err. When this world is ephemeral, do not rest with it, rise higher and above it because reality is like the navel bladder of the musk deer, and the pleasures of the world are like perfume emitting from that musk navel. The perfume of the musk does not last for ever as it is fleeting. But clever is the man who by pursuing the perfume seeks out and attains to the musk, the source of the perfume. He who lingers with the perfume errs, because he sticks to a fleeting thing. Perfume is only an attribute of musk. So long as, the face of musk is towards the world, you experience its perfume but if that musk (Reality, Lord) hides itself or turns its face away from this world to the other world, the living ones will die. The perfume ever subsists with the musk. Wherever the musk will go, the perfume will follow it. So fortunate one is he who transcending the perfume reaches the source-musk (the Reality, God), and gains union with Him, and becomes one with Musk (eternity, or God). Having attained to that state, he will impart perfume to the world and the world will be alive and gain life from it. His former existence will subsist in mere form (not in reality) and he will be totally transformed. Take an instance, he will be like the animal who is thrown in the mine of salt, his previous form (name) alone will remain, whilst he will be transformed into the river of salt. His acts and effects will become as of salt. How can, then, his subsisting former name cause him harm? It cannot take him out of the salt. If you change the name of the salt mine, even then, he will not cease to be salt.

It is, therefore, essential for man to discard all sensual happiness and tastes which are mere shadows of the Reality, and should not rest content with them but rise. above them, although this world, too, is the reflection (image) of God's beauty and His mercy. If we consider it in relation (as offspring) with God, we shall have to admit its eternity and constancy, but if we consider it in relation with us, it is non-eternal. In relation with this creation, it must also court death like the sunlight spreading in the house. Although the rays belong to the sun, yet they are so, as long as they are connected with the sun. But when the sun is set, the light is gone (dead). So we must turn, verily, to the sun, so that the pang of separation may never be our lot. The real thing is to win the victory in the game. Some people are charitable but lack in discrimination. They lack in the faculty of recognition; whilst others are discriminative possessing the faculty of recognition but lacking in charity. But he who posseses both these qualities is of exemplary character. He is enlightened and peerless. There is a person treading the path but he does not know whether it is the correct road or not, he is merely going on like a blind man. He may, perhaps, hear the crowing of the cock, which will be a sign that he has neared a habitation. But he does not stand in comparison with the other person who is acquainted with the path and is treading it. He needs no direction or sign to guide him. It follows that in the pursuit of the spiritual path the most important and foremost thing is *mārfat* (knowledge).

## CHAPTER 14

"The night is long. Do not shorten it by sleep. The day is bright, do not cloud it by our sins." To divulge the secret, the night is so long for making prayers to the Lord and seeking favour from Him. It provides a place of satisfaction and solitude away from the disturbance of the people and annoyance caused by friends. What a veil has the Lord spread whereby the good works are protected from pretension and display, for they are done only for the sake of the Lord. The rogue is distinguished from the honest person only in the night. In the night, everything is hidden behind the veil, the day unveils everything. The wicked person is revealed in the night. He thinks that no one sees him in the night and so he says that none sees him then but he fails to notice that He, Who is the Lord of the universe and Who sees all is seeing him but he cannot see Him. Only when one is defeated or suffers from ailment or pain in the ear or teeth or elsewhere one cries to the Lord calls Him and believes that He hears one's plaints and remedies one's pain and fulfil one's wants for, the Lord distributes charity–stealthily, hiding from others. Often to gain health the people feed the poor and have faith that charitable act will bring good health and remove ailment. But when they become healthy, that faith departs from their heart and doubt arises. Then, they say, "O God! Where are those days gone when we prayed to Thee with a pure and true heart?" Seated in the corner of the prison, how often do you not repeat, "He alone is the Lord" and utter it in all humility, pray to Him and never get tired of doing it. We say, "Thou hast fulfilled all our wants and we are now released from the prison, yet we are such prisoners as, when we were in prison previously, we prayed, "O Lord, You should take us out of this dark cell of this world and usher us in the bright and lighted world of the prophets." Now I cannot understand why I do not cherish the same anguish and pang of separation for Thee as I nurtured when I was down with suffering or in the prison house. Many thoughts arise now and I do not know whether they are leading to laziness or are beneficial.

As a result of these thoughts, I feel tired and lazy. They make it impossible for me to do anything. Where has disappeared that faith which used to set fire to my thinking and urge me to work hard.

The Lord answers the prayer, and says, "Have I not told you before that your carnal self is your foe? Never make this enemy of yours and Mine your companion and friend. Always keep this enemy confined within the prison house of penance. When it is thus imprisoned, you will shine in your virginity and strength. Many times you may have noticed that pain in your tooth and in your head or ailment in your body has been the harbinger of a flash of truth in you. Then, why do you engage yourself in comforting your body and worrying yourself about it loading yourself with cares? You should not overlook your own work, never forget the great secret and never cherish any earthly desire in this ego of yours. Then, will follow the fulfilment of all your eternal hopes, and you shall be released from this dark dungeon, the world, "He who checked his self from harbouring desire and remained desireless attained to eternal paradise."

## CHAPTER 15

Sheikh Ibrāhim said that when Saifuddin Faruq ordered some body to be lashed, during the period of the whipping he remained engaged in conversation. So nobody dared to intercede with him or claim for mercy on behalf of the criminal.

The Maulānā said, "Whatever you see in this world, is the replica of the next world, in other words, all the works of this world are samples of the other world. Everything found in this world we have got from the other world and everything is found there." We have got treasures of everything but we bestow them on people according to their capacity to hold them."

The grocers stock articles in plenty but display only in small samples which they keep in show cases for display. Take for instance, chilies, gums etc, which they stock in plenty but since all cannot be contained in the glass almirahs used for display of samples, so they place there only fractions of their stock. So is the condition of man like unto the grocer's or the chemist's shop. God has kept some attributes from His treasure in man with a view that man may act in the world according to his capacity. So on him is bestowed by the Lord a little of the power of hearing, a little capacity to talk, a little attribute of charity, and a little knowledge. So man can, in a sense, be styled the druggist or dealer on behalf of the Lord. He is filling the stock day and night, whilst you go wasting and emptying it. In the day you empty them and in the night He fills them, giving you new strength. Just as, you witness light in your eyes, in the other world (with Lord) there are innumerable eyes, and sights of various kinds. A sample or a fragment is bestowed on you, with a view that you may utilise it in seeing the objects of the world. With Him the stock of, 'sight' is immense but on man has been bestowed that little quantity which is enough for beneficial use by him. He is given that much of burden which he can easily carry. The Lord says, "With Me there are treasures of everything. These attributes, too, are available with Me in immense quantity. But of these infinite attributes, I bestow only definite quantity. Consider, for example, how many millions of people are born century after century, from that very river, and ultimately, they pass away. From this, you can imagine how great must be the store with Me. He who has knowledge of that world knows how-puny is man (himself)."

Consider this world as proceeding from that mint and again disappearing in it. "Verily, we are for and from God and shall return to Him." All our limbs are samples of that place. They have come from there and will reutrn there. Compared to this world that world is very subtle. All the animals and beings of this world are of kin, bearing similar forms and skeleton, similarly constituted and they are visible because they are formed from this world material which is gross whilst that of the other world is subtle and invisible. How surprising it is that when the cool breeze of spring blows, all the plants, vegetables, shrubs, gardens and flower beds turn green and blossom forth! You consider that all this is due to the spring breeze but if you visualise the breeze itself, you will not notice any of these effects in it. Does it follow, then, in that spring breeze, such refreshing sights and gardens are wanting? Yes, it embodies them all. The effects that we see outside are merely its reflection, although in it the garden with its bloom is not visible to our eye. The reason is clear. It is because they are so subtle (impressions) that they are not visible to eyes. So also is man in whom are hidden many virtues which are not visible by external and internal appliances, whilst they make their appearance during conversation with anybody, or when causing trouble to anybody, or when quarrelling or settling terms with anybody. You do not see them in man. Likewise, the virtues that are in you cannot be seen by you, if you look within yourself, but you consider that you are devoid of those virtues. This does not mean that your original self is changed. The fact is that virtues lie hidden like the water of the river. The water of the river is not born of the river, but it is transformed into vapour. This transformation takes place due to a kind of upheaval (motion) in the water, and is visible often in the form of waves also. Emotion is something that proceeds, likewise, from your mind within thee and without any apparent visible cause. But this agitation is not visible in the river, so long as, it lies still, and even if you stand close to the banks, you can see nothing. Likewise, your life is like unto a river, in which there dwell thousands of snakes fish etc, and many kinds of creatures, which make their appearance for a moment and then again disappear in the river. All thy attributes, anger, envy, etc., make their appearance out of this river. You, therefore, know that all the qualities are in love with God and being very subtle are not visible to the eyes, only if they are properly clothed, they will be seen. Divorced of this dress, they become invisible due to their subtlety.

## CHAPTER 16

Man within himself carries, love, pain, insatiate desire, anguish and tense yearning, which cannot be allayed and satisfied even if he becomes a monarch of a million worlds. All the people are busy in acquiring knowledge following different professions and crafts and trying to gain efficiency in various sciences like astronomy etc., or rising in their services. And these they are pursuing with all assiduity, taking no rest because they have not yet attained to fulfilment of their wishes. These things they desire but they do not call it their Beloved. For, on working restlessly for the Beloved, rest and peace must come to them. So all these joys and pleasures and vocations of the world are mere ladders, not the goal, mere means to take us to the goal. The ladder is not a place where we can dwell as in an abode it is a means to cover the distance of the journey. He who starts on the journey early so that the long way may become shorter for him and all life may not be wasted merely in climbing the steps of the ladder, is a wise and clever person.

People asked the Maulānā (Rumi), "How was it that sometimes the invading Mongols carried away all our goods whilst on other occasions gave us some of articles. What did it mean?"

Maulānā replied, "Taking away by the Mongols is like taking by God and His sealing it in His treasury. Just as, you take a jar full of water from the river, then, so long as, the water is in your jug, it is your property. No body else can claim it or have a lien upon it. If somebody takes it away without your permission, it will be per force and he will be styled as criminal. But, if you again pour the water in the river from your jug, it leaves your ownership and becomes the property of everybody. It means that our property is unlawful of the Mongols but their property is legal for us."

"Monasticism is unknown to Islam." "Living in community is an act of grace." Prophet Muhammad tried for living in association, because living in company is productive of great benefit. Living in society is beneficial, whilst living alone does not confer profit. That is the secret underlying the building of mosques. In that institution, all the people dwelling in a quarter of the town assemble together so that they may gain greater benefit and grace of the Lord. The houses which are exclusively and separately built hide one's sins and defects and cause distinction. The benefit of bulding the Jumā Masjid is that people from different parts of the town assemble there. The object of Kābā (Meccā) is that the people from various countries and towns may collect there.

Amir said, "When the Mongols arrived here, for the first time, they were savages and lived naked. They used to ride the bullocks and for arms they used wooden staffs. Now see how rich they have become and lead sumptuous lives. They ride on the best Arabian horses and use the best weapons."

The Maulānā said, "When their hearts were broken and they were weak and they had no strength in them, God helped them and accepted their meekness. Now, as they have become so wealthy and strong, God will crush them through the instrumentality of an extraordinary weak man. So, they will, then, understand that what they had achieved and won was not through their own strength but through the grace of the Almighty God. In the beginning, these people used to live in jungles, away from the people. They were naked, poor and full of wants. Some of them proceeded to trade in the kingdom of Khurzān Shāh and started carrying on bartering business. They used to purchase rough coarse cloth. Khurzān Shāh prohibited them to carry on business in his kingdom and beheaded many of them and taxed them heavily and stopped his merchant subjects to trade in the Mongol territory. The Tārtars went to their king and complained to him that they were dying and were maltreated. He sought to be excused for a few days, during which period he went into a secluded cave and started to fast, and in all humility, with tears, prayed to the Lord to help him. A Hidden Voice was heard, "I accept your prayers. If you raid the country, you will be successful in your raids." This was the reason that whatever country they raided, they were successful by Lord's grace.

The Amir said that even the Tartars believed in the Day of Judgment when a great court would be held and people would be questioned about their acts and examined.

The Maulānā said, "They are liars." Their sinister motive is that they may show that they hold beliefs similar to the Moslems. People asked a camel wherefrom it was coming. The camel answered that he was coming from a bath. They said, 'It is apparent from thy heels.' Now, if they believe in the Day of Judgment, what evidence they have to support their belief. They are piling their sins and tyranny as layers on layers like that of snow. When the sun of repentance shines, develops in them the fear of God and gives them the news of the other world, the layers of (sins) will melt as the sun melts the snow. If the snow says that it has seen the sun and that the hot sun has shone on it, yet it is left unaffected, it still remains frozen, no wise person will believe it for, it is impossible that the ray of the sun may fall on ice and it may not melt.

Although God has promised that the consequences of good and evil acts will follow on the day of Judgment, yet He gives some samples of those fruits even in this world. If a man feels happy at any time, take it that it is the consequence of his having pleased somebody here, at some time previously. If, however, he is unhappy, he must understand that this is the punishment for his having displeased somebody. Such effects are like presents received from the other world, and the foretaste of the day of Judgment so that by small pain he might comprehend the great agony of that world. Have you not seen that a handful of wheat, a sample serves to show the quality of the whole mound of wheat?

How great and noble was Prophet Muhammad! Yet one night, he suffered from great pain in his head. By kindness of the Lord, he learnt that it was due to get his uncle Abbas bound hand and foot, when he was taken a prisoner of war with others. Although it was in pursuance of his commands that he was taken a prisoner, yet he had to undergo the fruit of his action. Unpleasantness, sorrow and trouble that you have to undergo are the result of your having sinned or pained somebody else although you might not remember the cause thereof. This ignorance and forgetfulness on your part is due to the contact and companionship with irreligious people. It urges you to perform evil acts without giving a thought to what you are doing. You do not remember that your evil association is responsible for your leaning towards transgression of religious tenets. You must see, every time, how much pain or joy you are experiencing as a result of your actions. If there is discontent and sorrow in you, it is the consequence of some sinful act of yours, and your joy and happy moments are the consequences of your living prayerful life.

Once, the Prophet just turned over his ring in his finger. Atonce a message of displeasure came from the Lord, "You are not born to indulge in such idle play and to waste time like this. Do you imagine that you have been created for doing no work and without any purpose?" Therefore, you should be constantly watching how your time is being spent, in prayers and pious works or in sins." God entangled Moses in the affairs of the world. There was purpose at the back of it. He kept prophet ever engaged in contemplating and remembering Him. He first engaged Prophet Muhammad in His contemplation and then, commanded him to draw people towards religion and instruct them. The Prophet began to weep and requested the Lord to enlighten him as to why He had drawn him from His perpetual presence. He begged Him not to engage him with the people. The Lord replied, "Do not lose heart, O Prophet, I shall never forsake you and get you entangled in the world so as to forget Me while associating with the people of the world. I tell you that you will be working in the world whilst constantly you will be thinking and remembering Me. As you are today, so shall you be always with Me in all your worldly activities."

People asked Prophet Muhammad, "Can there be any variation in the dictates of fate and any change in what is predestined?"

The Mualānā replied, "The law laid down at the beginning of creation, that the return for good is good and evil for evil, is eternal and unalterable. For, the Lord is like physician who will never say to return evil for good. How is it possible that one should sow wheat and reap barley or the converse be true viz. one should sow barley and reap wheat? This is impossible. All the saints have said that the return for good is good and for evil is evil. Whosoever does the least good, shall have good in return and whosoever does the least evil shall have evil in return." It follows that what is writ on the day of creation is unalterable. But, if you want that the effect of good be increased and that of evil be lightened, you should know that the more of good you will do, the more good will follow and the more evil acts you perform, the more will be the evil consequences that you will have to face. There might be a slight alteration in this but the principle enunciated above is unalterable.

The Amir said, "We see that the bad ones become good and the good ones turn bad, the sinners turn pious and conversely."

The Maulānā replied, "The bad one thought of good and he turned good, and the pious one who thought of evil turned a sinner. 'Just as Satan took exception to the superiority of man and said, 'Lord! Thou created me from fire and man from clay, why should I bow to him?' This led to his expulsion from the presence of the Lord, inspite of his being the preceptor of the angels, he became the recipient of Lord's reprimand. I also say that the consequence of good is good and of evil is evil. So, he who was not of the company of the good at the outset (in eternity) is condemned for all times like Satan. But, it is never possible that the faithful ever becomes a heretic. Where such a thing happens, it follows that in eternity he must have been unlucky, for he who is created (at the time of creation in eternity) lucky can never fall into heresy. If such fate comes temporarily, he soon turns a believer."

The Amir questioned, "If someone promises before the Lord that he will keep fast, and then breaks his promise, will he be punished for that or not?"

The Maulānā replied, "According to the commentary of Shafi, it would be a breaking of the law and he shall be liable to be mulcted because such a promise becomes an obligation (an oath) and breaking of it is liable to recompense." But Abu Hanifa does not accord to this abligation, the status of oath, therefore, its breach does not make him liable to a penalty. Obligations are of two classes; one is that which does not insist on fulfilment and the other which is considered a duty. An obligation devoid of duty does not insist on fulfilment. The other insists on fulfilment, for it is a duty. The illustration of the first is, 'I shall fast for a day.' The illustration of the second is, 'I shall perform such an act if that person comes.'

The Maulānā said that a person lost his ass. He fasted for three days with the object that he may be able to discover his ass. After three days, he discovered the ass but found that the donkey was dead. He was very much grieved and irritated and raising his face towards the sky said, "If instead of these three day's fast, I do not observe six day's fast in the pious month of Ramzān, I may turn impotent. O Lord, You play a trick on me."

The Maulānā said, "Prayers, obeisances and blessings are all His grace and blessing. They are all His property for if the Lord does not confer health on us, we can never perform His worship and never gain deliverance. The Lord is their Master, we have no right over them. If He is pleased, He can confer them on us. Just as, in the spring season people carry on cultivation, come out in the fields, go on travels, start building new constructions. It is all due to the blessing and grace of the spring season. Otherwise they were lying in the houses or in the caves shut up from outside world. So it is due to the spring season that so many amenities of life are provided, viz., carrying out cultivation, going on picnic trip and enjoying other pleasures and sights.

People keep their attention riveted on the causes and think that all acts result from some cause or other. But this matter is revealed to the prophets that all causes are mere veils and they should, therefore, try to discover the Creator who has laid all these veils, which are all mere magic show. It can be illustrated and understood thus, it is as if some person were talking behind a curtain and people assumed that it was the curtain that was speaking. They were ignorant of the fact that the veil was a mere useless thing and a mere pretext and when the speaker behind the curtain would come out, everything would become clear that the curtain was merely a deceiving device. The Friends of God have seen many miracles of which no cause can be traced, just as, from a mountain, a camel came out, or the staff of Moses was converted into a dragon, and from a rock twelve springs gushed forth, or the Prophet Muhammad by mere motion of his finger split the moon into two bits or Adam was born without any parents, Christ had no father, and for Abraham, the fire was turned into a garden. These and many such things have led the friends of God to conclude that there is no cause for those things traceable, the Maker of these is some One else. Causes are mere pretexts the Creator of all these is somebody else. The Creator acts behind the curtain. The ordinary person keeps his mind fixed on the curtain and is ignorant of the actor behind the curtain. Prophet Zakaria was promised a son by God, but Zakaria was surprised how it was possible since he and his wife were both very old, so how could they give birth to a child. So, he praying to the Lord, asked "How can a child be born to us who are so old?"

The answer came, "Zakaria! Have you forgotten My ways? Have I not told you so often that My actions have no connection with causes. They do not depend on the causes. Do you not know that causes are mere pretexts, I, the Creator, am Omnipotent and can create before your eyes a million babes without the instrumentality of a woman or womb. By a sign from Me, millions of people can be born in the world, and all of them shall be wise. Did I not create you in the spiritual world without a father and mother, and prior to your birth in this world how many acts of kindness did I not confer on thee?" Prophets, saints, good and bad men are born according to their intrinsic merits thus, just as children were carried away from the land of the heretics and were sold in the markets to the Moslems as slaves. Some of those were five to ten years old. He who is brought so young, when he grows up and gets old forgets everything about the country of his birth and does not remember any mark of that country. But if he is of mature age, he remembers some details of the land of his birth and even more, if he is brought in an advanced age. So also when these souls were in the presence of the Lord (in eternity) and God asked, "Am I not your God?" They answered, "Of a certainty, You are our God." At that time the food of these souls was remembrance of the Lord and no words were uttered by them and no sound was made when mutely they praised Him. The very young souls who are brought in the tender age to this world and when they are taught the Book of the Lord, do not remember their past in antiquity, and they think they have no relation with the words of God. Such are those on whose intelligence are cast heavy veils, and they are sunk in slavery and ignorance. Other souls are those who remember a little their antecedents, and who sometimes experience the breeze and emotions coming from that world (of souls). These people are called the faithful. Lastly, there are the developed souls. When they hear the Holy Book of God, remembrance of past comes before their eyes and atonce they know who they were in the past. All the veils are removed from their vision. They enter the union with the Lord with Whom they were united in eternity (at the time of creation). These people are called the Prophets.

I advise my friends that when the spiritual secrets begin to dawn on them, they should not relate their experience to any body nor tell the reality about them to any one, nor should they tell others that I have thus warned them to keep their spiritual experience secret. Spiritual experience should not be told to others, because it is said that the divine mystery should not be taught to them who are incompetent to learn. If you teach them, you will cause injury to them, whilst you must impart that knowledge to them who are capable to follow it, for, "if you do not teach them, you will be tyrannising over them," If your beloved comes to your house and hiding himself in a corner, tell you not to reveal his identity to anybody and then, he shall live there as your own. Does it, then, behove you to take him to the town and parade him in the market place? He will never like it but He will leave you and go away. So, the Lord has made all these aforesaid things unlawful.

Just as, those in hell pray to those in heaven most plaintively to confer a little of the blessing and joy that have fallen to their lot, for their generosity they will praise them and be grateful to them whilst this generous act will not any way cause deficiency in their pleasure.

"In the cup of pleasure (lot) of the generous dwellers of heaven, there is a drop, as share of these people of the world too." The dwellers in hell will say, "We are being extremely tortured and suffocated here, a few fruits and cold water conferred by you will not any way cause you deficiency. They have all been bestowed on you by the Lord. Be generous." The dwellers of heaven will say, "All the gifts of the Lord bestowed on us, are banned for the heretics. The seed of the grace conferred on us here was in the world, but you did not sow it there and took no thought of it. That seed was honesty, faith, truthfulness and good deeds, then, how can you reap their fruit here? If we become generous to you, since you are condemned by the Lord for heresy, our gifts, will burn your throats and you will not be able to swallow them and if you pocket them, they will make hole in your pocket and escape from there."

One day, a group of *munafiqs* (pretenders whose external talk is opposite to what they cherish in their hearts) approached the Prophet and began to talk on the spiritual secret topics and also started praising him. The Prophet warned his companions to hide their vessels (spiritual experience). He said to them, "These people are impious and harmful animals, so beware that they may not fall in your vessels and make the water impure. Then, if you drink it, you will suffer harm spiritually." Thus, he advised and warned them to keep their tongues tied and their wisdom hid. They were rats and were unfit for this pious learning.

The Maulānā said that the Amir who had just left that place, although he did not follow his talk in detail, understood the purport thereof and knew that he (Maulānā) intended to draw him towards the Lord. His humility, his nodding his head and his loving attitude towards him, all testified that he followed what he (Maulānā) said, just as, the rustic when he was coming to city, heard the Muezzin's call to Namāz and followed the purport of that, although he did not follow the actual words of the Namāz.

## CHAPTER 17

The Maulānā remarked, "That the Beloved is beautiful is true but the converse is not true, viz., everyone beautiful needs not be the beloved. Beauty is only a fragment of the beloved, the real thing is beloved. The beloved must of necessity be beautiful too, for, the nature of the whole cannot be different from its component, it is rather mixed up with the whole. Do you not see that there were many beautiful persons in the days of Majnun, even more beautiful than Leila, but they were not beloveds of Majnun? People said to Majnun, "There are many beautiful women superior in beauty to Leila, we may bring them to you so that you may give up infatuation for Leila." He replied. "I am not the lover of the form of Leila. Leila is not a form for me. Leila is like a cup in my hand, and I drink wine out of it. So, I am really the lover of the wine which is held in that cup from which I drink. But you have riveted your attention on the cup and you are not cognisant of the wine that it contains. So if you bring to me a cup bejewelled or made of gold, and it does not contain wine but vinegar or any other liquid, of what avail is it to me? To me, wine in a broken clay cup is more enjoyable than a gold cup that does not contain wine. It demands love, a passion and discriminative faculty that may distinguish between wine and an empty cup."

Take an illustration. There is a person who has had no food for the last ten days and there is another person who is taking food five times a day to his fill. He whose stomach is full sees the loaf as a loaf of bread, but the other does not see the form of bread but in it, he sees life itself, for, this loaf is like soup and it is tasteful like milk. That being so, it is not possible to look upon it from another point of view but that of hunger. Now, try to develop hunger and craving so that you may not remain content with the form but probe further and notice that everywhere in this universe, you may see only the Beloved.

All the objects you see in creation are like so many cups and the arts, learning, crafts etc., in this world are like the engraving on those cups. Have you not observed that when the cup breaks, all the engraving and etching on it is also lost? "So, the thing of value is the wine in the cup and he who knows this and drinks that wine is the wise man. All the practice that is lasting is worthwhile."

He who wants to interrogate a person must bear two things in his mind so that he may be a worthy interrogator. The first thing is that he must believe that there is some error in his way of thinking that prompts him to put the question and the other is that there is some higher knowledge with which he is not acquainted. "Half the art consists in framing the question." It is this proper question that draws the attention of another person to the question. The object of every question is to enquire into 'TRUTH', and the whole life is spent in this hope (to get a reply). But there must be some such a one who amongst the people with the sense of discrimination highly developed in him should be able to discern who is amongst them treading the right path and has capacity to realise Truth. Such a one bears the king's impress (insignia) on him and has only one thing to say for he is a believer in Unity of God.

We shall call him whom water may turn as it likes, immersed in water whilst he himself has no control over water, but he whom water cannot carry where it likes is riding over water and controlling due to his capability to swim. It follows, therefore, that whatever act is performed by the drowned person and is manifested by him (his body), in fact, is the act of water. He is simply an intermediary instrument. Suppose, a wall becomes vocal, you will atonce say it is not the voice issuing from the wall but he who has made the wall vocal is somebody else. Similar is the state of the Prophets who have died before death (their ego being dead whilst living) and have become the instruments of Lord's expression, like the wall of the above illustration. Not a grain of their self (ego) persists in them. They are like unto a shield in the hands of the Lord. The shield by itself cannot move. This is the interpretation of the saying. "I am Truth." The shield says, "I am nothing, not even an instrument. The hand of the Lord moves me. You must accept this shield as instrument of Truth and should not take up the cudgels against the Lord, for whosoever has raised blow at such persons has, in fact, raised a quarrel with the Lord. You know how much have the lovers of God suffered from the days of Adam up to the present time, at the hands of Pharoah, Shaddad, Namrud, and the Saamuels to name a few. But the shield survives as such till the Day of Judgment and continues to live through the ages, sometimes, it assumes the form of the Prophets who have passed away, sometimes the form of saints who are living to-day and sometimes it will be in the form of saints to come in future. The reason of it is that it may be possible to distinguish between the sinners and the pious ones and distinction may be drawn between the friends and enemies of God. To the people of the world, every Prophet is the proof of existence of God. To the extent, the people love the saint, to that height they attain to. If people quarrel with him, it is like their fighting with God and friendship with him is friendship with God. God says, "He who met the Prophet, met Me (God), and he who was inimical to him was inimical to Me (God)."

The favourite servants of God are His Privy councillors (keepers of His secrets). God has sapped off their existence (self) the veins of their desires and the roots of all evil. This is the reason why they have become masters of the world, and the knowers of mystery which is revealed only to the pious and nobody else.

## CHAPTER 18

"If I have forsaken the education and upbringing of my friends and relations," says the Maulānā, "the reason of it is not my laziness or coolness of heart but because I have riveted my attention upon the culture and development of their souls for whatever I tell them is like unto life to them and if they become unmindful of their body and rivet their attention on their soul and direct their soul towards me, they will never suffer.

It is one of my traits that from my heart, I ever wish that no one should suffer injury at my hands. Just as, now, a concourse of people is knocking at the door and my friends seated here do not open the door. I do not like this. How often have I not warned my friends, that they should not reprimand any body on my account for, in whatever the people give me pleasure, I am so far anxious to please them and I am ever taking care that nothing which may annoy them should happen. For them, I sometimes indulge in poetic effusion. There is, therefore, no other reason for indulging in poetry. God knows full well that I have no inclination for poetry. In fact, I consider it my bane. I consider it the worst thing for me. My entertaining my guests with poetry is like a person entertaining his guest by taking out his entrails and washing them to feed his guest with them. My object is simply to entertain them. A dealer always enquires what the goods that are needed in a particular town are and he takes that kind of goods to that place irrespective of the fact whether they are of superior or inferior quality. With great effort and perseverance, I acquired knowledge with a view that very learned critics and men of understanding and wisdom would seek my company and I should entertain them with novel and delicate topics. It is God's will that

He has collected all the sciences here (with me) and made them of such a high order that I might pursue them. Then, what can I do? The pursuit of poetry was the meanest occupation in my country, and if I had continued to live in my country I would have followed and acted according to their wishes, and would have taught them as my people wanted. I would have written books to suit their taste and preached accordingly and pursued a pious life."

Amir Parwānā questioned, "Is not practice the main thing?" The Maulānā replied, "Where is found a person who is inclined to practice? If one can be found, I shall impart to him spiritual knowledge and teach him spiritual practice. At present here, I find that people only want enunciation of rules and only want to hear orations (with no desire to practise them.) If I remain silent, they feel pained. If you want to practise spirituality, I shall teach you that. But since none who wants to practise is found all only want talks, so I talk to them. What do you know of spiritual experience since you have not undergone the *sādhanā* (spiritual practice). Only by actual practice can one learn the value and profundity of the practice. Wisdom is acquired only through practice. Exterior is recognised by exterior practice and interior by internal practice. Since none is found treading this (spiritual) path, it lies forlorn. When we do not practise religion and do not tread the path, how can we see it crowded?

Fast and orisons are not practice. They are mere forms of it. Practice contains a hidden import. Since the days or Adam to the time of Prophet Muhammad, in every age, there were orison (*namāz*) and fast (*rozā*) but its form was not such as is today. It was a mere ceremony or formality. The real *amal* (practice) is something internal. As it is said that the medicine produces an effect, but effect (*amal*) has no visible form. But effect has meaning which is apparent, for example, in a certain place there is an *amil* (practiser or officer). There is no external form of the office he holds, but from the activities relating to practice, we call him an officer. So, what people call practice is not real practice. It is something besides, because if there is a *munāfiq* (pretender) who visibly follows some practice but in his heart is dishonest qua it and faithless, no benefit will accrue from that practice.

The reality of all is word. You do not know the import of word and expression. You consider expression as meaningless and unreal. Words proceed as fruit from the tree of practice. The Lord has created the world from word-KUN-(let the world be created). Faith is something of the heart. Do not express it in language. It will not profit. Orison (namāz) is an activity, if while performing it, you do not utter the necessary words of the *Qurān*, it will not be correctly performed.

One amidst the audience inquired, "While performing a pious act, if we desire some beneficial fruit out of it from God as a result thereof, is it bad on our part to cherish such desire, and shall we lose something thereby?"

The Maulānā said, "It is not so, I trow, Because faith is another name of this fear and hope." A person asked me, "Hope is a healthy thing but why is this fear?" I answered, "Give me an illustration of hope that does not carry fear in its womb. Both these things are inseparable. Never separate one from the other. Why should you, then, put this question? Take an illustration, say, a person sows wheat and he hopes that he will reap wheat but he fears lest drought or any calamity should come and wheat may not appear. It follows that there is no hope without fear, and the converse is equally true. Therefore, if a man hopes for better results, he will have to be more alert and persevering in his efforts." Hopes are like the wings to him. As the stronger are the hopes, the higher will he fly, but if he loses hope, he will turn lazy and he will be unable to do any work or perform prayers. Just as, a sick person, in the hope of regaining health, abstains from taking sweets and takes bitter pills of medicine. If he did not cherish hope of recovery, he would not do so. Man is an intelligent being (animal). He is constituted of animality and discriminative faculty. These are found in him at all times. They may appear dormant at some time but, in reality, they are always present there, just as clay or mud is always mixed in the water of the tank. The clarity in the water is like man's discriminative faculty whilst like the mud in the clear water is his animality. This animality is, like mud only a temporary thing, so, the bodies etc. may not or otherwise may be disfigured but his cleverness, wisdom knowledge and efficiency in brilliant conversation never suffer loss.

A man with an open heart is a complete man. If you meet such a one, you have met all. All the people are parts of that great soul. The people are fragments, he is the whole.

"All men good or evil are parts of the Dervish,
If this be not so, he is no dervish."

If you have seen him, who is the whole, you have seen the whole world. If you have heard him and his principles, what you will hear in future time will be mere repetition of it. If some one has seen the Dervish at some place, he has seen everybody at every place.

"O thou, that art he copy of the Book of God,
O ye that thou art the reflector of the beauty of God,
Whatever there is in the world is not outside thee.
Whatever thou seekest, find it within thee.
Because That thou art (you and you alone are.)"

## CHAPTER 19

The Junior Amir said, "In the former days, the heretics used to worship and pray to idols, and offer them obeisances. We are also acting similarly at the present day. For, what does it mean your going to the Mongols and offering obeisances to them, and you consider your ego as the real self. Besides, we nurture within ourselves many idols, viz., envy, avarice, pride and obey their order and offer allegiance to them. This means visibly and in secret and both the ways our conduct is the same as of the heretics of bygone days, whilst we pride in calling ourselves Moslems."

The Maulānā said, "There is, besides, another thing. When your heart tells you that a certain effect is bad and unpleasant, your heart's eye has surely witnessed a more beautiful and charming effect which is responsible for the present dislike of the object before you, for, he who has tasted sweet water alone can call salt water saltish.

The real shape of things can be understood by their opposites. That is why God has placed in your soul the light of faith. That act which looks bad presumes that there is something good compared to which this looks ugly. Otherwise, why is not this sweet pain in the lot of others? They are satisfied with themselves and say that whatever they are doing is the only work and there is no work besides it.

God shall bestow on you that which you want and that which you consider to be good. Wherever it may be, you shall find it. The bird flies with both the wings and the faithful one does so with his strength.

Creation is divided into three classes. Some are angels who are pure intellect and they praise God and pray to Him and these are their food and their life, just as the fish lives in the water and the water is its life. The water is its bed and bed-covering. The water does not cause it any injury. Similarly, these created beings do not affect the angels who are without desire and pure and there is no surprise at this as they are so constituted that they can have no desires. So, if they have no desires, they cannot be praised for practising restraint. If they offer obeisance, that too, is not a thing of praise for that is their nature and they cannot live without it. The second kind of creation is the animal world which is pure unadulterated desire. They have not the discriminative intellect which sifts the good from the evil. The third class is man, a poor thing, combination of discrimination and passion, half angel and half brute, half snake and half fish. The fish draws him into water and the snake to dry earth. Thus, the scuffle is going on. He whose intellect dominates his heart, rises above the angels and he whose passion dominates over his intellect falls below the animal state. Man by his intellect is an angel and being swayed by ignorance, he is an animal. Betwixt the two enemies, he is dragged this way and that. Some have become so much developed in intellect that they have verily, become angels and pure light. They are the prophets and saints.

They are exempt from fear and frown. They do not suffer from pain and are not victims to fear. While there are others whose desires sway over their intellect. They become slaves to their animal passions, while there is another class always in a state of strain. Within their heart pain is constantly swaying them and they are never satisfied with their condition. They are the faithful ones. The Prophets who are like the fish of the sea await the arrival of the faithful ones that they may take them with them to the goal, the Highest Abode (Paradise), where they desire to make them like themselves. While the devil like the serpent in this world is very alert awaiting to find an opportunity to drag the faithful ones to the hellish nether worlds.

We also cherish some desires, so do the others nurture opposite desires,

Nobody knows who will be the lucky person and his fate will crown him with success.

## CHAPTER 20

The commentators of the Holy Scripture (The *Qurān*) say that the Prophet was very anxious to convert the whole world into Moslems and make them tread the path to the Lord. He was very sad as his end approached, for he did not get so much time to preach his gospel to the world. The Lord told him that he should not feel sorry as he would see that many countries and cities which were to be won by sword turned without the force of weapons, by free will into faithful (Moslems). He would be satisfied, for, at the end of his life, he would himself see that the people coming from far off countries were adopting the Moslem faith and groups after groups following suit. When that happened, he should know that it was the sign that his time for departure from the world had arrived. Then, he should praise His (Lord's) piety and repent for sins and thus, he would go purified to Him (the Lord).

But the investigators of the above sura question the correctness of this interpretation. They say that the meaning of the verse is that a person who thinks that by effort, practice and penance, he can do away with his bad habits and tries those means to subdue his ego, ultimately, feels hopeless, and he does not succeed in his efforts. Then, the Lord addresses Himself to him saying, "O My slave! Do you think that whatever you desire to achieve, you will achieve by your effort? But I have made a law that you will first have to spend all that you have, in My way, then you shall find way and entry into My faith (religion). Try to walk in this endless path (to Me) with your weak arms and feet although I know that with your weak limbs, you will not be able to traverse the path. Covering the path is, of course, out of question. Even in a hundred and thousand years, only the first stage will not be reached by you. I ask you to continue to walk on the path because when you will be tired traversing it and no more strength will be left in you to continue further and will feel helpless, then I shall succour you. Just, so long as, the child is in the sucking stage, people carry him in their arms, but when he grows up, they leave him to walk on his feet. Now, that these efforts have forsaken you, you shall experience My grace, more abundantly. When you carried on these austerities, at that time, sometimes, in sleep and sometimes, in your wakeful state, I used to shower My mercy now and then, on you whereby the desire to meet Me increased in you and you felt hopeful. But, when your strength is spent up, you shall find that My blessing and mercy are showered in abundance on you. When your condition becomes such that your ego is totally effaced and you find that without guidance and instructions, you cannot proceed further and there is no more strength in you, My attraction and mercy shall befriend you and raise you in its arms and you shall have hordes of blessings which would never have come to your lot, had you depended as before on your efforts solely. When such helpless state of yours is reached, praise Me your God and sing My praise and seek My forgiveness and repent." You are proud and you think that acts are performed by you, with your strength; you do not see that the real actor is the Lord Himself. Now that you see that He is the Doer, you repent, for He accepts your repentance.

I do not like the Amir for his literary achievement or practical acquisition, for which people love him. Such people look at the back and do not cast their eyes on the face. The Amir is like a mirror and his virtuous traits are comparable to the jewel studded at the back of the mirror. They, who are in love with the jewels look at the back but they who are in love with the face of the mirror do not cast a glance on the studded gold and jewels. They always gaze at the face of the mirror and are friends of the shining surface of the mirror because of its power of reflecting beauty and they admire it when their beauty is reflected therein. They are not perplexed and do not look at the back of the mirror, its jewels etc., but if the person whose face is ugly looks into the face of the mirror and sees his ugly reflection, he atonce turns to the back of the mirror and is engaged in seeing the gold and jewels studded therein. If a hundred thousand classes of engraving exist at the back of the mirror or it is studded with jewels, how does it affect the face of the mirror? God has mingled man's humanity (angelic nature) with his animality within him, so that the two by contrast become visible. "The genuine state of the thing is known when it stands in contrast with the other." Since there is no opponent of God, so He says, "I was a hidden treasure. I wished to be known and recognised. So I created this world so that in its inertness and darkness I may shine as light and for the same reason, I created the Prophets and the saints, so that My attributes, may become manifest before the world through them." These Prophets and saints are the witnesses of the Lord, so that the enemies and friends may be distinguished as also His own people and strangers because the essential nature of God stands without a compeer; so comparison is tried to be manifested by external forms of Prophets just as the devil stands in contradiction to Adam, Moses in contrast to Pharoah and the Prophet Muhammad in contrast to Abu Jehal; so you can go one finding new illustrations, which are many.

Thus, by creating the Prophets, God has created his compeers (likeness) and they are, in effect, not His opposites. The more the enmity was shown by obstructers against the Prophets, the more did the latter make progress and earned fame. "The heretics desire to extinguish God's light by blowing it out but God shall see that this light spreads all round however much the heretics try to throttle it."

The moon shines and the dog barks at it. This is no fault of the moon but it is the nature of the dog. With the light of the moon sparkle forth all the four corners of the sky. What status has a dog, a despised creature of the world! In the world, there are many people on whom God bestows rank and honour although their soul always tries to run away from them. A Faquir once saw an Arab Amir coming towards him riding on his horse. His forehead was shining with the divine Light. The Faquir said, "Holy is the Lord Who confers on His slaves wealth, honour and along with it ignominy."

Somebody told the Maulānā that such and such a person read the Qurān correctly. He replied, "True, the outer form of the Qurān is correctly recited by him but he is ignorant of the inner import of the words of the Qurān because when he sees another person reading it correctly, (out of jealousy) he raises objection against its correctness. So, he reads the Qurān as a blind man. It can further be illustrated thus. Suppose a person holds a little sugar in his hand. When an other brings sugar of better quality to him, he does not like it as he cannot discriminate the qualities of the two. He is holding the sugar in hand because some one has so asked him to hold it after telling him it is sugar. His case is similar to that of the children who are playing with the nuts. If one gives them its kernel they refuse to take it telling him it cannot be a nut because it does not make a cracking sound like the nut with covering. After all numerous are the treasures held by the Lord, infinite is the number of knowledge proceeding from Him. So, if the reader of the Qurān fully understands what he is reading, why does he object to the reading of another and dislike it?

I, once, said to the correct reciters of the Qurān, "At one place, the Qurān says," Prophets tell the people that if all the seas were turned into ink, and all of it was consumed in writing the praises of the Lord, the seas would dry up, ere the praises would be completed. But the whole of the Quran is transcribed in ink worth fifty dirhams. So, this is the secret of His knowledge. A druggist dispenses medicine wrapped in a piece of paper. If you were to remark that his whole shop was contained in it, it would be an error. So, the whole of the knowledge is not this (in the Qurān) alone, for, even before Muhammad and his Qurān there were Prophets like Moses and Jesus Christ and others and the words (knowledge) of God ere in existence then (in their books.) That was not in Arabic. I was trying to explain this to him but unfortunately, he could not follow it and no effect was produced on him. So I abandoned the effort. In the days of the Prophet, if one remembered even half the verse of the Qurān, people used to look at him with great honour and pointing to him said that he remembered half the verse of the Qurān, because he used to digest it. To eat a seer or more of food and go on masticating and vomiting it is not a great thing. That you can do with hundred of seers of food.

Do you not notice that there are some Qurān's readers whom the Qurān condemns. This is said about such a person who does not follow the meaning underlying the words of the Qurān. Anyway, even then, the reading of the Qurān (by such a one) is also a good thing. God has tied the bandage of ignorance on many people so that they may keep this world existent by their ignorance. If some people were not ignorant of the other world, who would keep this world going on? Then, this world would cease to be, for this world subsists on ignorance which prompts people to construct buildings and populate places. Watch the child. He grows in ignorance but when he is developed in intellect, his growing physically ceases (in advanced age), and he does not grow taller. This proves that the cause of the growth of population is ignorance, and the cause of depopulation is watchfulness and intelligence.

What I mean to say is that the Qurān is read in two ways. There is no other way besides these two. I say so out of love, not prompted by malice or envy. It cannot be malice on My part for the simple reason that we envy that which is worth envying but never that which is not worth it. So in my case, it can never be envy. But, because of excess of love and kindness in me, I do want that I should draw my friends to the meaning of the Qurān and they cease to read the Qurān ignorantly.

A story is narrated that a person on his way to pilgrimage to Meccā was passing through a sandy desert. From a distance he saw a small hut and he directed his course towards it. Seeing a slave girl seated there, he shouted that he was a guest, got down from his carrier and asked for water. He was offered water which he drank. The water was extremely saltish and hot like boiling water, and his lips, mouth and throat were all burnt. Out of kindness and prompted by pity, the gentleman, said to her, 'As you have entertained me, you are entitled to have some gift from me. I pity you, so I want to tell you something on which you should ponder well. Know that close to this place is Baghdad and close to it are big towns like Kafa and Wasat. Even if one is sick or hungry or thirsty, one can reach the places rolling on one's back (that is, they are so near,) and there you will find plenty of cold and sweet water, dainty dish, houses with beautiful hot baths, delightful delicacies and other objects of comfort.' He narrated many virtues and gifts available at that place. Shortly after that her Arab husband arrived and the wife narrated to him all that the stranger had told her. He had brought with him a few wild rats he had hunted in the day and handed them over to her to cook. When they were ready, a share of the food was offered to the stranger who somehow swallowed the food and went to sleep at midnight outside the hut. The woman told her husband all that the stranger had told her. The Arab replied, "Beware! never give a moment's thought to the words of the stranger because the world abounds with envious people, who envy those who are more blessed with a few comforts of life and want to deprive them by banishing them from the town."

This, then is the attitude and way of the people. If you, out of kindness give a piece of healthy advice to them, they take it as being given out of envy. But, if the adviser is related to them, they give thought to it and follow it. If he has been blessed with a drop on the day of creation, that drop will take him to the ocean of reality and relieve him of many troubles and inconveniences. After all, how long will you evade us and run away from us and dwell as a stranger from us and be engaged in futile thoughts? What avail telling them such things as they have never heard from anybody even from their teachers? How can they accept, then, such things?

When saintliness is unknown to his family, how can he, then, relish the good things told by the saints?

Although he is a little startled when he is drawn inwards, yet as he proceeds further, his inner self feels sweetness and enjoys better those things which he resented formerly. But, howsoever much company you give him who has no leaning towards spirituality or who may be even your friend, the more you will get benumbed. Great is the difference between the external form and the internal meaning of the words of the Qurān. Do you not see that the moment, the inner self (soul) of man departs in spite of his exterior (body) appearing in good form, not for a moment, is he (dead body) kept in the house.

## ILLUSTRATION

"A big caravan," said Maulānā Shamsh Uddin, "was proceeding towards some destination. On the way, they found no habitation nor water was available anywhere. Luckily, they saw a well. They tied a rope to a pan and gradually lowered it into the well. However, the rope broke in the way and the pan fell. They again tied another pan to the rope and again lowered it in the well. It also fell as if cut down by somebody. Thereafter, they tied an intelligent man to the rope and lowered him into the well. Time passed and yet the man did not come out. Then, the very wiseman amongst them offered to go into the well. He was, likewise, lowered. On reaching the bottom, he met a frightful dark-complexioned negro. The wiseman felt there was no chance of his surviving then, so he collected his senses and waited. The black man said, to him, 'You are my prisoner. You can be released from imprisonment if you can correctly answer the questions I put to you or else you will have to remain in confinement here. 'The wise man agreed to answer him. The black man, then, asked, "Which is the best place to live?" The wise man thought if he praised Baghdād or Egypt, it would be interpreted that he was casting slur on house. He replied that place which interests any body, let it be at the botttom of a well or the hole of a rat, is the best for him. Hearing the reply the black man jumped up with glee and praising him said, 'Words in which to praise your intellect fail me. In the world, if there is a man, it is you. I release you and out of gratitude I release all others who are imprisoned here. Henceforth, I shall kill nobody and for your sake free everybody I have taken prisoner in the world.' He, then, offered water to the caravan to drink and for sundry purposes. This is the story. The meaning behind it is not what its exterior form displays. But it cannot be described differently.

## CHAPTER 20

Maulānā said, "Tajuddin Qabai says, 'These commoners come to us, Faquirs, and turn us faithless. Since, they are not naturally of us, so, it is never possible that they become ours.'" This can be illustrated thus. Suppose, you tie a collar of gold in the neck of a dog. Due to that collar merely, we shall not call that dog a hunting dog. Hunting is a peculiar trait which is found in the hunting dog whether you put round his neck a collar of gold or of wool. Merely by donning a gown or a hood, one does not become a man of learning. Knowledge is a quality particular to a man of wisdom. If that knowledge is in the gown or the hood, where, then, is the difference between the man and his clothes? Just as, in the days of the Prophet, to bring infamy to Faith (Islām), the pretenders used to don the dress of the faithful ones, used to so mix with them that they might ruin and weaken their faith and meddle with the faith of the Moslems by externally putting on the Moslem dress. This they did because if a Jew or an European were to abuse Islām, the Moslems would never hear him. "Condemned are the Moslems who are lazy in offering prayers or merely make a show of it and are miserly in trifling matters." The real thing is that which is light within thee but thou art lacking in human understanding. Discover the human element within thee and do not waste time in decorating words, for, know that he who desires to embellish his conversation often misses the import thereof.

A shopkeeper used to love a lady. He sent a message through her slave girl that he was deeply in love with her and was being roasted in the fire of separation. Every day he was suffering from the pang of separation as the time passed. With difficulty he could pass his time. When the slave girl reached that mistress, she told her only the purport of the talk in the following words, "The shopkeeper sends you salutations, invites you to himself for such and such purpose." Although the shopkeeper had sent a very long message, yet the purport was simply this. The purport alone matters, all else is futile talk.

## CHAPTER 21

The Maulānā said, "You are all the time quarrelling with others and are trying to teach good manners to women, and attempt to remove their impiety. It will be far better, if, instead of that, you try to reform your own self and turn more polite and mannerly. Go to that woman and follow her directions, even if, in your eyes, you find them impossible to follow. For the time, forget your zeal for honour or modesty, although it is the virtue in men. Due to this trait of yours, virtues will find a place in you." It is for this reason that the Prophet said, "Monasticism is unknown to Islām," because the monks dwell in the secluded caves of the mountains, do not marry and renounce the world. The Pure Lord has disclosed a very secret and delicate path to the Prophet. What is it? It is that Muslims should marry and bear with patience the tyranny of women, and give ear to their impractical demands and try to fulfil them and make them mannerly. "O Prophet, really you are a person with very refined manners." To bear up with the tyranny of other people means that you cast your dirt on them and become purified. By patience, you improve your habits. Endurance makes you well mannerly. Try to purify yourself and your endeavour. Consider women like a piece of cloth (towel) with which a person cleans his body of impurity. If your habits do not endure it, try to exert your mind and through intellect, try to console your self saying, 'Consider women as such as you approach them to satisfy your passion when you get passionate.' Thus should you soothe your passionate self and calm your agitated mind. This is with a view to prepare thee for ascetic practice and learn endurance by the inordinate demands of these women and proceed in the righteous path. Thus you will see that putting up with atrocity has been beneficial to you.

It is narrated that when the Prophet returned with his companions from the crusade to his town, he ordered that the bugle of victorious return be sounded, and that night they should stay outside the town and enter it in the morning. People asked him why he passed such an order. The Prophet replied that if they entered at that hour, they might find their women seated with some other persons and that might cause them pain and lead to a quarrel. One of the Prophet's companions did not hear this warning and he entered the city at that late hour. He found his wife seated in company of another person. The teaching of the Prophet was, to bear with trouble and banish honour, modesty and the passionate nature. You should put up with the worry of providing women with food and clothing and drink many bitter draughts of trouble like syrup so that you may follow the import of what the Prophet taught and may experience it.

Jesus taught that devotees of the Lord should pass their lives in solitude and kill their passion. Prophet Muhammad, on the other hand, taught the scripture saying that men should bear women and other trouble. If you do not follow the path outlined by Muhammad, follow that of Jesus so that you may not be totally deprived of the benefit. It is necessary that you follow some precept. If you are pure and determined, you will have to undergo much disappointment and you will see much benefit accrues from it. If you have faith in what is taught to you, you should accept it literally and pursue it to the letter and wait with patience till that time when the benefit of which we were apprised in the beginning will accrue to us. Then, you will see what has been the result of your determination. Many treasures will be to your lot, and you shall gain more than you had thought. This talk of mine is impressing you a little at this time but when your faith will grow, it will produce greater effect on you.

What is a woman and what is the nature of the world? Whether you answer these questions or not, they are what they are. You should carry on your work. To express an opinion on this matter spoils it. Suppose, you pick up a leaf and hide it under your arm pit, and start saying that far from giving it, you are not prepared that any person may cast a glance at it, then although that leaf is like hundreds of those which are before thee lying on the floor and which even the dogs will not like to touch, yet because you refuse to show that leaf to anybody, everybody gets curious and wants to have it. If you thus hide it up the sleeves for a year, the desire to have it will grow keener in the people because the desire to enjoy a thing which is probibited is heightened due to that prohibition. "Suppose you order a woman to put on a veil. Her desire to show herself will grow even keener in her. Other people will also become more eager to have a look at her. Whilst you are quietly seated, by your order to veil, you have actually brightened the fire of desire on either side. So, you think you have done a good act, but in fact, you have caused injury. Really, if by nature a woman is pious and hates evil deeds, whether you order her to veil or allow her freedom, she will insist on pursuing the righteous path. You will also pass your time without any anxiety or fear. If, however, the woman is of opposite nature, she will pursue her rash course. The truth is, "Prohibition entails waking up desire."

People say that they saw Shamsh Tabraiz. But, how can they see (recognise) him? They who cannot see a camel from the roof of their house dare say that they saw the eye of the needle and passed thread into it. Therefore, the people have rightly said that they smile when two things are told them. First, that they say a negro was painting his fingers black and secondly, that a blind man took put his head out of the window to look at the objects. Likewise, there are these pretenders who are blind in heart. By taking out their heads from the window or the skeleton of the body, what will they see? Then, what worth is their styling a thing good or bad? Their judgment is of no value as they lack in the power of discrimination to distinguish good from bad. Foolish is their talk. First, they must develop the faculty of discrimination and then, seeing things and passing remarks about them will be of some value. Besides, faculty of discrimination, they must also have the power of understanding.

In the world, there are many saints who are wise and far-sighted and of attainment. Besides them, there are also other saints whom the the Lord has kept in hiding from the world. The former saints pray bitterly to the Lord to disclose the identity of those latter saints to them. So long as, they will not entreat pathetically to God, they will not possess the eyes of discrimination and they will not see them. Do you not see unless these women of the town do not wish themselves, can any person approach them? So also, these saints in hiding can never be seen, unless they themselves want them to see them and how can one recognise them unless one has developed faculty of discrimination? Very difficult it is to recognise them. Even the angels err and seek them in vain and feel helpless. Therefore, they say, "We praise Thee, O Lord, call thee and style Thee, Pure Love. We are pure love, spirit and light whilst the men of the world are slaves of their stomach, are wretched, are born out of the womb and shed blood." All these things are with the purpose that man may always remain in fear of the divine angels who are careless of all wealth and dignity and are always in the presence of the Lord and see Him. They are of pure light and their food is the vision of God and pure love and are far-sighted and have keen vision and are always engrossed in this trouble as to what they have to say and what not, what they have to accept and what not, their understanding fails to decide; then where does man, who does not know who he is and who lacks the faculty of recognising Truth stand? If, per chance, a spark of light kindles in him and righteous spiritual emotion is suddenly awakened in him, he should offer a thousand obeisances to the Lord in gratitude, knowing that he is a mere gnat and the most unfit.

This time, you will derive great benefit from the words of Shamsh Uddin, because faith is the sail of the boat of human existence.

If the boat has a sail, the wind will carry it far, but if there is no sail, all words will fall flat on him. They who are frank are great lovers of the beloved. All formality subsists with strangers but betwixt genuine lover and beloved, except the talk of love, all else stands condemned.

I wanted to talk, at length, on this matter, though the subject is a single one, yet I shall have to dig deep and make many canals before the water will reach the tank of the heart. Either the discourser is tired or the hearer is fatigued or the discourser is finding excuses, else, the conversation that does not remove all sorrow is not worth two pence. The lover cannot prove by arguments the excellence of the beauty of the beloved, nor can anybody offer arguments to convince him of the shortcomings of the beloved. It follows that argument has no place here what matters is desire for love. If we try by a poem to exaggerate greatness of the beloved, it will be no exaggeration on our part. We know that the disciple offers his spirit to the teacher because that one mark of his is replete with a thousand meanings and any disciple who approaches the teacher, forgets his self (importance) but becomes a beggar at his door.

Bahāuddin said, "The disciple does not give up his self and lose sight of it for the sake of the teacher, rather his self starts desiring and craving for the self of the teacher."

Maulānā said, "It should not be like this. If this is the case, both will become of the status of teachers. You should try to gain the light within you that the fire of doubts may be extinguished there and you may be relieved of it and turn fearless. In the heart of the person in whose self the light has appeared, all the offices. dignity and ranks of ministers shine like lightning and disappear instantly, just as in the hearts of the wordly people the fear of God and passion for the spiritual world of the saints appear like the lightning and disappear. The lovers of God have become totally of God, they are all the time facing the Lord and have turned their back to the world. The desire for the objects of the world arises in them just as the carnal desire arises in an impotent person, only to pass away and hold its place no longer there. But, the worldly people are quite different in spiritual matters. (For, if at times, a spark of spiritual world comes in their mind, it disappears soon and does not stay for long.)

## CHAPTER 22

Pasokhta of revered memory has written:

He, the Bestower of gifts, cares not for the world,
He is the life of all and Himself needs no life,
Of all things, you think of
He is the Goal of them all. Himself He seeks them not.

This is an unpleasant talk uttered neither in self praise nor in the praise of the king. After all, O man! what are you to gain, if He expects and accepts nothing from you. Such a conversation does not behove a friend. It is uttered by enemies or, to enemies, viz. 'that we do not care for you and we do not need you.' Just notice that this lover and vigilant Moslem, in the state of intoxication, is telling his Beloved that he does not care for Him. Such an attitude can be compared to that of a sweeper attending to the privy (latrine) saying that the king cares a little for him but has no need of other sweepers. How does this fool sweeper enjoy these words, that the king does not care much for him? He ought to have said that as he stood on the roof of the latrine, the king passed that way. He prayed audibly for the longevity of his life. Hearing this, the king kindly looked towards him and for a long distance went on casting a kind look at him. This is an enjoyable talk. What do the words mean that the king does not care for sweepers, and this is no praise of the king nor something which is enjoyable for the sweeper.

"Beautiful are the words that come in imagination." But, what benefit can thy imagination confer on a fool for the people are equally careless about thy imagination and condition. If you talk about your fancies, they will shun you and run away from you. What worth has fancy that the Lord should care for it? This verse is meant for heretics. This can never be said to the faithful. To be grateful to God is an open secret. If thy act is such, that it deserves praise, the Lord will confer on thee blessings according to the merit of thy act and shall not forget thee. Our conduct bears similarity to that of the heretics of bygone days whilst, we pride in calling ourselves Moslems (the faithful).

The Maulānā said, "There is something besides also. When your heart tells you that a certain thing is bad and unpleasant, your heart's (internal) eye has surely witnessed a beautiful and pleasant thing which is responsible for your present dislike of the object before you, for he who has tasted sweet water alone will call salt water saltish.

The genuine forms of objects are revealed by their opposites. That is why God has placed in you the light of faith that act which looks bad presumes that compared to it, there is some good thing that makes it look ugly. That is why many hearts do not cherish agony of separation and leaving God are happy and engrossed in ephemeral things of the world. They think that the vocation in which they are engaged is the best vocation. God shall bestow unto you that which you want and which you consider the best and shall bestow it on you at the place where you dwell. "The bird flies with two wings and the faithful flies with his faith (effort)."

The creation is classified under three heads. Some are angels who are pure intellect and worship, remembrance and prayers of the Lord are their food and life, just as the fish lives in the water and water is its life, its bed and covering. The water does not cause it any injury. The created beings (the angels) are devoid of desires and are pure, then, if they are not subservient to desires, it is no praise of them. Or if no carnal desires sway them, they cannot be styled to be practising austerity. It they offer obeisances, no praise will be bestowed on them, for all this is their nature and they cannot live without performing those pious offices. The second class of creatures is the animals which are pure, unadulterated desire (carnal). They do not possess discriminative faculty and cannot sift good from evil. The third class is man, a poor being, combination of discrimination and passion. He is half angel and half brute, half snake and half fish. The fish draws him into water whilst the snake draws him towards the earth. Thus a scuffle is ever going on within him. "When his intellect dominates over his passion, he rises in esteem over the angels even, and when passion domineers over his intellect, he falls below the scale of the animals."

"Man through his intellect is an angel, and swayed by ignorance he turns into an animal. Man is dragged this way and that by these two." The head of the village was shouting, "Interview is the first and primary thing and thereafter comes talk, just as, the king is seen by many persons but a few gain audience and talk to him. He who holds conversation with the king is the honoured person." The Maulānā said, "This is an inapt and useless statement, rather its converse is true. Moses wanted that after his talk with the Lord, he might be blessed with the vision of the Lord. The status of holding conversation with the Lord was reserved for Moses but the vision was bestowed on Prophet Muhammad. So that the head of village said cannot be correct."

A certain person told Sultān Shamsh Tabraiz that by convincing arguments he had establihed the existence of God. Shamsh said, "It is true; last night the angels came and said to me, 'All praise to that person (you) who has established the existence of our God. May God confer on him long life! He has performed a great deed for the people of the world. Fool as he is, he does not know that God stands Self-proved. Where is, then, the need and occasion for proving His existence? It does not require any argument to establish His existence. In creation, is there anything that does not praise His purity?"

There is no gainsaying the fact that those learned in law are clever people and in their own branch of learning, are farsighted. Between these people and the people of the world, a wall is raised to distinguish between what is legal and what is illegal because if the walls were not there as curtains, they would never study Law and would remain ignorant of it. Take the illustration that the spiritual world is like a river, compared to this world which is like foam and fret over water. God wishes to keep this little foam populated; so He made some people ignorant of the river so that they might preserve the foam (the world flow). If they did not remain engaged in that work, they would destroy others and that would mean confusion in the world. Suppose, a tent is set up for the king and many people are kept engaged in its upkeep. One of them says, 'If I do not make the pegs, where will the ropes of the tent be tied?' Another says, 'If I do not prepare the ropes, how will the tent be raised up?' Everyone of them knows that he is a servant of the king who will reside in it with his consort. So, if the weaver were to give up his profession and try to become the minister, the whole world would go naked. So he is born with passion for his work in which he is engaged and he enjoys it. It follows that men are born to keep the show of this world (of foam) on and to maintain its discipline and order. But, who can praise the dignity of that man for whom the whole world order is created and he is not created to keep the world in order. God always bestows on every person one or other desire which keeps him engaged and happy, even if, he were to live a million years, he would enjoy and continue to carry on his profession and go on advancing in it. "In the world, there is nothing that does not praise the purity of God." In other words, every one is created for some work or other. The rosary of the rope-maker is one and of the peg maker another. So also, the weaver and blacksmith are engaged in separate service and he who is seated in the tent takes rest there. He is the beloved of God. He counts beads of a different kind.

When people come to me (to converse) and I remain silent, they are pained and grow sullen. If I talk to them something beyond their capacity to follow, they become angry and start defaming me, saying that I am displeased with them and desire to keep them off. But, this is incorrect.

Why should I run away from them? Does the fuel run away from the vessel, kept on it? Yes, the vessel runs away because it cannot bear the fire beneath it. So, the getting away of the wood and the vessel is not running away of it but when it sees that the vessel is delicate, it removes itself. Really, to get away is the nature of the vessel at all times. So, our running away from these people is really their running away from us. We are like unto mirrors. If their tendency is to run away, we reflect that nature of theirs in us and for their sake we run away. Mirror is something in which the people see their faces. If we look sad to others, it is their reflection seen in us (like a mirror) because to be gloomy is great weakness and it has no place in our nature. Why should we ever be sad?

Luckily, I met Sheikh Sālah Uddin at a public bath. I was very polite to him and he was equally considerate to me. I felt uneasy at his display of humility and I thought to myself that I should not have shown so much humility all at once but would have done it gradually. Rubbing first the hand and then slowly the body by and by so imperceptibly that the other person might not be even conscious of my service and he might have felt it as an ordinary matter. It should not happen that for my sake he might be put to trouble, to render service to me for the service rendered by me to him, for, if I gradually accustomed him to such feeling from my side, he would not take it as humility but an expression of friendly feeling. Both for the sake of friend and also for the enemy this method of serving gradually should be adopted, for example, in the case of an enemy, give counsel politely first, but if he does not hear, rebuke him and remove him from your place and still, if he persists, beat him. The Qurān says, "First counsel them, thereafter do not meet them and lastly beat them."

The world goes on like it. Do you not see how conciliatory is the approach of spring first? First it informs its coming by displaying a little of the fresh colour, removing the cold winter's touch and displaying warmth. The trees also grow in the same way. They display new buds which sprout out and smile greets them, then, they don the garment of flowers and leaves. The Sufis interpret it as so many ways to reach the Beloved and after all, they possess Him. Whether it may be the work of the world, or of the spiritual (next) world if the man wholly throws himself in the work at the outset and puts all efforts into it and if even then he can not gain victory over it, he gives it up. So also, the way of worship is stated in this way. He who is accustomed to take a seer of food a day, should reduce the quantity of meals little by little by degrees every day, then, he will find that after two years, his appetite will be reduced to half and no sign of weakness will appear in his body. So also, should he grow and make his progress in worship, in living in solitude and offering prayers. When someone starts a spiritual life, let him first be content with offering orisons (namāz) five times a day as it is ordained. Later on, he should gradually go on increasing the number, till he attains to the state of the adepts about whom it is said, "Those people are engaged all the time in prayers."

## CHAPTER 23

He must keep in view the account of Sheikh Alāuddin, son of Chaush. From it, he will derive benefit, and the veil of darkness that conceals his heart will be removed. The son of Chaush, perhaps, imagines in his heart that since many people abandoned their hearth handsome, their children, friends and country and started on a pilgrimage to Sind in India putting on iron sandals which even broke, so arduous was their pursuit in that travel, and all this they did in the hope that they might meet a saint who carries with him a little perfume of the next (spiritual) world. Many people died in the search after enduring much hardship. Fortunate art thou who has found one such person in thy house and you are trying to avoid him and is running off from him. This is thy mistake and the cause of thy misery. Maulānā always praised Sheikh Salāhuddin often before me and called him a great personality. This is a minor but an important matter for, ever since I have met Maulānā, I have never heard him call Sheikh Salāhuddin by name but always respectfully as "our leader, our master, God's elect."

Is it that his evil habits have cast such a veil on his eyes that leads him to say that Salāhuddin is worth nothing. After all, how has he injured the Maulānā that leads him to tell his son not to fall into the blind wall (Sheikh Salāhuddin). He says that out of his kindness towards his son, but the son does not value this advice and does not consider it blindness. Why is it so? It is because when you perform an act which does not meet the approval of Sheikh Salāhuddin, you become a source of his displeasure and annoyance and when you are under his displeasure, all spiritual experience and visions are barred to you. The more you grow black in the smoke of hell, the more, he will be advising you and rebuking you that you should not be a victim of his anger and displeasure and invite you to good acts and ask you to enter the palace of kindness, pointing to you that it shall follow as a result of your good acts, for by these good acts shall shine your heart and you will become the effigy of light. Sheikh Salāhuddin advises you in your interest and for your benefit. You, however, interpret this kindness as prompted by some ulterior sinister motive. So you ponder, after all, why should such a great soul be inimical to you? Suppose, you get strongly addicted to prohibited wine, music or dancing and be intoxicated, will you at that time-reconcile with your enemies i.e., will you excuse them on that occasion and will you express the desire to kiss their hands and feet and will both the heretics and the faithful become equal in your eyes?

Therefore, know that Sheikh Salāhuddin cherishes real spiritual enthusiasm and fervour. A very river of this fervour is ever welling out of him. How can he, then, be inimical to anybody! God be praised, it is impossible that he should ever bear grudge to anybody. He is always kind and merciful to God's creatures, and is always imparting salutary instruction to all. Otherwise, what relationship is possible with him, a veritable king of spirituality and master of saintliness of these mouse-like and frog-like creatures? What is the worth of these insignificant people before him?

It is stated that nectar is located in darkness. It means that the saint's body dwells in darkness whilst within them is nectar (water of life) hidden. So, if you despise the darkness (body of saints), you will really despise the water of life (the spirit of saints). How will you than get it? If you desire to learn the art of the eunuch or the ways of the wayward women from them, you will have to face many troubles and endure many unpleasant things and will have often to act against your natural instincts. If you are not prepared for that, you will never succeed and your hope will never be fulfilled. Then, why do you doubt that to attain eternal life which is the privilege of the saints and prophets, you will have to exert much or persevere a lot and in its search endure many troubles and forsake many desires? Only then, shall you achieve the goal.

The Sheikh does not say that you should abandon your wives, renounce your children and wealth as was the practice in times of yore, and the teachers used to advise their disciples thus and when they had done so, they used to take over their wives and children for themselves and the disciples used to put up with it, and look at yourself you are commanded to obey a certain order but you refuse to follow it. "May be, that you like a thing which may be detrimental to you." These people, blind with foolishness and ignorance do not give a moment's thought to it that if a man loves a woman, how obedient he becomes to her and verily, becomes the dust of her feet. Sacrificing all his wealth, he wants to woo his beloved and tries to bring the beloved under his control and runs all day and night at his beck and call. Now, if some disciple loves his spiritual teacher or God, but disobeys his little commands and abandons him on simple pretext, know that he is not a lover, or a seeker. If he had been a lover, he would have endured far more troubles, and considered misery as sweet as honey and sugar.

## CHAPTER 24

Maulānā said, "Let us go to Tufan, as it is a suitable health resort for summer. Although Antioch is also a good place to pass summer, yet it is populated with many Turks (Rumi) and they do not follow our language, although a few can grasp the purport of our conversation. I was discoursing on a subject to people amongst whom were some heretics, who were weeping in the midst of the discourse and were much affected by it."

Some one remarked, "What can they follow of the discourse when it is such that even among thousands of Moslems, a few can follow it? Why should they weep when they cannot fully follow it?" Maulānā remarked, "What matters, is not the form of the words but the real thing is to follow the spirit and purport. Do you not see that every one accepts that the Creator and Sustainer is the same God. He is the Supreme over creation. We have to return to Him. To forgive or to condemn lies in His hands. When they heard these things and found them related to the praise of God, His remembrance awoke in them. Restlessness and desire for the Lord captured their heart, for in the discourse, they smelt the fragrance of their Beloved. Although the paths are different, the goal is one just as, the roads that lead to Meccā are various, some are by the sea, others by the land, some through Turkey, others through Syria, some are long, whilst others are short. Apparently, you find that all the paths are different from one another but the goal of all is one and the same, so all roads are the same because they are all going to one place. Hence, if you keep sight on the goal, they all are one and the same. The hearts of the people are closely related to Kābā, because there is no place for opposition. That relationship is neither heresy nor faith. There is no particular thing because it has no particular affinity with any path or practice. All the people reached the same destination although they travelled by so many different paths detailed by us, then all quarrels of the path of being long or short vanished. On reaching Kābā (Meccā), when they saw that the goal was one, all discussion and all quarrels related to the paths ceased.

If the cup had life, it would have become a veritable sacrifice and slave of the potter who had made it and would have fallen in intense love with him. Some say that the cup should be placed on the table, others say that it should be washed from inside, some others say that it is not necessary to wash it. The difference in opinions is about this extraneous matter viz, washing, but all agree on the point that its maker is one person and it is not made by itself. Now, consider that all the people in their hearts love God and are in His search. They ever pray to Him, seek everything from Him, and do not consider any one else other than Him as God, the Supreme Lord over everything. This inward thought within the heart is neither heresy nor faith, and no term can be assigned to it within the heart. But, when it flows out from inside through the passage of the tongue, it is transformed into words of the alphabet, a, b, c etc., and at once it is classified as heresy or belief, or good or bad. Now, consider the case of vegetable. In the beginning, when it comes out of the earth, it is beautiful, delicate and without any definite shape or form, but the more it grows, the more it becomes big, stiff and uncomely and its colour too is changed. If the heretic and the faithful one were seated together, until they open their lips, they will look similar. It is not possible to brand their thoughts. Within the heart, there is the rule of freedom because thoughts are made of subtle stuff and submit to no authority. "We can put restrictions and rules on the externals. God is, however, the Master of the hearts." Whatever thoughts God sends in your heart, cannot be removed by effort or condemnation. They who say that God needs no instrument or means (to act) are quite correct. Watch, how without any pen, instrument or colour, He has given birth to innumerable thoughts in your heart. Even those thoughts are like free birds and deer of the forest whom you cannot confine in cage or keep tied by ropes, nor can you sell them, for you will have to gain possession (i.e. confine them) ere you can sell them. How will you transfer their possession until you first get possession over those wild deer and free birds? So, their sale and purchase are not permissible by scriptures. So also, with the thoughts. As long as, they are confined in the cell of the heart, they have no name or form and are amenable to no order. They cannot be styled heresy or belief. No judge can say you have no right to think in that way, nor can he call on you to swear that you will think in a particular way. In short, none has a right to rule another person's heart.

These thoughts are like the free birds and wild deer. When they are uttered, they are encaged in words and sentences and are subject to be condemned as heresy or praised as belief. Just as, this is the world of bodies, so there is a world of ideas, and imagination. But, the Lord transcends all these worlds. He is Pure and is neither outside, nor inside. Now, consider the almightiness of the Lord Who without any pen or instrument, gives these thoughts and imagination form as they come out through the tongue. Now, if you tear open your heart and cut it into pieces in the hope that you may be able to discover those ideas and imagination, you will not find them. In the blood or in the veins or in no other part, you will be able to discover them. Neither they will have a condition or direction nor will they be above or below. They will be only ideas, so, if we search them outside the heart, we shall not be able to find them or see them. So, like the realm of ideas, many subtle traits of the Lord whose excellence is difficult to describe are working. All this goes to show that He is the Creator of everything. Now, consider, how Infinite, and Unknowable must He be! Just as, the skeletons of men are gross compared to their souls, so also these incomparable and subtle meanings which have been described above, in relation to God are gross like the bodies and forms. If that Pure Soul manifests Itself from behind the veil, the intellect and soul of man will be like body (gross) in relation to the Lord.

God cannot be contained in the world of ideas nor in any other world, for, if He had been contained in the world of ideas, the ideas would have encircled Him from all sides and God would not have been called the Creator of ideas. It follows that His nature is beyond the realm of ideas and imagination.

God turned the dream of the Prophet true, namely, "If God wills, they will enter the true mosque." Everybody says that he goes to Kābā, but a few say 'If God wills, we shall enter Kābā.' They are lovers, for, the lover never considers himself the doer and free to act because he knows that he has no freedom and power. For him, the Beloved is everywhere and for him He is all, so, he says, 'If the Beloved wills, I shall enter Kābā." Apparently, the people think that pure mosque means Kābā, but the lovers of God and the select few understand by pure mosque union with the Lord, although they say, 'If God wills, we shall meet Him and enjoy His vision. This is the state of the lovers. But rare will be the occasion and very secret shall be the import if the beloved says, "If God wills"; only a rare personality is wanted to follow this mysterious statement.

There are some Lord's devotees whom God loves and does for them all these acts which the lovers do for their beloveds. Just as, the lover of God had said, 'If God wills, I shall attain to Him,' so also does God say to His beloved slave 'INSHĀALLĀH' (If God wills). If I disclose the meaning of this, even the advanced saints will not follow it. So, how can this be expressed before the ordinary people? The pen refuses to write further. He who cannot see the camel at the top of the minaret, how can he see the hair on the mouth of the camel? I again start the old discourse. When the lover says, 'If God wills,' it means that they have no freedom, all power rests with the Lord. If He wishes, he will enter Kābā. They are those lovers who are drowned in the love of the Lord and none besides Him has any place in their eyes, they consider it blasphemy to remember any one besides. Not to speak of others, even he has to efface his ego. Until this happens, entry into the presence of the Lord is impossible. "There is none besides Him in the two worlds."

The Lord says that the dreams of the Prophet are like those of the lovers of God and the true people who will manifest their truth in the other (next spiritual) world. Rather all manifestation of this world is like unto dreams, the reality of which will be found in the next world. If, in the dream, you see yourself riding a horse, it means that you will obtain the fulfilment of your desires. Now, what is the relation of this horse with your desire so that such a meaning is ascribed to it? So also, if you see in the dream, that some money is given to you, it means you will hear some nice discourse from some learned person. Now, what is the relation of money with your discourses? So, we say all things of the world are like dreams. "This world is a dream of a person who is asleep." The meaning of these dreams and their interpretation in the next world will be different. They will not be as they appear in the dreams. Their interpretation is given by the learned one (Prophet) who is appointed by you, for everything is revealed to him. Just as, on entering a garden, a gardener, at once, on seeing the trees, tells you the name of the tree although there are no fruits on it. He tells you that it is of date, it is the pomegranate, this is the fig tree and so on. This is because he is acquainted with that art. The Day of Judgment is not necessary for him to interpret the dreams and find out their meaning. He shows from the outset what a particular dream connotes, just as a gardener knows what fruit a particular tree will bring forth. All the luxuries of the world i.e., clothes, wealth, family, property, are not the real purpose but with some ulterior motive, they are brought forth. Suppose, you had a million rupees with you in cash and you were to feel hungry and no bread was available, will you allay your hunger by eating your money? So, is the desire of a woman for a child and satisfying her natural craving, just as cloth is necessary to protect against cold or heat, so every article is needed for a particular defined purpose and satisfying necessity and its connection goes to the Lord and He is the real object (Being) sought.

So God should be sought for His own sake, not for any other reason because He is the Supreme of all, Omnipotent Delicate and Subtle, the desires which are for anything besides Him, are low and not befitting. All desires ultimately end in Him.

When God is realised, the goal is attained. Beyond it, there is no other way.

At this time, man is enveloped in darkness, doubt and difficulty and there is no way out for him but when he will turn a lover, all doubts and difficulties will disappear for him. "The love of some one makes you deaf and blind to all others." Satan did not pay homage to Adam and disobeyed him and said, "O God! You have created me out of fire and man is made of clay, how can one of higher order bow before one of lower degree?" This was the sin of the Devil, his effrontery to the Lord and he picked up a quarrel with Him. He was, therefore, turned out of paradise. He said to the Lord, "You put me to trial and now you rebuke me." The Devil sinned and the Lord turned him out of Paradise. Adam sinned. God rebuked him and turned him out of Paradise. Adam stood silent. Addressing God Satan said, "O Lord! Just as you have deluded me, I shall beguile all the progeny of Adam. "(Qurān), Lord asked Adam, "When I rebuked you and turned you out of Paradise, why did you not argue with Me and said like Satan?" Adam replied, "I was conversant with the argument but how could I be impertinent to Thee and my love for Thee prevented me from raising any objection."

The Maulānā said, The ethical code is like a washerman's place of washing. It can be illustrated thus. The king has one court and one law for all plebians, and patricians but count is not taken to the law court. The law is full of benefits. The work of the world is carried on through it. If there were no law, the work of the world would suffer. But, the case of the dervish is different. They are like the counsellors of the king. They always associate with Him. What is the need for them to know the law or the judge? No knowledge of them is necessary for him who is the companion of the king. There is a mightly difference between these two things. In a school, there are many teachers. The head of the institution pays them according to their ability. To some, he pays ten dirhams to another twenty and to the third thirty and so on. Likewise, I talk to everyone according to his capability to grasp my conversation. "Hold converse with the people according to their capacity."

## CHAPTER 25

A person entered the assembly. Maulānā said, "He is our beloved and the discourse of today will be principally directed to him. When a branch is laden with fruits, it bends down. But, the one without any fruits holds its branches high like the cypress tree. When the branches are laden with fruits, they are held up by sticks so that they may not touch the ground. The prophet was very humble because he was laden with fruits of this world and the next. "Never did anybody excel the prophet in the exchange of greetings." This was so because he always greeted a person ere the other raised his hands. Salutation was done with a view to show honour to a person. If, perchance, he forgot to greet first, even in reply, he greeted with great humility. People first learnt the art of exchange of greetings from him. All mannerism has been learnt by the people from him. All are like his shadows. Just as, if a man's shadow first enters a house, it must be deemed as if the person himself has entered it. The shadow is after all a shadow and cannot precede the body of which it is like a branch. Mannerism is kneaded in man from the days of the Prophet, when he was in so many particles. In the various parts of man entered these particles, some were very shining and others were not, while others were very dull. Now, they are manifesting themselves. But this shining quality is extant in them from before and their particles excel in their light, shining quality and manners even Adam.

There are certain classes of people who look to the beginning of an act whilst there are others who keep their eyes on the end (result). Of the latter class those who keep their attention on the end are to be respected more for, they and belong to a high order because they keep their eye riveted on the end, and on the Day of Judgment. There are, however, special class of people who hold the view that they should not fix attention on the result, but they should look to the beginning, for, if wheat is sown in the beginning, in the end wheat and not barley shall be reaped. Therefore, they keep their eye on the beginning. There is still another class of people, very dear ones, who care neither for the beginning nor for the end, even the remembrance of beginning and end never occurs to them. They are merged in the Lord. Whilst, there are another class of people who are drowned in worldliness. They too, are neither cognisant of the beginning nor of the end. They are deep in ignorance and are the fuel of hell fire.

This shows that the Prophet was the real personality. So has the Lord said, "Had you not been born, I would not have created the sky (Heaven)." Honour, humility, sobriety and dignified manners all are gifts and his shadow, because they are born of him, just as the act by the hand is really the act of mind (intellect) because the intellect dominates it.

Mind has no reflection and casts no shadow but the Prophet did cast a shadow, although not apparent, just as, there exists a spiritual world but it is not visible to the eyes. If reflection of the mind (intellect) was not cast on the limbs, they would all become useless, unable to function. Hands and feet will refuse to move and eyes will refuse to see and ears will refuse to hear. Owing to the intellect's reflection on them, they are all working. If you look to reality of everything, you will notice that in reality, the intellect is working and doing every act. These hands and feet are merely its instruments. In a way, the saint is the representative of God on the earth, and is perfect intellect and all other (ordinary) people are like his feet and hands. Whatever they perform is done by them as reflection (direction). But, if any evil act results from them or some mistake occurs, the cause is that perfect intellect has ceased to cast its reflection on them. Just as, if some one turns mad and begins to act rashly, everybody will come to know that there is no intellect in his head, it is not casting its reflection on him and he has travelled beyond the jurisdiction of the latter.

Intellect is of the nature of the angels. The angels have wings, feathers and a form but the intellect has no wings, no feathers yet both are of the same genus and both act in similar manner, and are of similar nature. We should not cast our looks on the form, when, in spirit, they are working similarly. This means if you melt the forms of angels, they will become mere intellect and their wings, feathers etc., nothing will be left. Thus, they demonstrate to us that they are nothing but intellect which had assumed a form and which could be styled as the effigy of intellect. Suppose, you make a bird of pure wax, make its wings and feathers. All of them will be pure wax. You melt it and all will be wax, neither there is head nor foot nor arms in it. It is clear, now, that it is all wax and it had adopted a form or body of wax. So also, when snow melts, it becomes water and when it was frozen it was called snow but even then, it was water. The only difference is that when it was frozen, the water, had assumed the form (of ice).

So a man might become an angel living in the company of an angel because it is possible for an ass to become an angel by following an angel. Christ had the feather of intellect with him, so, he flew to the sky. If that person had half the feather of an ass, he would have ceased to be an ass. There is no wonder that an ass may turn into a human being in the end because God rules everything and is Omnipotent Lord over all. Do you not see that when a child is born, he is more ignorant than an ass even. He puts his hand in dirt and puts it in his mouth. The ass has intellect, he extends his feet when he makes water, in order that urine may not fall on his feet. When a child grows by God's grace and He bestows intellect on him, he becomes an intelligent man. So, if God turns an ass into a man, it is not a matter of surprise.

On the Day of Judgment, every limb of man will become vocal separately. The Philosophers interpret it thus. They say, how is it possible for the hand to talk? Therefore, it means that there will appear some sign which will reveal something. Just as, if a boil were to appear on the hand, it can be said that the hand is saying (is vocal) that it is suffering from axcess of internal heat, or if the hand is turned black or is wounded, it is saying that it has come in contact with a black pot or is injured by knife. The limb will express itself thus. But the Sunnis interpret it literally and state that this is not the way in which they will express themselves, rather, they will talk as we do and that conversation will be understandable. Man will say that he did not steal. The hand will interrupt him and in plain language contradict him saying, 'Indeed I did hold the stolen article.' Surprised, the man will say, "How is it that these hands and feet talk so plainly now but formerly, they never did so. The hands and feet will reply. "God has now blessed us and bestowed power of speech on us." He bestows that power of speech on every one. He can make the stones, the pebbles, the houses, the doors and the threshold—all vocal. He has given your tongue the power of speech. Tongue is a piece of flesh, so is thy hand. The piece of flesh called tongue can speak but the hand cannot, how does thy intellect accept this? But, since you have ever seen the tongue talk but never the other limbs, so, you feel it is impossible (that on the Day of Judgment all limbs will be endowed with speech). But in the eyes of the Lord, the tongue is a mere pretext for speech. He ordered it to speak and it became vocal and whenever He orders it to speak, it speaks. Speech is in proportion to the capability of man.

Our speech is like the water in a drain, through which it flows. What does the water know which way the drain will take it whether towards the garden or towards fallow land. We know when large quantity of water comes flowing through the drain, we conclude that it is going towards a large tract of land and when the flow is meage, it is going to some garden or small piece of enclosed land. "God endows the preachers with that amount of speech which is in proportion to the capability of the audience. If I am a shoemaker with large quantity of leather in my possession, I only cut that amount of leather piece that will be enough for a shoe.

"I am the shadow of a person and his scale (measure),

As is his body so much am I (his shadow)."

There is an insect that lives in the ground, in darkness. It has neither ears nor eyes. This is because where it dwells there is no need for eyes or ears. As he does not need them, so he is not given them (by the Lord). Although there is nc scarcity of ears and eyes with Him. He has infinite effulgence (of light) with Him. But He bestows only that much as is needed because if He bestows excess of it, it will be a burden on him on whom He bestows, Whilst His kindness lightens his burden. Why should He burden a person with excess of load? Just as, if you bestow on a tailor the carpenter's tools and ask him to work with them, this will become a source of trouble to him. How can he work with them? So, whatever God bestows, He does so according to the capability of a person.

Just as, the insect of the above illustration dwells underneath the ground in darkness and does not feel the want of another world, neither craves for the Divine vision. If it was conferred the ears of intellect and eyes of heart, what will they avail of and what purpose shall they serve to it. The work of the world goes on with the external eyes, so they are bestowed on creatures. They have no thought of after life and the next world, so what is the use of conferring on them a wakeful heart (full of intellect)?

> Beware, never think that there are no pilgrims on the path,
>
> Nor think that there are no perfect saints with signs of perfection,
>
> Just as, you are unacquainted with spiritual secrets,

Do not think there are no others who are not conversant with them. You must know that this world is maintained by ignorance. The world would cease to be if there was no ignorance. The desire to meet the Lord, the passion to remember Him, the intoxication of His Love are all things of the next world and inhabit it. If all the people were gifted with these attributes (of the next spiritual world), they will cease to dwell in this world but will inhabit that world. But God wants that we should remain here so that the two worlds may continue to exist. He has, therefore, created two officers—ignorance and enlightenment (wakeful- ness), so that both the houses may remain inhabited.

## CHAPTER 26

The Maulānā said, "For all these—kindness, effort and grace, that are offered to me in my presence and behind me, if I fail to express my thanks and praise you for your excellence and express my apology, you should not think that it is due to my arrogance or carelessness. The fact is that I do not know how to express my gratitude and give good in return for kindness done to me. I know full well that you cherish full faith in me and your treatment towards me is at the prompting of the Lord. I, therefore, present you to the Lord that He might give good return for the good done to me by you. After knowing all this, if I should thank you by tongue and praise you in words, it means that I have diminished the amount of good turn that the Lord would have otherwise conferred on you (if I had remained silent). This humility, this apology and this kindness are the way of the world. If in this world, you undergo trouble for another or bestow wealth or render service to him due to your office or do some other good turn, the best thing is that God should give you a suitable return for it. I, therefore, do not thank you. Thanks giving is a formality practised by the worldly people.

Just as, you know that wealth is not a thing that can be eaten by itself, it is useless for that purpose, but it is true that through its instrumentality, articles of food and other things of comfort, slaves and other articles can be purchased and even dignity can be obtained. Through it, the people will praise them and bow before them if they have money. They get the return in the world in the form of dignity and honour and praises of the people (then, what remains for them to get in the next world?)

Sheikh Nasāj of Bukhārā was a great saint, a man of heart. The men of learning and wealth used to visit him and sit respectfully before him. The people used to learn from him the meaning of the secret verses of the Qurān and the traditioṇ. The Sheikh answered, "Gentlemen I do not know Arabic. You translate the passage to me and I shall explain its meaning to you." When they translated a verse to him, he critically commented on it at length and also told them that the particular verse descended on the Prophet at a particular place in such and such condition, and stated the various stages and pointed, in detail, the different ways by which progress could be made in that direction.

One day, some descendant of Hazrat Ali praised Qāzi Marif before the Maulānā very much and ended his praise by saying that never, at that time in the world, there was a greater Qāzi (Judge) than him. He did not accept any bribe and had attachment for nobody. In God's name, he dispensed justice to everybody. Maulānā replied, "You say that he does not accept bribe. It is a perfect lie. You are from the line of Hazrat Ali and belong to the family of the prophet. Is it not itself a bribe that you are praising him? What greater bribe than it will be that you offer praise in his presence?"

## CHAPTER 27

Sheikh Ul Islam Tarmuzi said one day, "Sheikh Burhan Uddin discusses the spiritual mystery with excellence and the reason of it is that he has critically studied the works of the saints, their tenets and their sayings and their inner experience." Somebody retorted, "You too have studied those works, why do you not explain matters with the same excellence? The Sheikh replied that he cherished agony in his heart, put effort in his spiritual exercises and was a practical man. The person, thereupon, remarked, "Then, why do you not deal with the subject thus rather than praising his study?"

The truth is that Sheikh Ul Islām Tarmuzi did not cherish the learning for the next (spiritual) world, his affection centered on this world. In this world, some are born to eat meals and others to enjoy the world. This is ever their wish that they should first acquire knowledge and then sell it. This discourse is like a bride, a beautiful beloved, a delicate slave. If she knew that her master wanted to dispose of her, she will never fix her affection on him. But the merchant enjoys his trade. He does not keep the slave for himself and has no such carnal desire that he should keep her for himself. So, if some eunuch is presented with a nice Indian sword or a fine heavy bow, of what avail is it to him except that he should go and sell it; for he has not the strength in his arms to hold it or to pull the bow? He is the lover of something else. He will purchase from the price he will get, delicate decorating things, perfumes etc. What a surprise that by selling such a nice thing he purchases such trifling ware!

This conversation is in the Syrian language. Never say that you follow it. That talk which you have followed is far from the real import hid in it. If you could have followed, it would have been a grand acquisition. Alas! you have not the understanding to follow it. Only if ignorance had left you, you would have been able to follow something. You say that you have filled your water-skin with all the water of the river. This is impossible. Yes, you can say that your water skin is drowned in the water of the river, then, it would be a correct and true statement.

Only that much of intellect which may lead you to the door of the king is sought and is enough. When you have reached the king's threshold, bid good bye to your intellect, because the intellect will now be injurious for you. It will be like a bandit for you. You have reached the king. Surrender yourself to him, and remain in his possession. What concern have you now with little one here and there take an illustration. Suppose, you desire to make a head-dress or gown out of a cloth. Then, your intellect urges you to approach a tailor. Intellect was serving good purpose till it took you to the tailor and you handed over the cloth to the tailor. Now, divorce your intellect and leave the cloth with the tailor. He will prepare the right kind of gown. Leave giving your suggestions to him. So, the intellect of a sick person is good as long as it takes him to a doctor; beyond that it is of no use, for, when he has reached the physician, he should surrender himself to him and follow his advice.

Your mysterious words are heard and understood by the enlightened saints that cherish love's agony in their hearts. Others, less competent, cannot follow them. Do you not notice that amongst the camels, he who is love-mad (intoxicated) can not hide himself? He is easily recognised by the foam issuing from his mouth. "The love-intoxicated devotees have marks of obeisances on their foreheads."

Whatever food the root of the tree draws from the earth nourishes the leaves and leads to sprout the fruits at the top. The root that does not draw its nourishment from the earth gets dried up. How can a fact remain suppressed?

The secret behind this is that these dervishes who are making gesticulations and crying loudly, have learnt many secrets from knowledge of one thing and by understanding a single word many secrets have been revealed to them, just as, if someone has studied many commentators on a text book, and if a single word of the text book is quoted before him, from a single word, he will be able to follow many genuine secrets and principles because of the various commentaries he has studied. As he goes into esctasy on one word, it means that he knows the depth of the subject. He says it is the very thing that he has learnt undergoing much trouble and keeping night vigils. Then, he has gathered this treasure. He says "Have we not ripped open your heart?"

He who have studied the commentary will, by a simple hint, follow a lot. But a new-comer will understand only one word from a single word. He knows nothing besides and does not make any gesticulations or gyrations of ecstasy. Only that number of words which the audience want come out of the lips. So long as, the hearers enjoy this syrup, do the meaningful words go on issuing from the tongue. The moment, they stop drinking, the philosophical and mystical words cease to issue forth from the mouth. If a child wants milk, the paps of a mother issue the milk, and the moment, he stops drinking milk, it stops coming out. If someone objects and says, "Why will the words not flow out?" tell him, "Since you do not drink, so the words do not come out." Know that He who confers on you the power of hearing, imparts to the discourser the power to deliver discourse.

In the days of the Prophet, there dwelt a kind-hearted heretic. He had a Moslem slave. One day, the master of the slave ordered him to carry the pails of the water with him to the bath. On the way, fell a mosque in which the Prophet with his companions was saying his prayers. The slave addressed the master, "Please hold these pails for a moment, so that I may join the Prophet in the namāz. Thereafter, I shall accompany you." He entered the mosque and even after the companions of the Prophet had left the mosque, the slave stayed on. As the time passed and the heat of the day grew, The master shouted to the servant to come out. He replied "How can I come out since He is not leaving me. The master peeped through the chink of the door and found there was nobody with the servant. He was alone. So he asked the slave who was holding him back? He answered, "He who is holding you back from entering the mosque, does not permit me to come out. He is the very same Being. Only you do not see Him. A man is always in love with that which he has not seen, heard or understood and is everyday and night seeking it. "I am the slave of Him Whom I do not see." The man runs off the thing which he has seen and understood. The philosophers who do not accept the traditions, say that if you see a thing once, your desire for it will be satisfied and you will get tired of it. This, however, is not correct. Rather ,the seeking should be kept alive. The Sunnis, however, say that they will be surfeited if they continue to see God in one form throughout and if they see a hundred forms every moment, they will not. "Every moment he shines in new grandeur," If He were to manifest Himself for millions of years, every menifestation of His will be very different from the other, ever new and never resembling the one previously seèn. You are seeing God in many signs and in variegated forms, none resembling the other. His one form is seen by you when you are happy, another form when you are in tears, a third varied form when you are in fear and a fourth different form when hope lingers in you. When illumination of the attributes of the Lord is varied, illumination of His acts, also must be His own illumination (of His Being). You can guess His (Beings) illumination from the illumination of His attributes. Not to speak of the Lord, watch yourself. You, who are a particle of His, change your colour hundred times a day and never remain steady in one state. There are some men of God, His devotees who attain to Him through the teachings of Qurān. There are some other His select slaves who find the Qurān on arrival in this world, and know that it is revealed by God.

God says "I have revealed the Qurān, this Book of instructions. It has descended from Me and I see to its due preservation." The commentators say that this verse

is revealed and relates to the Qurān. This is a good statement. But the truth of the matter is that God says, "O man! I blessed thee within thyself with such capability, understanding, craving, yearning and passion that prompt thee to investigate such things, and I am the Protector of that inner power of thee. I shall never permit it to become useless and I shall take thee to the destined places where if once thou callest Me God and wait, I shall remove all trouble that falls in thy lot."

Somebody approached the Prophet and said "I love thee." "The Prophet said, "Be cautious ere that word comes out of thy mouth." He repeated the same remark, "I love thee." The Prophet said, "Now, you should not run away for, I am going to kill you with my own hands. Alack thy misfortune!"

Once a person came to the Prophet and said to him, "I do not accept your faith. By God, I do not accept it. Pray, take it back from me. From the day, I entered your religion, I have never passed a quiet day. I lost my wife, my children, and honour, in short, I am ruined." The Prophet said "How can religion be taken back? For, whosoever adopted our religion broomed his house, till then, it did not leave him. None who is not holy can enter it. He who will allow a hair-breadth of ego to remain within you, is no Beloved. He will not appear before you and you will not be fit for union with Him. First, become miserable with your life and turn your own enemy and feel the world as your enemy, then you will witness the charm of His beauty. So also in our religion, the case is similar; Until our religion, which makes a place in man's heart, has led him to Truth and has dispelled all unbecoming longing in him, it will not let him turn his face from God. The Prophet has said that the reason why you did not get peace and remained involved in sorrow was the result of the vomit-like-enjoyment of the world in which you were previously indulged. As long as, the least particle of that remains in your self, you will get nothing (no spiritual experience). Just as, when a person vomits, nothing is given to him. Of course, after the vomit, he is given something to eat. So you should go on enduring trouble without demur.

This undergoing pain is like the vomiting. After this vomiting, you will find that joy which knows no sorrow. You will get the rose which has no thorns. You will get that wine which shall ever inebriate and never diminish intoxication. You constantly seek relief from pain in this world and find comfort but (real) comfort is a misnomer in the world. In spite of it, you are constantly seeking after that comfort which is as short-lived as lightning, which brings with it shower of rain, hailstorm and snow-fall which confer further trouble on you. A man bound for Antioch is, by mistake, proceeding on the road that takes him to Qaisaria. Do you think that person will never reach Antioch? If he is going by that route, he will ever reach Antioch. But, if he pursues the route that leads to Antioch, he will reach there howsoever weak he may be and even lame. When you find that the work of this world cannot be completed without undergoing pain, why should you not work hard for a happy end (and successful entry in the spiritual-next world) that this life may not be wasted? The person said, "O Prophet, take back thy religion from me. It is a source of worry for me." But, consider, how can our religion leave a person, until it has taken him to the goal?

A learned person was so poor that even in bitter winter, he was putting on a shirt of fine linen. A bear was brought down in its current by a river from its source in the mountain. The head of the bear was surrounded by water, only a little of its back was visible above the surface of water. The disciples of that learned teacher said to him, "Look, Sir, there goes a coat of skin in the current of water, you need a warm clothing, why do you not take it out and don it? The teacher was shivering with cold, so, he jumped into the river and waded to catch the skin when the bear caught hold of him and he remained struggling in water. The disciples began to cry, "Leave it Sir! and come out." The teacher replied, "I have left it but it does not leave me." So also is the craving for God. How can the craving for the Lord ever leave you? It is an occasion of thanksgiving that we are not our masters but are subordinate to the will of the Lord, just as, a child in infancy keeps nothing with him and wants only milk and that too he

gets when he weeps. Did the Lord forsake the child in that condition? Not so, rather He let him grow and developed him till he began to take food and learnt to jump and play and He led him to that stage where he developed discrimination and wisdom. So also you should understand that our worldly condition is like that of the child (and our grown up state like entry into the next world.) That world is like unto a garden where, when we shall reach, we shall feel this world as the infant state of ours, "I am struck with wonder when I notice the people are forcibly dragged, fettered and bound towards hell." About them, the Lord has said, "Those people, then, put fetters in their feet and chains and burn them in the fire of hell, then, roast them in the fire of union and then burn them in the fire of beauty and effulgence." The fish is not entrapped all .at once. When the hook enters its throat, the string is let loose a little and thereafter, it is pulled again and then again let loose a little and again the string is pulled, till the fish is tired and becomes weak. Then, the fisherman pulls it towards the bank. When the thorn of Love pricks the soul of a man(s), God in His mercy removes his dirty thoughts and waywardness by degrees." God creates both narrowness and expansiveness. "Lā Illāh, Ilillāh (there is none deserving of our obeisance and ownership except God). This is the common belief but the extra-ordinary faith says, "God and God alone exists (Lāilā Allāh hu). As a man sees in his dream that he is seated on a throne and the ministers and nobles stand in audience on either side of his. He, in his heart, says that he is the king and none besides him. This he says in the dream. When he wakes up, he finds himself alone in the house, there being no one besides him. He says, "I am alone here and no one else." To follow this, a wide awake eye is needed. It is not the business of a sleeping eye. Every fraternity disbelieves the other. Everybody says that he is on the path of Truth and holds the charter from God and the others are in error. The others also think in the same strain about their faith. Of the seventy two religions, every one thus refutes the other. When they collect together, they say that the voice of God

descended on none of them. That means all of them agree that none is the recipient of the Divine Message. However, all are agreed that, at least, there is one religion on which descended the Divine message. Now, such a faithful believer who should point out the religion on which the Divine Charter is descended is needed. Faith, after all, is the name of belief and discrimination.

Somebody remarked, "The number of those who do not know is large and those who know are very few. If we start discriminating who knows and by what virtue he knows and also who does not know and by what deficiency he does not know—this will engage us for a long time." The Maulānā said, "Although those who do not know are very many, yet if you recognise some of them, you will be able to recognise all of them, just as, by taking a handful of wheat from a big stock, you know what class of wheat the whole stock is, or by tasting a small quantity of sugar, you will know all the sweets are made of sugar. If, after tasting sugar candy, he says that he cannot recognise sugar, we shall call him a man with horns (beast). Since you do not follow our discourse, we have to repeat it twice or thrice.

God has said "Alhām dullālah rab ul lālmin (all praises are for Him Who is the Sustainer of all the universes)." I also said the same thing. This is not said because there is shortage in the gifts, benevolence and food. There is immense quantity of them. But no appetite is left and the stomach of the guest is full. Since after taking meals, we say Alhamdullah (all praise to the Lord, so we also repeat the formula. But real praise of God is that the food and things of the world are not left with us because food and water can be taken even when you have no hunger and you are not thirsty. That is a lifeless thing which can be taken wherever you like. It has no life and so it cannot refuse coming in your possession and to follow you to the place you want to take it too. But contrasted to them, the spiritual gift of God is a living gift which can fall to your lot only when you have developed great yearning for it. You will get it if you are thirsty and hungry for it. But you cannot exercise any force on

it. If you have no desire for it, you cannot perforce bring it under control. It will hide itself and you cannot find it.

Mulānā was talking about miracles. He said, "If someone flies in the air with speed, it will not be a great surpirse nor would be a great miracle. Even the fast wind can travel with that speed. It can reach any place it likes in an instant. Real miracle consists in your being elevated from an inferior (spiritual) status to the higher one, and transcending the state of ignorance, reach the stage of intellect and instead of remaining mere earth and stone, evolve into life and attain God. God brought you first in the vegetable kingdom. You evolved and entered the realm of the creatures who are formed of blood and flesh. From there, you evolved into the human kingdom. The miracle is that the Lord shortened such a long path for you into such a small and simple one. You passed through those stages and routes although even in your heart and imagination, these matters were not present. Now imagine the path that you traversed and how you came into existence and now, clearly you see that you are here. So you will have to travel to the other worlds (scales of creation). So, do not deny these things and believe them as authentic.

Some people brought a cup of deadly poison to Hazrat Umar and respectfully presented it to him. Umar inquired about the attributes of the contents. They answered when an enemy is not sought to be killed openly, a few drops of this are administered to him to serve the purpose. The enemy who cannot be killed by sword can be easily disposed of by a few drops of it. Umar appreciated the gift and drank the whole of it, saying, "Within me there dwells a deadly enemy (nafs=ego) which defies all sword-thrusts and that deadliest enemy cannot be killed by any arms. He is not a single one. He is an enemy equal to a thousand ones." When Hazrat Umar quaffed it off, all these present turned Moslems, saying that his faith was true one. Thereupon, he said, "Brethren, you have turned Moslems (faithful), but that heretic within (nafs) me persists in his heresy and is not converted."

Hazrat Umar did not mean the faith that the ordinary people possess. He had already attained to the higher

faith of the honest and true people. What he meant was that he wanted to achieve the faith of the Prophets and the saints and that faith should grow into a stern belief. He was desirous of it. As, in a forest, a rumour spread that a great lion dwelts in it, many people travelled to that jungle coming from far off lands after travelling for a year and passing through various stations. When they saw the lion from a distance, they stood aghast and bewildered and did not proceed a step further. The people of the place said, "To see the lion is not enough, since you have travelled such a long distance. The lion is so docile that if you approach and caress him, he does not injure you if this is done in a fearless spirit. But if anyone fears him and hides himself from him, he gets annoyed and attacks him thinking that this person doubts his intention. When you have travelled this long route for a year to come here, what does your standing here mean? Why are you not taking a courageous step towards him?" They said, "All the steps we took were easy but this is the real but most difficult step which is raised to reach the lion. It matters much."

By faith Umar meant—this very step, the step of belief, so that they may take this one step towards the lion. There are very few who are bold enough to take this step. This step is the property of the privileged few who are very close to God and of no others. Really, this is the step that alone matters and who else but the prophets possess the strength to take this step? This step of faith comes in them who have washed their hands with the life (are prepared to sacrifice their lives for faith). Very rare is the true friend. Mere thought of the friend gives strength to the friend. He proceeds on being impelled by that thought and gaining strength and new life all the time. Where is the occasion to be surprised in it? Do you not see that it was the thought (recollection) of Leila that infused strength in Majnun? It became his food and by thought he lived. When the thought of the beloved is so effective in the world that it instils such strength in the lover where is the occasion to be surprised in respect of the Real Friend.

Who must impart strength to his lovers whether present before Him or absent from His eyes? You may not call it mere thought. It is the life of reality. All this world subsists on thoughts and the world is called a reality. It is so called because it is visible to the eyes and is felt. You consider that real world of meaning, of which this world is merely a shadow (branch), is conjectural. What a folly it is! In fact, this world is a mere conjecture. That Reality produces hundreds of such worlds and never gets old. He is beyond the opposites—new and old. Only the branches emanating from it are called new or old. He creates all the creation and creatures and has no attachment to them. He transcends them all.

An architect first thinks of the plan of a house in his mind, of its length, breadth, its height, plinth, courtyard etc. Will you not call it a mere thought although that reality (house) is produced from that thought? If that plan had not come in thought, how could the reality have been born? If, however, these thoughts come in the mind of the architect, they are mere conjecture and not reality.

## CHAPTER 28

It is the best not to ask any question from the Faquir, for questioning him means that we want him to fabricate a falsehood. This is so because if a worldly man puts him a question, he will have to answer him in a way most favourable to him, because the truth cannot be told him as he is unfit to receive it and that morsel is not fit for his mouth and throat. So, according to his aspirations and habits, he should get a wrong reply. An untruth will have to be coined so that he might leave the place although what the Faquir says is ever true and never untruth. The same words are real words and true, even though they may be untruth, because the hearer always considers them true.

A teacher had a disciple who used to beg the whole day long and feed the teacher with it. One day, the disciple brought in alms, some food of which the teacher partook. In the night, teacher had a bad dream. He inquired of the disciple from where he had brought the food. The disciple

replied that he had brought it from a beautiful girl. The teacher said, "By God, I say I never had a dream for the last twenty years. Last night, I suffered from it the cause of which was the alms given by that girl."

Thus, a faquir should avoid things and should not partake of food offered by everybody. As the Faquir is subtly constituted, he is very soon affected and many effects appear on him, just as on a clean sheet of cloth, the minutest mark of even ink is distinctly visible, but if the cloth is dirty, the mark will not be easily visible. So, the Faquir should not dine at the places of the tyrants, ungrateful beings and worldly people. That morsel affects immediately and gives birth to evil thoughts as the food given by that beautiful girl had spoiled the Faquir's thoughts.

## CHAPTER 29

The ways of the seekers and religious adepts are that they are constantly engaged in prayers and spiritual exercises. They distribute their work on appointed hours. Take an example. They get up very early, for early morn is the best time for prayers. At that time, the mind is pure and stable. At that time, everybody, according to his bent of mind, prays to the Lord, as well as he can. The angels say, "We stand alert in rows and we always describe the holiness of the Lord. There are millions of such rows, and as the people in rows develop in worship more and more, we advance them in the first rows. We send back those who err to the back rows. We send them to the back rows when God makes them slack in their worship. This is the divine order. This is a very long story but there is also no escape from it. He who will shorten this tale will reduce his life and suffer. "Yes, it is for the Lord to save any one whom He likes." That is besides this talk.

Now, I shall describe the manners and ways of the spiritually advanced souls. They are such people that very early in the morning the pure souls, angels and those persons who are known only to the Lord and have been hidden from the eyes of the people, come to pay their respects to them since they are so advanced and spiritually elevated. "You see that the spiritually advanced ones are

in numbers visiting them along with the angels." But alack! you are seated close to them, yet you do not recognise them and do not hear their conversation nor pay the salutations that are offered to them. There is nothing to be surprised about it. Such sights as even people seated close to him do not see nor hear their talk, appear before a man who is ailing and is on the point of death. The thoughts of the advanced souls whom I have just stated are far subtler than that of the man who is on death-bed. How can, then, others see the visions which they see? So long as you are not likewise ill and nearing death, you will hear or see nothing of the kind. To see and hear those visions during normal life is impossible for you. The people who are acquainted with the spiritual status of those advanced saints to whom very early in the morning, the angels and great saints visit, do not go to meet them in the morning lest their activities, orisons and worship should be disturbed, and the Sheikh should suffer unnecessary trouble, just as, at the gate of the king, every morning, arrive various slaves to whom are assigned various duties. Some of the slaves cannot approach the king very close and the king sees them from a distance in such a way as if he had not seen them for such is their duty. But there are other slaves who come very close to him. Such are offices and duties assigned to them. But when the king is in the public Hall of Audience, all his servants are free to come close to him from all directions because there is no specified duty assigned to every one of them. "Try to adapt yourself to the nature of God." Establish yourself in this stage. "I become His ears and His eyes," to this stage they attain. This is a very high spiritual state. Very difficult it is to realise the true import of that state. It transcends the state of self and non-self, of existence and non-existence. "With the excess of illumination of God, the city of existence will be consumed" "When the kings enter a city, they annihilate it." If an elephant places his foot in the hole of a mouse, it will be ruined. But fortune of innumerable treasures will become the lot of that deserted hole.

In the deserts are discovered treasures,

In the towns are found dogs.

We have discussed and discoursed a lot on the devotees. Now, what should we say about those who have attained to the Lord. About the Saliks (Mystics), it can be said that they have attained their goal, namely, union with the Lord. But the limit of attainment of those who have attained to Him cannot be described. It is infinite. Yes, it is a union in which no difference remains (with God). That grape which has once ripened does not again become raw and unripe.

I deem it blasphemy to talk on worldly people.

But when the talk turns about you, I cannot restrain myself.

By God, I tell you I do not desire to lengthen the talk. I shorten it.

I am drinking blood and you consider that I am tasting wine.

You are taking away my life and you think you are infusing life in me.

He who will try to shorten this talk, will be acting as if he leaves the correct road and proceeds towards forest of death.

## CHAPTER 30

A Christian surgeon said, "Once a group of the disciples of Sheikh Sardār Uddin visited me. They drank wine and whilst intoxicated, they said to me. 'What you say is true. We also accept Christ, the Son of Mary as God. What you say is truth. But with a view to keep our religion and faith intact, we suppress this fact and deny it openly.' " Some of the audience said, "This Christian is a liar. What he says must never have been said, for, this statement issues from a man who is drunk with the wine catered to him by the devil and the devil himself is strayed from the right path and deludes others. He is condemned and leads others to condemnation. He is turned away from the presence of God. How is it possible that a weak person who being persecuted by the Jews in sheer annoyance, ran from one town to another, and who was in height no more than two yards, should be the sustainer of the seven heavens which have a circumference that requires five hundred years to cover it, and the distance of one heaven to another requires one to walk five hundred years? Their earth requires five hundred years to traverse it and each earth is separated from the other by a distance coverable in five hundred years and under the highest heaven, there is the sea equally deep and there is an angel so high that the deep sea reaches up to his knees and so on. How will the intellect accept that the preserver of these things is such a weak person as it is described above? Next, it is said that Christ is the Creator of heaven and earth. Whatever the people say is really the praise of God and He is by far the Highest and Holiest of all. Next, the Christians say, "The earth element passed into the material elements and holy spirit into the Spirit." Maulānā said, "If the soul of Christ is God, now tell me to what region has his soul departed. The soul returns to the Creator after it leaves the body. If we accept Christ's soul as God, it is the Reality. Now, where will this Reality go?" The Christian said, "Thus has the teaching come down to us and we have accepted it as our religion." Maulānā remarked, "Tell me, if you get in inheritance from your forefathers, bad coins of gold, will you not exchange them with the genuine ones or will you go on insisting, that what you have got (the bad coins) you will have them and none besides." Or suppose, on the death of your father, you became maimed in limbs and when the physicians came, who could cure you of your disease, will you refuse to be treated and prefer to remain with deformed limbs and say, 'I do not want to have them changed.' Or if the water of the town where your father died and where you were born, brought up and grown, was saltish and then, you learnt of another village where there was sweet water available and vegetables grew in plenty and the people of the place were healthy, would the desire be not aroused that you should shift to that new village and by drinking that sweet water be cured of your illness? Or you will insist and say that since that village with saltish water had fallen in your inheritance, you would not leave it. How is it possible that a wise man with senses should talk such nonsense and act accordingly? God has given you an intellect distinct from that of your father; so also your sight and power of discrimination is distinct from his. So you should not cast aside your intellect, discrimination and observation and follow that other intellect which will lead you to extinction or away from the righteous course.

A person who was the son of a shoemaker gained audience to a king who got him trained in the use of arms and appointed him to a high office. Would he say, 'Our ancestors were shoemakers, so I cannot accept this high office,' and would he wish that the king might give him a shop in the shoemaker's market? Even a dog who is such an insignificant creature, when he is trained as the king's hunting dog, leaves the company of its parents and forsakes the mounds and dirty dead stuff on which he used to live earlier and accompanies him in his hunt. So also the hawk when he is trained by the king, does not say that it has inherited from its parents the habit of living in forlorn hills and eating dirty meat and it is not going to answer king's bugle and follow him in his hunt. When even an animal, renouncing its paternal profession, adopts the better life as he gets the opportunity, what a great mistake that a man though being possessed of discriminative faculty superior to all creatures should fall lower and lower in the scale? May God save us from it! Yes, if some one were to say that God conferred honour on Christ, loved him and drew him close to Himself and made him one near to Him, and anyone who would be obedient to Christ would, in effect, be obedient to the Lord, and service of Christ would be God's service, it was correctly said. But if God has sent a prophet who is greater than Christ and who has performed miracles superior to those performed by Christ, it is necessary to follow that Prophet, because he is the Prophet of God and he is not God Himself, nor he desires that he should be worshipped (in place of God). Rather, he himself worships God and loves Him and if he loves another, that too, he does in the name of God and for His sake. "There is no gainsaying the fact that the highest destination of yours is God." If anything is loved so that it may be the means to reach the highest and last destination, God, the love of that other thing too, is love of God.

It is a useless formality to don Kābā with the cloth, for the display of its beauty, it is necessary that Kābā should remain exposed. Just as, torn and dirty garments hide the richness and nobility of the nobles, so nice dress and beautiful clothes hide the excellence, virtue and capability of the faquirs. The heart of the Faquir opens when his clothes are turned into rags and are torn.

There is a head that is decorated by a crown, and yet there is another head whose beauty of the lovely curling locks is veiled by the jewelled crown it wears because it is those curly locks of the beloved that attract lovers to him. Their hearts do not care for jewelled crowns. The crown is decorated with stones whilst the wearer thereof is a living entity, the beloved one. We searched for Solomon's ring but found it ultimately in poverty. Many tricks I played on my Beloved and much humility I practised but He was pleased only with my poverty. Although, since my childhood, I have sought this secret, yet only now, I have learnt that the remover of all obstructions and destroyer of all veils and the root of all worship is poverty. Everything else is mere a branch of it. If you kill a goat and then, try to blow wind in its carcase, of what avail will it be? Fast tries you, yet the effect is that you are spiritually elevated. "God dwells with those who endure and remain patient." All the things that are sold in the market or many professions prove that they are created to satisfy some want of man.

This want is a thing which is not visible to the eyes and is totally hidden in man. So long as, this desire does not make itself manifest, that other thing will not come in the market. So, all the religions, prophets and their miracles have a latent cause behind them. That cause is related to the soul of man. So long as, the chain of his head, does not make a motion, that thing (in the market) will not be brought. "We have enumerated every thing in an open book."

Is the doer of good or evil, one person or two persons? The reply to this query is that when the doer is in doubt what he should do and what he should not do, of course, there are two persons for, a person cannot oppose himself. Judged from the standpoint of the doer of good and evil, man is the same person and good and evil are the same things, for evil is not separate from good. Goodness is the name of the act of leaving doing evil and if evil is not there, what is to be given up. The proof of the statement that the name for leaving evil is goodness, is that if there is no desire to be good, there will be no desire to leave evil and it will be a bad thing. As the Fire-worshippers say that the creator of good is Yazdan and that of evil is Aharman. I answer them that the good things cannot be separated from the bad ones. If the bad things do not exist, the existence of good things will be an impossibility. A thing will be liked when that which is disliked is removed from its way. Happiness is the name for the removal of sorrow and if sorrow does not exist what will have to be removed? It follows that evil and good are one and the same and they cannot be separated. I have stated that unless a thing effaces its self, its virtues and good effects cannot be known. Just as, it is the case of one's discourse. So long as, the letters do not efface their identity in talk, the hearer gets no benefit from it.

If a man calls a wise man bad, he is, in effect, praising him because a wise person hates praise and runs away from it lest he should someday receive censure. The wise person is the enemy of that attribute. But, he who calls bad habit as bad, will be stating that the enemy of the wise man is bad and it will be the praise of the wise man. The wise man runs away from that bad thing and he who runs away from that bad thing is praiseworthy. The reality of a thing is revealed from its opposite. The wise man really knows that he who calls him bad is not his evil-wisher or enemy because he knows that he himself is like a blooming garden round which is raised a fencing wall and on it are placed brambles and thorns and dirt heaps. Those who pass that way see the dirt heaps and not the garden within. Only the wall and the dirt are exposed to their view and they call it bad. Why should the garden be annoyed with them? But, he who blames the garden is in error and injures his interest by speaking ill of it. For, it is meet for him to make friends with the garden so that he can enter it. Now, that he talks evilly of the wall, he cannot enter the garden. The Prophet Muhammad said, "I am the smiling tyrant." It means "I have enmity with whom I am angry." He kills the heretic in one way so that he may be prevented from killing himself in hundred ways. It naturally follows that he should smile whilst he is killing another man (heretic).

## CHAPTER 31

The Police Officer always seeks the thieves and they always fly away from him. But here (in spirituality), the process is reversed, the thief himself is searching the police officer and prays that he may arrest him. 'God asked Ba Yazid what his desire was. He replied, 'I desire desirelessness.' A person has one of the two states, either he cherishes some desire or else he is without desire. It is never the attribute of man that he should desire nothing. It is the trait of that person who is empty of his ego i.e. who has totally effaced his self. To the extent, ego persists in a person in the least degree, to that extent, he is a human being and that human element in him desires, or does not desire. God wants to make him perfect and transfoms him into a perfect teacher so that in the end, he should attain to such a state as there may be left no scope for duality or separateness, and there should be complete union and oneness. All pain arises from this—you desire a thing and you do not get it. When no desire is left, where will be the occasion for sorrow? On this point, there is much difference of opinion in the various schools of thought and various are the stages reached by them. Many people, by efforts and perseverence, attain to those states that they satisfy whatever desire arises in them, by internal strength and intellectual argument. This is in the power of man. But it is beyond the power of man that neither desire may arise in his heart nor doubt may appear therein. Except the love of God, nothing can do it in man. "Tell the Prophet, that Truth dawned and unreality faded."

"Get away O faithful one, for thy illumination is quenching my fire." When the faithful one turns faithful from hand to foot genuinely, he performs that act which God wishes. What does it matter if that desire arises at his instance or at the instance of God. They say that Divine messages did not descend on any one after Muhammad. This is not true. Why should not others receive the message from God? The messages have come to many others although they were not styled divine messages. "The faithful one sees by the eyes of the Lord." When he sees from light of the Lord, he shall see everything from the first to the last, the past and the present, for, nothing is hid from God's light nor can it be hidden from it. For, if anything remained hidden from it, it cannot be called God's light. Even today divine messages do come. Only they are not so called although they convey the same thing as the divine messages of old (that came to the Prophet).

When Hazrat Usmān became Caliph and ascended the pulpit, all were impatiently waiting as to what he would say. He, however, was gazing towards the people and was silent, although the assembly was so much affected that they were not even conscious of themselves. Such was the ecstasy caused in them that they could not stir, neither could they recognise the others nor knew where they were seated, nor could accost any body. That condition they had never previously attained even after hearing a hundred discourses, even after undergoing a hundred penances and following a hundred instructions. They enjoyed many experiences and revelations and learnt many secrets. Hazrat Usmān was simply casting his glance at them but spoke not a word. When he was descending the steps, he simply said, "Your Imām (leader) who acts is superior to him who simply discourses." He stated the truth because for the people who had achieved the fulfilment of their hopes by hearing discourses found that through silence (of their Imām) they were totally transformed. So, whatever Hazrat Usmān said was totally true. Usman styled himself a doer, although to all appearance, he did not perform any act visible to the external eyes. Neither he offered prayers, nor he went to Meccā, neither offered obeisances, nor discoursed about God nor read out from scriptures. It follows that practice or action is not the name of these apparent forms but practice or action means that internal reality of which these are mere apparent forms. The Prophet said, "My companions are like the stars. Whichever star you take as a guide, shall take you to the destination." Does the star talk to the person who follows its guidance? Never, he, however, looking at the star corrects his mistake as to whether he is taking the right course or wrong and thereby, reaches his destination. So also, it is possible that you look at the Prophets of the Lord, and they shall take you to attain the goal without much asking and without great trouble.

"He who desires to see me, let him see me.

For my features shall agitate a person who thinks love is a simple affair."

In the world of God, nothing is impossible and harder than to put up with impossible versions. It can be illustrated thus. You have read a book and revised correcting it making the necessary dotting the is and cutting the ts. Now, a person seated by you is reading it incorrectly, will you bear it without demur? This is not possible. However, if you had not read the book, it would never have occurred to you whether he is reading it correctly or incorrectly. However, after reading the book, you have begun to discriminate the correctness or incorrectness of the work. It follows that it is very difficult to bear with impossible things, and such endurance is the greatest penance. Even the prophets and the saints cannot escape such impossible things.

The first austerity in the path of God is that the seeker should kill his carnal desire (nafs). This is the greatest crusade. The saints successfully underwent it. When they reached the destination and attained the abode of peace, everything right and crooked was revealed to them. Even thereafter, they were involved in still greater struggles, for, all the acts of the people of the world are either crooked or evil, and the Prophets see them and put up with them. If they do not bear them and blurt out the truth, no one will honour or greet them. But the Almighty Lord has bestowed on them a high place of honour, a great heart and a mighty soul. Therefore, they endure even on seeing all crooked things. At the most, they disclose a fault or two so that it may not be heavy on them and they may not be disturbed, rather they praise them saying that the crooked thing is the right one and by degrees remove their faults one by one, just as the teacher teaches a child in the school to write out a line which, when it is completed, the child shows to the teacher. Although the teacher knows that what the child has written is curved and crookedly written but to keep up the heart of the child, he praises him that what he has written is right, only points out a letter or two in the writing as curved and writes them correctly to show him the right way in which they are to be written. Thus, he shows him the correct way to write. He says the rest is correct so that the child may not lose heart and give up writing altogether. The child feels elated by the teacher's remarks. So, by degrees, the teacher teaches the child and he thus progresses. If God wills, we are sure, He can fulfil all the wishes of the Amir, and also others of which he has no knowledge. He will bestow on him all of them. Amongst those things which he does not know that they are to be prayed for, there are things that are like roots of the most valuable things i.e., even those valuable things will be bestowed on him. When these will fall to his lot, the Amir contrasting them with the earlier one that he had sought and received, will feel shy that he was seeking nothing, whilst he got everything. He will then, feel he has got those things and why he was in their face, seeking for those smaller things. The divine gift is that which a man cannot conceive of and it can never come in his imagination because man can only conceive according to his capacity, whilst the bestowal of God is according to His Status and Omnipotence. So, His Bestowal will be according to His Omnipotence and not in accordance with the imagination of the devotee. "So, it is said, "I bestow that thing which is never seen, heard or even conceived by the devotee. Man conceives and expresses desire for things that are according to his capacity and conception, but My bestowal is wider and greater in scope."

## CHAPTER 32

Belief is like a perfect teacher and pious and right thoughts are his disciples. There is only the difference of stages and degrees in it viz., good thoughts, better thoughts and the best thoughts. So the best thought is the nearest approach to belief and is far from heresy. If you can weigh the belief of Hazrat Abu Bakar, all right thoughts like milk from the breast of belief, will develop thereby. Drinking milk or the growing of those thoughts means that the knowledge and practice develop these thoughts into faith. Fancy or surmise or thought does not remain as such after it has merged into belief. In the world of matter. All these teachers and disciples are the impressions and prints of those teachers and disciples. In these prints, there has been transformation in every age and in every century. These teachers (beliefs) and disciples (fancies) have existed in every century and in every age. This is easily shown by arguments. Those thoughts that are undesirable and take us away towards wrong path and which the teacher (belief) has condemned are thrust far away every day and fall back every moment because every moment, he is persevering to develop that power which will give strength to his holy thoughts. "Disease existed in their hearts, so the Lord prolonged their disease."

Just watch that the rich people eat dates and camels feed on the thorns. The Lord says, "Do you not see the camel?" But, God will transform the evil traits into good ones of those people who repent and who developing faith act righteously. That thing which was responsible for spoiling his fancy will now help him to reform himself and turn good, just as, if a confirmed thief repents and vows that thenceforward, he will not steal and is made a police officer, all the tricks he used to employ in stealing will help him in doing justice and good to the people and he will be the far more efficient police officer than those who were not previously thieves because this police officer is fully acquainted with the profession of stealing and with the ways of the thieves and he will at once recognise what class has been responsible for what class of theft and he will uproot the institution of theft. So also the erstwhile deluded man of bad character who adopts the righteous course and who is constantly trying to attain purity of heart and faith, will of certainty become the great teacher and perfect guide and will show the path to the world and will be recognised as the leader of his age.

## CHAPTER 33

He said to us, "Pay your respects to us and retire, do not come close to us."

When you are my hope, how can it be that I should remain away from you?

Remember always that a person, wherever he may be, carries his desires, with himself. Never is man away and far from his desires ideal. This is the case with all creatures. "Man's wants are more closely attached to him than he is attached to his parents." 430–Those very wants are his fetters, and like a noose in his nose. They drag him hither and thither. It is never possible that he should improve himself by himself because everybody desires freedom and does not like imprisonment. It is evident, therefore, that someone else has tied him up. Suppose, a person desires health. He will never try to court illness. It is impossible that he should seek health and ailment simultaneously. When it has become clear that want is sticking to a person, it becomes necessary that a man should also be with him who has entangled him in the desire. But as his attention is only directed to the noose, he is condemned and is lowly. *If his attention is riveted solely upon the puller of the noose, he will never feel the need for the noose.* The noose has been kept, for otherwise he does not move without it and does not see it. God says, "I put the noose in his nose and drag him towards Me, contrary to his desires because without the noose, he does not come to Me."

They say, "After one attains the age of eighty, is it possible for one to be childish and indulge in play?"

I remark, "Is there any occasion to be playful before the age of eighty?"

In His grace, God bestows such youthfulness on old people, so much so that even children are unaware of it.

The youthfulness confers on old men boon of gaiety, frisking and frolicking and laughing. All these come in its wake and they feel that the world has put on a new garb for their sake. Seeing the world new, the old man does not fear it, because he has already seen the world and has enjoyed worldly satisfaction. This spirit of playfulness and youthfulness develops strength and freshness in him.

> Great is the problem of old age (and great its value)
>
> As soon as age advances, he should make it a horse of interesting things to ride on.

By the grace of God, even dignity of old age is magnified, because it displays the charm and beauty of the spring of the greatness of God, at a time when the autumn of age is lording the old man. The treasure of the charm of life has run out its course. It follows that it is the grace of God that diminishes the glory of spring. The spring of smile is gone on the decay and fall of the teeth and with the whitening of the hair, the plant of the grace of God turns green. With the weeping of the shower of autumnal rain, the garden of reality loses its fascination. "God is much Higher than the tyrants describe Him to be."

## CHAPTER 34

I saw the shape of a wild animal. It wore the fox's skin. I tried to catch it, as it was peeping behind the casement of the window. It raised both its arms and began to grin at me. Then I looked at....Uddin. He appeared to me in an ugly shape. Agitated, he ran off. I caught hold of him. He tried to bite. I put his head under my foot and pressed it so hard that all that it contained came out of it. Then looking at the beauty of his skin, I remarked that it was so beautiful that it should be decorated with jewels and diamonds and even with costlier things than them. I added that whatever I wanted I had taken out of it. I said, "Now, you despicable world, you may take it away wherever you wish or cast it away in whatsoever direction you want and run away." It was frisking and frolicking to escape from being caught, although in his being captured lay his good luck. There was no doubt that his face was composed of very fine particles of meteors, and a desire was injected in it, and it desired to own everything and every person, in this very same way that it tried to escape. He loved such vocation, and besides that, he could do nothing because the heart of the mystic cannot be entangled in such traps, nor overpowered by tricks, howsoever cleverly the whole may be manoeuvred. It is within the power of the mystic to flee from a person or be entrapped by him. Man has not the strength to capture him by his ingenuity. To hunt him you will have to build a hiding place. He sees all your ways and is acquainted with all your technique, whilst he has full control over himself. Very many and varied are the ways for him to escape. He will not escape through the way where is located your hiding place, rather he will choose to escape that way he has made for himself. Very vast is God's land. His knowledge cannot be circumscribed except that much that He wills. When you understand the delicate words that are stated above, they will cease to be difficult for you. But coming in your understanding those matters will lose their beauty, just as, whatever good or bad things fall into the mouth and the mind of the saint lose their original form and are transformed into some new form, They are encircled and wrapped up in new wrappers of grace and miracles. Did you not see how the staff in the hands of Moses change its essence? It did not remain a staff, but was transformed into something else; in the same way, the talking column and staff in the hands of the Prophet and prayer in the mouth of Moses and iron in the hands of David and the mountains in His presence lost their nature, their original state was transformed and they became something else. So also, when prayers and the mystic formula fall into the hands of a dull and ignorant person, they lose their original form and nature.

So long as, the ego persists in thee,<br>
Thy worship has turned Kabā into a tavern.

The heretic eats seventy entrails, and the mat he makes his bedding. The ignorant one will be styled as eating with seventy entrails although he may be eating with one. Just as every atom of a despicable thing is despicable, so every particle of a pleasant thing is pleasant. If this mattress had the power to protect me, I would have sat on it and would have loved it and would not have left it till it would have removed me. But this removal will not have been caused because it ruins man's religion, soul and body, but since he indulges in drinking wine and does unbecoming acts so his removal is just. But this person has obtained the graces of good people. But he has spread the prayer mats all over the place. Would that he had wrapped them up and got himself wrapped in them and then he were cast into a corner of the house so that the bedding were purified from his malpractices and evils. He is creating distrust in his benefactor. The benefactor invites him to his presence, but that person keeps silent, and is suffering pang of life. He has made himself a hunt of the worship and orisons in the hope that some day, he may try to see what are the things that have drawn him away from his Benefactor. Then, he may strike Him and say that it is He Who has practically killed him. Just as, my misdeeds and my sins are encircling me, so the saints have seen in their intuition that their bad deeds and deluded imagination are seated collected behind their house in a corner, and I am myself hiding them from my Benefactor. He says, "Why do you try to hide them from me? I trow, by my God, the Lord of my life, if I call all those effigies of my sins and evil deeds to my presence, they will appear fully embodied before me and disclose their identity fully and also their secrets. May the Lord protect the oppressed people from these dacoits who obstruct the path that leads to the Lord, and who by fake worship delude the seekers.

The kings play football in the open grounds so that their subjects who have never been to the battlefield may see how the enemy is pursued and fought with and conceive how the heads of the enemies are cut in the war and how they battle with them. This game is a sort of drama that depicts the scene of a battlefield. Those who have the warrior instinct in them are drawn by those dramas to go in for actual battlefield. So also this music, worship and orisons are a device to draw people to God. The principal singer of spiritual songs is like the Imām in namāz. All follow his dictation. If he raises his voice whilst singing a song, they, too, start singing loudly and dancing and if he lowers his tone, they also sing and dance slowly. It depicts that they are following what the internal monitor is dictating them and following his advice and instructions.

## CHAPTER 35

I am surprised at the scholars of the Qurān (who have learnt it by heart) that they are ignorant of the attainments of the saints. Look what the Qurān says, "You should never follow him who swears often and is of a mean temperament always expressing himself in sarcasms. He who condemns a person that he should not hear the recital of another person is himself condemnable because such a person is obstructing him in the pursuit of a spiritual practice. The Qurān is such a miraculous thing that he who hears it, howsoever opposed he may be to it, becomes an admirer of it and with love starts hearing it. He who understands it becomes unconscious and he who does not fully understand it, too passes into ecstasy.

God has put His seal on it. "Very subtle is God. There is pleasure in His frown which is enjoyable. So also He has put on a lock of peculiar kind. It is a lock that can not be opened as ordinary locks are opened. It is very extensive. So also the excellence of the Lord is beyond description. Even if I cut myself into shreds, I cannot describe and enumerate His infinite kindness and the pleasure I enjoy in opening (the secret) His locks.

If I fall ill or even die, I shall not say I am ill or dead. This, too, is a pleasant and unparalleled gesture of my Hidden Slaughterer. The dagger that is employed in killing me is with a view that some bad luck may not attack my limbs, and others may not even be aware of my slaughter.

## CHAPTER 36

Form is a branch of Love. With love, all forms are futile. A branch is that which cannot appear without a root. So we shall say Allāh has no form because form is never the real root. It is merely a branch. God is Real. He cannot be called a branch. Somebody says that without seeing the form, love is impossible. Therefore, love is born out of form.

Our answer to it is that love can be born without a form. Rather it is love that gives birth to form. Millions of forms are born out of love as its result both in thought and in reality. Is it true that engraving is possible without there being an engraver at its back? So also, without an engraving, an engraver cannot be discovered. But the real thing is the engraver, and the engraving is his branch, just as, a ring is in motion with the movement of the finger. As long as, there is no love born for a house, no engineer will be able to plan the building, so also, sometimes wheat is sold dear (as gold) and sometimes cheap as earth. The form of the wheat remains the same in both the cases but its value rises or falls according to the demand of it. So also, are all arts and crafts whose value increases and the people pursue and learn them. When there is demand for the artists and craftsmen, the people become their seekers and love them. When there is no love of art, none learns it or seeks it. They say, after all, love is that we should desire a thing and seek it. How is it, then, possible that what we desire should become the branch and the desire should become the real thing (root)? I answered him, "What you are saying is because of your desire for it. As you were inclined to this talk, so this talk was born. So, you see desire precedes the talk and is the first thing which leads to the birth later of this talk. Desire is born first and then follows the birth of the object desired. So it can be said that the desire is not the branch of the thing desired, rather, it is the essence. Apply it to love and the object loved also. The thing desired is always the branch and the desire, the essence or the root just as, the tree is the real thing and the fruit is a branch thereof.

## CHAPTER 37

First, the people approach the entrance, the threshold and then, the house. This world is like a house. He who will enter it, must come through the entrance first. So, the plan of this house, in which we are seated, came first in the mind of the architect. After that, this house came into existence. We have said that this world is like a house. That plan or essence which, you saw, being born in the beginning, must be taken to be born before the house.

All the objects, good or bad, born in the world, were first born in the beginning or plan and then, came in the house. When the Lord desires that various kinds of gardens, flowers goods, arts, crafts and works of learning may be born in the world, He creates a desire in the hearts that they start desiring for such things. So, know that whatever you see in this world, is in that (spiritual) world. Seeing a thing that is born in the sea, you are convinced that it must be of the sea. So the sky, the earth and the other things created can be conceived. The Lord had created a desire in the souls of people of old for these things, so this world (with these things) was created, because of that desire of theirs.

The people remark that the world is ancient. Who would like to hear this talk? Other say that the world is casual (just appearing). These prophets and saints are older than the world, more ancient than the birth of this world. The Lord created a desire in them to crave for the appearance of the world. Due to the craving in their souls, was this world created. So, these saints and prophets know that this world is casual. Therefore, they point to the Day of Judgment and keep their eyes riveted on it. Take an instance, we are seated in this house. I am sixty or seventy now. This house was built only a few years ago. But the rats and the insects that are born in its walls, see it populated on their birth. Then, if these insects say that this house is ancient, how can we accept this statement of theirs, because we have seen it built before our eyes? Just as, these insects born in the walls of this house have not seen the house other than this and know nothing besides, so there are many people born in this world. They have no spiritual knowledge. They are born here and will die likewise. If they state before the prophets that this world is ancient, will the prophets and saints admit it? They are born millions of years before the birth of this world, and they have seen this world being created as you have seen this house built.

## CHAPTER 38

Philosopher Gusti said, "How do you say that the world is casual? Where from did you learn it?" Why do you not ask him, "If you say that it is ancient, what is your authority for that statement? You say that the world is ancient. It follows that you mean that the world is not casual. That is, you deny its being casual. But have you ever pondered that to deny a thing is more intricate than to prove its existence? To prove its existence is easier than its denial. Suppose, just as you say that such a person never did this act. This is a matter which can be discovered and proved with difficulty that, in reality, he did not do that act, because only that person who has lived with him as his shadow all his life can testify to it. Even he may err because it is possible that at a time when he performed that act that man might not have been with him for some reason or other, say he might have gone to vacate at that time and he could not have accompanied him then. So it is incorrect to try to prove negation of anything but he who testifies to the positiveness of the thing says, "I was present when he did such an act," then this will be accepted as trustworthy.

So, he who says that the world is casual is right and easily understandable. But you, who say that the world is ancient mean that this world is not casual, that is, you have proved the negation. But the fun is that there is no argument either way to prove the ancient or casual nature of the world, for, no one has seen whether the world has just appeared or it is ancient. So, when you ask him why he says that the world is casual since he has not seen it such, he also can put you the question why you call it ancient. Your assertion is difficult, for, you, too, cannot urge any proof or argument in favour of your assertion.

## CHAPTER 39

The Prophet was seated with his companions when the heretics began to raise objections. The Prophet replied, "Gentlemen, you, too, accept that there is a person who has revelations and is subject to divine auditions, and that this is not in the lot of everyone. There are various signs by which such a person can be known and recognised. His acts, his features, his words and all things about him point to his being subject to such revelations. After seeing all this, why do you not hold fast to him and direct your attention to him so that he may help you?

The heretics, on hearing these words, felt ashamed and had no words to retort. They took out their swords and started fighting, and thus troubled the companions of the Prophet, and mocked at them. The Prophet advised his companions to forbear and endure with patience, lest those heretics should feel and say that they gained victory over them in argument. They desired to do that. But, God would, surely, manifest their religion. For long, the followers of the Prophet Muhammad used to offer their prayers in secret and disguise and repeated the name of the Prophet secretly. After a time, the divine message came that they should also draw sword and fight. The Prophet is styled illiterate because he did not know reading and writing. Another reason is that the knowledge which he possessed came with him from the womb of his mother. He never went to school, yet notice, that he who was unable to write the alphabet was capable of writing on the moon. What was it that he did not know in the world? All the people acquired knowledge at his hands. Could he be ignorant, then, of anything? His was a perfect intellect. A perfect whole is greater than a part.

Partial intellect cannot produce any new thing by itself. Neither these books that the writers have written nor the many houses that these architects have constructed are original productions. By looking at other books or buildings, they have produced their works adding or subtracting here or there a little. But they who produce new and original works themselves are possessed of perfect intellect. Partial intellect requires to be educated and schooled. Perfect intellect is itself the teacher and needs to be taught nothing. So also if all the source of world's professions and arts are inquired into, they will be found to have their beginning in divine revelation, and the people must have learnt them from the Prophets as they are perfect intellect. Consider the case of Cain (son of Adam) and Abel. The crow instructed them. Cain killed Abel. He did not know what was to be done with the corpse. Thereupon, he saw a crow killed another crow and buried it under the earth. So, he learnt from the crow the practice of burying. So also is the beginning of all professions.

Man of partial intellect requires to be educated. But the perfect intellect produces and gives birth to everything. This perfect intellect is possessed by the prophets and enlightened saints who have connected themselves with the partial intellect and have merged themselves into it, just as, the hands, feet, eyes and ears of a person acquire knowledge from the heart and the intellect. The feet learn to walk with the help of the intellect, likewise the hands grasp, the ears hear and the eyes see through the intellect. In the absence of the heart and the intellect, all the organs of sense are useless. In comparison to the intellect and the heart, this eye is gross. The former are subtle. The gross thing exists because it has joined itself with the subtle one. If it has some excellence and virtue, it is because of that subtle thing, otherwise, it becomes dirty and gross. So, for the partial intellect (fragmentary intellect), perfect intellect is a source from which it can draw great benefit. Compared to the subtle perfect intellect, this partial intellect is dirty and gross.

A person said to Maulānā, "Please remember me with fervour and perseverence. The main thing is perseverence. Expression is its branch. This perseverence was in the world of the souls and existed before this world of bodies. Not without purpose are we brought in this world of bodies. There is purpose behind it. So, there is need to discuss this matter which shall be useful. If you remove the husk from the kernel and sow it, nothing will appear from the ground but if you deposit the kernel covered with the husk, it will grow into a plant. It follows that form is also necessary, mere kernel (essence) will not do and will not be effective.

Namāz (prayers) are within man's self, but to be productive of result, it should be uttered externally also. When during offering prayers, he will bend down and fall in obeisance, the full benefit shall accure from it, and the goal will be reached. "They are always engaged in prayers. They are readers of the spiritual namāz. Their souls are always in orisons. The external namāz is performed at specified hours, not the whole day long. Soul is a river which has no banks, and the body is its bank and dry land. It is a limited thing. So except the soul none can offer the perpetual namāz. The soul offers obeisances but it should do it externally with the body also because the essence and the form are so intimately connected that they cannot be separated. If they were not connected, they would not be effective, just as unless seed is covered with the husk, it will not be able to germinate.

The statements that the form is the branch of the meaning (essence) and that the form is the subject while the heart is the king, are relative terms. How do you say that it is its branch? So long as, there is no branch, how can the name of the reality be annexed to it? A root is called a root because of the branch. If there is not a branch, none will give a name to the root, just as if you call Him God, it means there is His slave also and if you call someone an officer, it follows that there must be some subordinate to him. Khāsā Uddin of Arzanjān was a great controversialist before he associated with the dervishes. Wherever he went, he entered in hot discussion with the people. But, when he came in contact with the dervishes, he lost all taste for discussion and controversies.

One affection can be destroyed by another love alone. He who desires to meet God must associate with the Sufis. This learning of the world compared with the saint's spiritual experience which they are undergoing internally every moment, is merely a puppet-show and waste of time. What is this world? A mere play and show.

When a child grows into a youth and attains wisdom, he, no longer, indulges in children's plays. Even if he does, he does so secretly and is ashamed of that. This material and external world and all its aspirations are like the wind while man is like a particle of dust in them. When the wind mixes with the dust and enters the eye, the eye feels pain and the wind does not any way confer comfort to it, but it creates further ailment and worry. The eye weeps when it hears anything sad. Its tears flow like water. You will witness tears flowing from the eyes. But opposite is the case when rain water falls on dust. When the dust gains the gift of water, beautiful green grass, flowers of variegated colours and different kinds of vegetables grow out of it. The way of poverty is such that pursuing it, you shall attain to the fulfilment of all your desires viz, to destroy the armies and gain victory over the enemy gaining possession over countries and subjugating the people. You will also advance in glory and grandeur over your former equals. All your wishes shall be fulfilled by pursuing the path of saintly poverty. He who has travelled this path has never any occasion to complain. But in other hundreds of paths, thousands have travelled but strayed any one has attained success, even after extreme perseverance. Even after that achievement, the person does not gain peace. The reason for that is that, in every path, there are methods by which when duly performed man achieves his purpose. The path is long and thorny and replete with troubles. May be, these methods employed to reach the goal may turn faulty and the destination may not be reached. But, when you cross the threshold of poverty (faquiri) and adopt it, God shall bestow on you such kingdoms as had never entered your imagination and you will feel ashamed of your former ideals and desires and will say, "Fie on me that in the presence of an object of such high order I was running after trifles." But God, the Great will say, "Although, for My sake, you have renounced your former desire and now you dislike it but since, at one time, you had cherished it, so, I shall fulfil that desire of yours along with this new desire for Me. I shall confer on you both the things."

Just as, before the prophet attained to the high spiritual state and prophethood and gained such wide fame, he used to yearn for being an expert speaker and instructor. When he used to hear any famous saint, he wished for a time when he would attain to that eminence. But when the hidden spiritual world was revealed to him and he was full of God-intoxication, that desire left him. He submitted solely to the Lord and he did not care for the fulfilment of that desire, for, of what avail was it to him then? He had no need of it and did not care for it. God replied, "You will have both, this one and the fulfilment of your earlier desire too. Rest assured, no harm will come thereby to you." The Lord conferred on him such ability of discoursing that till to-day many people of the world are trying to write learned commentaries on his discourses. Even then full understanding of his talks is impossible. The Lord had said, "If those devoted to you lack in strength and your enemies surround them and create mischief for them, they take your name very secretly. I shall proclaim and progagate your name in all the countries of the world so much so that from the high minarets in melodious sweet voice, your name and your greatness shall be proclaimed, and you shall be renowned in the east and the west."

It means that he who loses himself in this (spiritual) way attains to all the gains of this world and the next, and he never complains that he did not gain anything by pursuing the spiritual path. All our conversation is current coin, most genuine, whilst what others talk is counterfeit and spurious. This counterfeit is also a branch of reality. The reality is like the foot of a person, and the copy of it is like the wooden mould of the foot. That copy or the wooden mould of foot is formed with the help of the real foot, and is prepared after seeing the real foot. If there was no real foot, how could this copy, the wooden mould of foot be prepared?

So, there are several things that are real whilst others are fake. Both these remain combined with each other. One should be equipped with the discriminative faculty to distinguish between the two, the real and the unreal. Faith is the discriminative faculty, whilst heresy confounds, and betrays. Consider the time of Pharoah when the staff of Moses was converted into a dragon and the ropes of the magicians also began to look like snakes. At that time, those endowed with the discriminative faculty, at once, recognised which was the genuine thing and which was the magician's trick. Those who were endowed with faith turned believers. But those who were devoid of faith could not distinguish between the two and to them both appeared as similar. Due to this power of discrimination in them, the believers became the faithful. It follows, therefore, that discrimination is faith. What is the root and reality behind these religious laws. It is the revelation, the Divine Word.

But when these were mixed up with the worldly matters and talks, they lost all that spiritual charm and subtlety, now they cannot be compared with the Divine word (revealed thing).

Just as, the water of the canal is going towards the town, see how clear and limpid is its source! But when it passes through various quarters of the city, the people wash their hands, feet and clothes in it, the beasts vacate themselves in it and much dust mixes up with it. If you examine the state of that water at the other end of the city (at its exit), although that water, too, allays the thirst of the people and is used in drinking, but he who has discriminative faculty developed in him will, at once, recognise that that water then does not possess its earlier deliciousness, because dirty things have mixed up with it. "The believer is a very intelligent and wise person."

If an old man who is one hundred years old, engages in play, he must be deemed to be a child. Here, age does not matter. But, the pure water which removes all the dirt and ugliness itself and remains unaffected even on entering the abdomen is the living water or nectar.

A person seated in prayers shrieked and wept. They asked the Maulānā whether the prayers of such a person would be acceptable or not to God and whether they would be in accordance with religious tenets. Maulānā replied that if he wept because he witnessed an inward world as distinct from the external world and witnessing or thinking of such a world as of the nature of prayers, completed his prayers (namāz), he achieved the purpose of prayers. His prayers were therefore, in accordance with the tenets of the Faith and were perfect. But, if, instead, some attraction of the world, some fear or envy or some such thing made him weep, his prayers were unacceptable and likely to cause injury instead of good.

It follows, therefore, that faith is a faculty of discrimination that distinguishes the truth from untruth, evil from good. He who has no discrimination is unfortunate. He who has discrimination will benefit by our discourses and he who is devoid of it will not be profitted thereby. Suppose, two respectable and learned people from the town were to appear as witnesses for a villager and speak in favour of him in evidence, and the villager in sheer ignorance were to interrupt them in the middle of their deposition with a silly remark or admission, whereby their deposition might become useless, it follows that the efforts of those people were wasted. It is for that reason that the saying goes, "the villager is his own witness." When a man is intoxicated, he is not conscious of what he is doing, nor can he distinguish the good person from the bad one, nor does he distinguish who deserves to be allowed to participate in conversation and who does not. Being unmindful of the audience he prattles on, with his idle conversation. His condition can be compared to a woman whose breasts, when they become full of milk, cause her pain and prompt her to go to the puppies of the street and get them sucked by them.

If such a gift falls to the lot of a person lacking in discrimination, it is like bestowig pearls to an ignorant child, unacquainted with their value. He will gladly part with the real pearl if an apple is offered to him for it. This is because he has not developed discriminative faculty in him. Discrimination is a great boon.

Bāyazid's father took him to school to teach him theology. Bāyazid asked, "Will this teaching lead me to God-realisation?" The people told him that it was the school of Hanifa whose teachings were imparted there. Likewise, when he was taken to school where grammar was taught, he inquired, "Will the grammar you teach lead me to God?" They answered in the negative. Bāyazid atonce said, "I have got nothing to do with this knowledge." Dissatisfied with his attitude, the father left him to himself. Bāyazid in his search for knowledge went to Baghdād. The instant, he saw Junaid, he cried, "Here is the Theology of God realisation." How is it possible that the kid should not recognise the mother goat? Similarly, he has taken his teaching like milk and developed discrimination and thought.

A teacher used to keep his disciples standing round him in reverence and folding their hands. People could not tolerate it and thought that that was display of vanity on the part of the teacher. They requested the Sheikh to let them remain seated as it did not behove a Faquir to keep the disciples standing. That display befitted the monarchs. The Sheikh asked them to remain silent and observed, "My object in keeping them in that position is to inculcate reverence in them. I confess that reverence is always an attitude of the mind and is an internal attitude but externals serve as an introduction to internals. After all, what is the purpose of an introduction (in a book)? Its purpose is that by its perusal, the people will guess the contents and the chapters of the book. By this apparent reverential attitude, and by standing like this with folded hands in an erect position, it appears to what a degree of reverence their heart has attained and how much they revere God. If they do not show respect externally, it is clear, that their internals are impure, for, they cannot show respect to lovers of God.

## CHAPTER 40

A servant of the Sultān named Jauhar asked, "When a person is on his death-bed and he is instructed five times prayer, of what will it be for him for, on death he will forget everything? I answered him," As people forget the instructions, so they are again taught to them as also new instructions are given to them. Do you not see that you are hearing my discourses for a long time? But some instructions you accept totally as you have heard them from others also, others you partly admit, whilst some you deny totally and begin to argue against them in your mind. None hears them nor is one acquainted with the discussions that are going on about these matters in your mind. It is not possible to put in practice internally what you are arguing there. Your ears are there but you do not hear what is passing in your heart and if you try to seek who is talking in your heart, you will find there nobody.

Your coming to meet me is your query which you are putting without the use of the tongue and lips. In fact, you come as the query personified itself seeking the way and you wish that the instructions previously given to you may be explained further. My sitting with you, irrespective of the fact whether I am silent or speaking is really answering all your hidden queries. When you return to the monarch from here, you will enter in conversation with him. The monarch talks with the slaves all day long mutely and he guages how they stand and cast their looks and finds the reply in their gestures. If there is crookedness in some slave, his words also betray his crookedness. He will not be able to give pertinent reply. If the tongue of a person stammers, howsoever much he may try, he will not be able to answer clearly. The goldsmith by striking the coin on the stone hears its voice and from that he discovers whether the coin is genuine or counterfeit.

When gold will be melted, the melting pot will tell whether it is genuine gold or counterfeit (contains alloy). Canine hunger is an index that some damage has occurred in the system (house of the body). So apply a little mud to it or repair it with placing a brick. That is the answer to the sign (hunger), and eating food is the answer of it. Not taking food means there is no new hunger. In other words, the first layer (of bricks) has not yet dried up so, the second layer of bricks must not be put on it. The doctor feels the pulse, and its movement is the answer to his query. To look at the urine of the patient is putting the question and silently, it is answering. Placing the seed in the ground is like putting the question, that I want such and such fruit. The appearance of the tree is the answer to the question. The tongue has no place here, all questioning and answering is carried on mutely. If the seed is rotten, it will not germinate. The question is put and the (rotten) seed answers that it has no wealth that it can offer.

A king read one application three times but gave no reply. The applicant complained that he had sent the application three times but had received no reply. The king had not given any reply whether he had accepted his application or not. On the back of the application, the king wrote, "Do you not follow that writing no reply on the application is the answer thereof. The reply to a fool is silence."

The refusal of the seed to sprout forth is like the seed

not giving the answer. Whatever movement a person makes may be considered as putting the question and whatever pain or pleasure that follows in the wake is the reply thereto. If the reply is favourable, he should offer thanks and thanks-giving means that he should, in future, put such questions so that similar good reply may fall to his lot. If he gets an unfavourable reply, he should apologise and desist from putting similar questions in future. "When My wrath fell on them, why did they not take recourse to seeking forgiveness bitterly? But their hearts became hardened."

They did not follow that the answer was in accordance with the question. Satan betrayed them by depicting their actions as good. That is, they considered that their query was very good and remarked that the answer, was in accordance with their query. This was a bad reply. They never knew that the smoke comes out of the fuel, not from the fire. The more the fuel will be dry, the less will be the smoke that will come out of it. You have placed a garden in the superintendence of a gardener. If the garden begins to emit bad smell, the blame will come on the gardener, not on the garden. Somebody asked a person why he killed his mother. He replied that he saw in her such a dirty thing that could not be described. The person asked him then why he did not kill the person who was the accomplice. The man asked him if he meant to suggest that he should kill a male every day.

Crush the ego so that every day you may not have to quarrel with new people (desires). If the people object on the ground that evil also emanates from God, my answer to them will be that for that very reason, they should, crush the ego, for, thereby they will save the whole world from its mischief, and this instruction also emanates from the Lord. Just as, a man climbed an apricot tree, shook it violently and ate some of the fruits. When the gardener reprimanded him for that act and asked him to fear God and beware of such act, the man replied why he should fear God because he belongs to God as much as that tree was also His. He was the servant of the Lord and he was enjoying His gifts. The gardener replied, "Wait a while for a correct reply." He, then, asked another person to bring a rope and with it, tied the man to the tree and lashed him severely telling him that that was the reply. Now, the man began to cry, "Why do you beat me? Do you not fear God?" The gardener said, "You are the servant of God, and the lash also belongs to God." The lash of the Lord is striking the servant of God (where is the fault in it?).

This world is like a mountain. Whatever sound is made before it, good or bad, you will hear its echo likewise. If you say that you said a good thing and the reverberation was bad, it is impossible. How is it possible that a nightingale should lament before the mountain and the echo may be the hoot of the crow in answer to it. Remember, you will get the answer in accordance with the sound you make.

Make a good sound when you enter a mountain,
Why dost thou bray like an ass before a mountain?
Whatever sound will proceed from the inverted bowl
(the sky) will represent your good voice.

## CHAPTER 41

We are like the cup afloat on the water. The cup does not float on the water by its will, wherever the water takes it, it goes. Somebody remarked, "This is a very ordinary (illustration) talk. Yes, some know this and others do not. The Maulānā replied that if it was very ordinary talk, how could that special thing be said, "The heart of the faithful is betwixt the two fingers of God!" This is also stated that God has taught the Qurān. It cannot be said to be an ordinary statement. After all, it is God Who has taught all the sciences (species of learning). Why is in the Qurān especially mentioned? "Likewise, the Lord has created the earth and the sky." Why do they, then, hold a special place and speak of it particularly? Popularly speaking, all things are God's creation. We have, therefore, to admit that all the cups float on the water by God's will. But if we attribute something bad to God, it would be disrespectful. Suppose, one were to address the Creator, "O ye, Creator of dung cake and bad odour," whilst another were to say," Thou, the Creator of heaven and the earth and of the intellect," Such particularisation will not be without beneficial results. Although it is a very ordinary thing, yet by particularising it, we show that it is a selected thing. The purport is that a cup is floating on the water and water is carrying it so that all other cups collect round it to watch it flow, whilst there is another cup similarly made to float on the water but other cups run away from it and feel awkward to go near it. It is the water that is conferring strength on the other cups that desire to run away from it. Just as, it is said, "O Lord! Keep us away from them." With regard to the other cup (first one) they say, "O Lord! Draw us close to it."

One who considers it an ordinary thing, thinks that both the cups are of similar status as they are controlled by one (water), to him, the water replies, "If you knew the virtues of this cup and its excellence on motion, you would not cast your eyes on ordinary qualities of the others (in the face of these specialities in it) and never care for them. Just as, man has his beloved who like all creatures contains in his abdomen filth as other beasts contain in their stomachs and like the beasts he shall also die some day. So, all these common traits are found in that beloved too. If somebody were to say that his beloved contained filth, and that he was subject to death and evil, that lover would never admit it but would consider that the objector was his enemy, and deluder. So, although this thing has entered your mind, yet, you keep your eye riveted on the ordinary phase, then you can never witness our special form. It is futile to argue with you because our arguments relate to beauty and to disclose beauty to an ignorant is tyrannical. "Don't impart knowledge to them who are not capable of receiving it. If you do it, you will be oppressing them. Teach wisdom to them who are capable of learning it. If you do not do so, you will be tyrannising over them."

In the autumn, fruits and flowers do not bloom because it is opposed to them. The nature of flowers is not such that they should oppose autumn. But when the sun impregnates them, in the temperate climate, they manifest their glory, otherwise, they remain secretly seated and revert to their source. The season of autumn says, "If you are not a dry branch, come in my presence in the field and show me your strength." The flowers answer, "Compared to you, we are dry and impotent twigs. We are not coming out, howsoever much you may taunt us."

> O Thou, king of the faithful, hast Thou seen any imitator,
> Who is dead with Thy being dead and living with thy being living?

Maulānā Bahāuddin! If any old woman with wrinkled face, toothless and with entrails peeping through the skin approaches you with the words, "Look here, the bed is spread, come and enjoy me, I am ready. Let me see if you are a man with strength and not impotent." Even if you are in full strength, you will reply, "I am impotent. May God protect me. Whatever people have told you about my strength is a lie. If I get a wife like you I shall prefer to remain impotent."

A scorpion approaches you ready to sting you and says, "I bite you to see how you smile because I have heard that you are always bearing a smiling face. Please smile a little as I want to enjoy that sight." You will answer, "Scorpion Sir! Since you have approached, all my laughter and glee have left me. What the people told you was a lie. At present, all my joy awaits the time when you will leave me and go away."

The Maulānā said, "You uttered a sigh and the whole effect was lost. Pray, do not sigh so that its effect may be preserved. The converse also happens at times. When a sigh is uttered, it is most effective. Varied is the nature of these experiences. If such had not been the case, Ibrahim would not have been styled soft-hearted and forbearing. You did expound your worship, but embodied it in such expression that it lost the relish. So, if the talk destroys the relish, it is futile to indulge in such conversation. It can be illustrated thus. A man is asleep. The people are trying to wake him up as the caravan is about to start on the journey. Others intervene and say, "Do not wake him up as he is enjoying the sleep." Hearing this, the people who want to wake him up say, "Well, this pleasure of sleep is like unto death and by waking him up I confer the pleasure of everlasting life." The others say, "Do not wake him up as he is in deep meditation." They will answer, If we wake him up, he will, then, enter into deep concentration and meditation, for, how can he who is sleeping enter into meditation? He will go into meditation and reap the benefits thereof when he wakes up and then, sits in meditation."

This waking up and call is of two classes. If the waker is spiritually more advanced, he will, by that call, gain and rise spiritually. If he who is the waker is an enlightened soul and is wakeful and alert, by waking up the man who is down in idle sleep, he will lead him to a higher spiritual state and he will grow in his meditation because he has been called by a voice stationed very high. But, if the matter is reverse and the waker in status is spiritually lower than the sleeper, on waking up, his eyes will look lower things, because the waker is of a lower degree. He will instruct him in a lower plane, and take him to lower regions, dragging him to abject worldliness.

## CHAPTER 42

Those people who acquire wisdom of the world think that if they associate with the Dervishes, they will forget what they have learnt. It is their mistake to think like this. In fact, by such contact, their knowledge will gain a spark of life. It will become apparent that carcases have gained life. The soul (root) of learning of the world is in the next world, and from that world devoid of medium of words and sound (mutely), it has come to this world.

In the Traditions, it is recorded, "The Lord held concourse with Moses." God did not converse with Moses through the medium of words and sound for, it first presupposes the existence of lips and tongue. Without these two, words cannot be uttered. The Holy and Pure Lord does not keep any connection with tongue and lips. So what the Prophets and saints say or hear is in that world where there are neither words nor sound. There, they talk with God. The partial, imperfect and fragmentary intellects of men (of this world) cannot reach there nor know anything of that world. But, the Prophets and saints come to this world from that world, where words and sounds do not exist, and turn into children for the sake of children here and state that they have been sent here as teachers. Although these children cannot follow the teachers as they have been brought up into this world of words and sounds, yet they draw strength from them and are nurtured by them at their hands. They, therefore, become acquainted with them as children. Though a child does not fully recognise his mother, yet he gains power and obtains peace from her or as the fruit rests on the branches of a tree and sweetens there but does not know (its relationship with) the tree and in spite of this ignorance, it grows held up by the tree. So also, the worldly children develop under the patronage of the teachers and with their help. Of course, they do not follow the words and the sounds and often are not aware of their existence nor can they understand them. But they profit by the knowledge they impart. It follows that whatever impressions are made by the teachers prove that there is a mightier world behind and beyond this world of intellect, sound and words.

Have you not seen that every body is anxious to see a God-intoxicated person and seeing him, says, "Here is one mad after God." What he says is correct. But the fact that has made him so does not come in his intellect. It does not mean that anything that does not come in the intellect does not exist. Take a nut. It is round in shape. But every round thing is not a nut. The sign is there. But its state is past expression. Still, it is fed and developed by the intellect. These mad men who are circumambulating about God are not doing so at their pleasure and do not suffer themselves. They think that they will gain comfort but we do not call it comfort. Their case can be compared to that of a child who has been forsaken by his mother. He gets little peace in the arms of another woman who takes him up for a short time. We shall not call it genuine peace and ease for he is a lost and ignorant child.

Physicians say that the appetite keenly demands whatever suits the temperament, and that will strengthen the temperament and cleanse the blood. This, however, holds good when a person is in good health and is not suffering from ailment. Suppose, a person who eats earth (dust) says he likes it. We shall not say that it will keep him in good health. It does not matter if he likes it. So also, a person suffering from bile likes sour things in comparison to sweet ones. His pleasure cannot be depended upon because this is all due to his ailment. Real pleasure is in a thing which is pleasurable in perfect health. Suppose, a man's hand is injured and it is hanging, because it has been cut. The Surgeon sets it right and the bone is settled in its original and proper place. Whilst he is setting it, the patient feels pain and does not like it. The surgeon says, "When, at first, your hand was uninjured, you were satisfied with it, if some one had twisted it, you would have complained of the pain. If you want that the hand should remain twisted as it is, this desire of yours is false and undependable. You must suffer a little pain in setting it right. So also, in the pure spiritual world, these pure perfect souls remain steeped in remembrance of God and enjoy happiness akin to that of the angels. Now, on coming into this world, their body becomes liable to suffer from the diseases of this world and they prefer eating the earth (sensualities). The saint who is the physician tells them that happiness of theirs in this world is false. They have forgotten the thing that was pleasant to them. That former thing is the most beneficial and suited to their temperament. The former thing was something healthy but the present one is the cause of ailment to them.

A mystic was seated by a grammarian who said that words can be classed only under three heads-noun, verb and letters. The mystic on hearing these words tore his garments, drew a heavy sigh and said "All my effort and perseverance of twenty years is wasted that I spent in my search to know if there was anything beyond the ambit of these three. "I performed many austerities but you have smashed all my hopes. Although the mystic had attained the goal of life, yet he wanted to teach the grammarian and wake him up to go in quest of Reality which lay beyond what he had learnt.

It is stated that Hazrat Hasan and Husain saw that a

person was performing his abulations in an unprescribed wrong manner. They said to him, "We are performing the abulations before you and tell us whether we are doing it in the prescribed correct manner," and saying this, they started to perform abulations. The man on seeing that said, "Yours is the correct way. I was wrong."

The larger the number of guests, the more is the space utilised in the house and the more it is decorated and a larger quantity of delicious dishes are prepared. Take the case of a child, he is tiny in stature and the thoughts that he has are also very small because the house (his body) holding them is small. He knows only the milk of nurse and nothing besides; but when he grows up, his thoughts, intellect, discrimination and wisdom all develop in him as his body grows.

The divine love is so vast that it cannot be confined to the body. When it enters a body as a guest, it destroys that house and turns it into a waste and deserted abode. Thereupon it builds now mansion, pitches kingly tents because the guest-Love with all his armies and accoutrements cannot stay there as the older curtains and doors are unsuitable for the new entrant. Very penetrating and infinite is the sight of Love. Fot it, very vast must be the place (which may accommodate it). When the curtains that accompany Love are hung, they cast beautiful effulgence and light, and all the old veils are shorn, and the hidden mysteries are revealed. On the other hand, the curtains of the world increase the veil and conceal the whole thing. The curtains of Love are quite distinct.

> I complain of many things but do not enumerate
> them, just as, the candle weeps but does not know
> whether its tears are shed because of its meeting
> and company of the flame or in pang of separation
> of the honey from which it has been removed.

Someone remarked that that poem was by Qāzi Abu Mansur. Maulānā said, "Whatever Mansur says is a mysterious and painful thing and ephemeral by nature. But Mansur cannot bear it, so he reveals it that the whole world is bound in chains by the order of God and the command of

God is in possession of the saint who is a witness of it and is unable to keep it secret, so he reveals it."

Maulānā then, said, "Read some verses of Qāzi." He read them. Thereupon, the Maulānā said, "There are certain God's servants who on seeing a veiled woman order her to raise her veil that they may see her face and know who she is. Otherwise, if she passes by veiled, there shall always be a doubt in their mind who she is. One of them says, "I am not of a class of persons that I should see your face and fall in love with you and start pursuing you. For long, God has made me careless of women and I am totally unattached to them. I do not fear, therefore, that if I cast my glance at you, my thoughts will turn impure. However, it is possible that if I do not see you, my thoughts may turn impure. For, if I do not see you, certainly, there will be this query in my mind, "After all, who is she?" "On the other hand, there is a group of people who are very passionate. If they see a beautiful woman, they fall in love with her and become very restless. In their case, it is best that woman should not appear unveiled before them lest they should fall in trouble."

A person remarked, "In Khwarazan, nobody falls in love as there are plenty of beautiful persons. If seeing one beautiful person, they fall in love, another who is more beautiful comes in sight shortly after and they forget the earlier one." The Maulānā remarked, "If it is impossible to fall in love with the beloved of Khwarzan, it is imperative to become a lover of Khwarzan because it is full of innumerable beloveds. He is the Khwarzan of Fuqr (devotion for Lord). In it, there are innumerable spiritual beloveds, and there is no limit to spiritual forms. Whatsoever form you will love, shortly after you will notice another even more beautiful form which will make you forget the earlier one and like that indefinitely. It follows, therefore, that we should be lovers of spirituality (Fuqr) which is full of such beloveds.

## CHAPTER 43

Every one likes a mirror, because it is clear and has many merits. Although it does not reveal the reality of a lady's face rather she through it corrects the veil on her face. Thus, the mirror corrects veil and the face of everyone is a mirror. You open your mouth and you will find me the mirror of your face. I shall prove to you that I myself am the mirror. Somebody stated, "I am convinced that the presumption of the saints and the Prophets, too, is based on an error otherwise, there is nothing except veil." The Maulānā inquired, "Is it a mere joke in which you are making such statements or this conclusion is reached by you after reflection? If this assertion is the fruit of your mature understanding, you have yourself proved that it is possible to see God in existence. This existence is the most adored thing with you. "Therefore, the Prophets have correctly stated that besides seeing God, "they have asserted nothing. You, too, have admitted the possibility of seeing God."

Again, consider that unless there is an object to be seen, it is not possible to see anything. Ponder that seeing is a transitive verb and for seeing, it is necessary that there must be a seer and an object seen. That thing which is witnessed (seen) is the objective (desired). The seer is the seeker, or its opposite. Therefore, in spite of your not accepting it, in existence, both seeker and sought are proved. Whether you admit or deny, both God and His servant are extant. So God's seeing is openly proved.

The Maulānā remarked, "Those people adore that fool as a teacher and respect him." The Maulānā further said, "The fool is not worse than a stone idol. The worshippers of the stones and idols worship them and eulogise them and have great expectation. They have great affection for them in their hearts and pray to them for the fulfilment of their wishes. They weep before them and pray to them for fulfilment of their desires. Although that stone is without any attributes, is divorced of all feelings and is motionless, yet in view of their strong faith, God makes the stone confer benefits on them because of their truthfulness. Take the case of a person, considering in darkness a column as his beloved, embraces it, makes plaints to it and weeps. He can never derive such benefit by clasping that stone column. When a person decides to go on a pilgrimage, he hopes to find many things of interest there and many activities to his liking, and he will improve and all his friends will be happy, and his enemies will fear him. He thinks in that strain but the Lord wills otherwise. On reaching that place, he makes many plans to get out of all difficulties but succeeds in nothing, even then, he has faith in his efforts and devices.

The slave makes many plans believing them fully but forgets destiny. Before the dictates of destiny, what place do man's efforts and devices have? His case is that of a person who in a dream visited a foreign country where no one recognised him. So he wandered aimlessly here and there none recognising him anywhere. He lamented and was very sorry why he went there where there was no one who knew him, nor any one inquired about his welfare. In sheer agony, he ground his teeth. But on waking up, he found that there was no city of the dream nor any person nor object. He felt that there was no pain or suffering for him and unnecessarily he was anxious. He wondered why he was suffering in his dream. He again went to sleep and again found himself in a city similar to one of his previous dream. Again, he started his lament and anxiety, and again started his repentance forgetting that on waking up, he had previously been sorry why in the dream, he had unnecessarily suffered because after all, it was a dream as the newone. So, is the case with the people of the world that often they have see that all their efforts and devices have borne no fruit and have been ineffectual and no desire of theirs has been fulfilled. God, in His mercy, casts a veil on their memory and they forget their previous failures and again start their futile efforts anew. "Certainly, God becomes an obstruction between his heart and Himself."

When Ibrāhim Adham was a Sultān, one day, he went out on hunting expedition. He, seated on horseback, started pursuing a deer. In a short while, he reached far in advance of his army and found himself alone in the jungle. The horse began to sweat profusely, yet he was galloping it. When he had exceeded the limits of his striving the deer turned his face towards him and began to talk in human voice, "You are not given birth to pursue this idle course. Never in eternity, were you directed thus to hunt me. Assume that you kill me in this hunt, what avail will it be?" Hearing this reminder,

Ibrāhim shrieked and got down from the horse. Finding a shepherd closeby, he entreated him and exchanging his costly kingly garments, arms and horse took over his blanket and wrapped himself in it and went out a wandering in the jungle. Now, consider that it was the intent of Ibrāhim that he should hunt a deer but God in His mercy through the deer's instrumentality hunted him.

Before he was converted to Islām, Hazrat Umar, one day, went to his sister's house. She was at that time reading the Qurān loudly, "We have revealed the Qurān." On seeing him, she closed the book and hid it and became silent. Umar drew his sword and asked her to tell him what she was reading or he would sever her head. His sister knew that he was a person of hot temper given to great anger. For fear of her life, she said, "I was reading the words that have been revealed by God to Muhammad." "Read them so that I might also hear them," remarked Umar. She read it on which he was terribly infuriated. Remarked Umar, "It will be very insignificant thing to kill you. First, I shall strike off the head of Muhammad". Saying this and holding a naked sword in his hand, he proceeded to Muhammad's house. The officers of Querish community saw him going to Muhammad's house on some errand. Umar was noted for his valour and was very fearless. He could singly face a whole army. So courageous he was! So the Prophet Muhammad was always praying to the Lord that He might make Umar or Abu Jehal his supporter in the crusades so that they might help him because both these persons were select amongst the contemporaries. After he was converted to Islām, with tears in his eyes, Umar used to pray, "O Prophet! what a precarious condition would have been mine if you had taken the name of Abu Jehal in preference to mine! For, if you had done so, I would have been deluded." As Umar was on the way to Muhammad's house, Hazrat Jabriel brought the message of God to Muhammad that Umar was on his way to his house and was going to him with a view to be converted to Islām. So, he should embrace him with affection. Umar had just stepped into the mosque when he expressly saw a light emanating from the body of Muhammad and entering his body like an arrow. He shrieked and fell down senseless and such love arose in him for Muhammad that he felt like melting into water, and effacing his individuality totally before him. He asked, "Prophet of God! tell me what is Faith, so that I may hear that noble word (Islām). When he was converted to Islām, he confessed that he had first gone there to kill him, then, he promised that for that error of his, he would repent in that way that if any one was insolent to Muhammad, he would sever his head immediately. Saying this, as he stepped out of the mosque, he met his father who reprimanded him saying, 'So you have turned a Moslem and changed your religion.' Umar at once cut off his head, and was carrying the same blood-drenched sword in the hand. The officers of Quresh said, "You had promised to bring the head of Muhammad, but we do not find it." He said, "Ye, I have brought the promised head." Saying this he pointed to his head. They remarked that that he had carried from there. He replied, "It is not the same head that I had carried with me from here." Do you watch now what Umar intended to do and what was done by the Lord? It follows, therefore, that what God wills, happens. Umar carried the sword to kill Muhammad but he was entrapped in the net spread by the Lord and destiny with smile claimed him to be its own.

"Similarly, if you are asked what present you have brought, say that of your head you make a present. If again, the people say that they saw that head before, you should reply that it is not the same head they had seen before. The head that treasures some secret is the true head, otherwise a thousand heads are not worth a penny."

The Maulānā read the following verse from the Qurān, "When I settled that Kābā was the abode for people to gather there and was a place where peace reigned and ordered that the people would offer their Namāz at the place where Ibrāhim stood, thereupon Ibrāhim remarked that I conferred on him, the garment of My satisfaction and accepted him and he prayed to Me to conquer on his progeny the same favour." God continued, "I do not say these words concerning the tyrants. It means that the sinners will not be participants of this honour." Ibrāhim, therefore, came to know that the tyrants, and these disobedient persons would not be recipents of God's grace. Then, Ibrāhim said, "O God, confer on the believers and the pious the gift of Thy food and do not deprive them of it." God said, "I confer food on all. All the people will derive benefit from this guest house but the garment of My satisfaction and acceptance and the crown of honour will be bestowed on the select few."

People apparently say that house means Kābā for the escapad who seeks shelter gets it there and no one then can cause trouble to him. The hunting or killing of animals is forbidden there. Pain cannot be caused to anybody there. It is the select spot of God. This is a fine and correct statement, but this is only the outward explanation of the words. The investigators after truth, however, say that the house here means the heart of man and the expression means that God should cleanse our hearts of evil thoughts and egoistic desires and should not allow bad thoughts to enter it so that there remain no danger lurking and peace should sway everywhere there. Then, that heart will act as a receiver of Lord's messages and the devil of doubt will not get in there, just as the Lord has created fire arrows on the sky so that the condemned Satan may not be able to ascend to that place and be stopped from the secrets of the angels so that nobody may get acquainted with the secrets of the angels and thus the angels are saved from all troubles. So we say, "O Lord! place the sentries of Thy grace on our hearts so that evil thoughts emanating from the devil and mind and the snares of Devil, the desires, should keep away from us." This is the matter of that relates to the advanced devotees and saints and everybody states that which dwells in his heart. The Qurān is like a silken cloth with two facets. Some people take advantage from one of its sides and others from the other. Both are beneficial sides. This can be illustrated from the case of a woman who has a husband and a sucking child. Both of then seek enjoyment and derive pleasure from her but the nature of the pleasure is different in either case. The child enjoys the milk of the breast whilst the husband has another kind of enjoyment from the wife. All the people generally are like children treading the path. There are others who are grown up and enlightened and who have attained perfection. They derive a different kind of enjoyment.

The place of Ibrāhim, where he used to say his prayers is located very near to the house of Kābā, and is a very small place about whose sanctity the watchers of externality say that it is profitable to say prayers there. But the genuine investigators of truth say that the place of Ibrāhim means that the devotees of the Lord should annihilate their ego for His sake and by efforts attain to that station (which Ibrāhim had reached.) They should undergo tribulations and even though they cannot attain to that high station, yet they may reach very close to it, for, had not Ibrāhim become a sacrifice unto Him? Such men will have no fear left in them for their lives. Did he shudder at the sight of any danger? Nay, he courted the fire even for His sake. Likewise, it is conducive to say a few rukāts (verses followed by obeisances in Namāz) at the place of Ibrāhim but those prayers should be so said that whilst we stand up in prayers in this world, we should kneel (offer obeisances) in the next spiritual world. Kābā means the Prophet's heart which is the spot where descends the message of God. This (worldly, external) Kābā is its branch. To what avail is Kābā if heart did not exist? The Prophets and saints have totally renounced their will and have made their will subservient to the will of the Lord. They feel sorry for those on whom the grace of the Lord does not descend and it does not matter if such ones may be their parents. Their sight worries them and to their eyes they appear as deadly enemies.

> We have handed over the bridle of our hearts in His hands, If Thou sayst a thing is ripened, we shall Go FURTHER. and say verily, it is burnt.

Whatever we say is an illustration. It is not an axiom. An axiom is one thing and an illustration a different thing. God has described His effulgence as candle light.

This is a sort of illustration, whilst the body of the Prophets is like a big lamp. This, too, is merely an illustration. For, His effulgence cannot be borne by the universe. How can the human heart contain it? But, if you are its true seeker, you will discover it in your heart. Not in this way that your heart is a vessel and the effulgence fills it but you will find it there just as you find your reflection in the mirror, for, in reality, it is not there. Yes, when you see the mirror, the reflection will be visible there because you will see yourself there although you are not there (in the reflection). These matters which are difficult to comprehend, become easy of comprehen- sion through an illustration. If once we comprehend them, we can feel them also, just as if you say that when a man closes his eyes, he witnesses many strange objects which are capable of being felt. But, when he opens his eyes, they are gone. No one will say that such a thing is capable of comprehension by intellect, nor can it be the subject matter of faith. But if you state them as an illustration, people will follow it and visualise what it is like, just as, a person sees millions of sights in sleep but on opening the eyes, nothing remains visible, or some architect makes a plan of a house in his mind, of its form, length and breadth, it will be difficult for us to know what he is imagining but the moment, he puts his thoughts on paper, they become understandable. If he fixes the details, every detail of it will become of the ken of intellect. When it becomes in a form capable of comprehension, the house will also be built and felt as it was well imagined. It follows that all these things which are not comprehensible by intellect can be understood through the means of an illustration. Likewise, it is stated that on the Day of Judgment, the record of Prophet's actions shall come flying into their hands (palms, of some in the right hand and of others in their left hands.) The angels will be present there. People will be resuscitated. There will be paradise and hell. Scales will be set up to weigh the merits of the actions of every one and accounts shall be taken. Till these matters are explained by an illustration, you will never be able to follow and grasp their import. It is also difficult to find their illustrations in this world, yet by examples it is possible to convey the import and fix their meaning.

The example in this world may be understood as follows. The whole creation goes to sleep at night. During sleep at night, the cobbler, the tailor, the king and the Judge, all being asleep, the thoughts emanating from their mind start floating in the void. No power of pondering and thinking remains in them at the time. But when the morning comes, like the sound of the trumpet of Ispharail (angel of Death) on the Day of Resurrection, the particles of the body of the dead are enlivened and rejuvenated and the dead bodies are revived. The scroll containing the reports of their past actions done in the world and the fruits thereof come flying into the hands of every individual respectively. No mistake occurs in this process. The thoughts of the tailor go to the tailor and of the blacksmith to the blacksmith. So also, the thoughts of every one (gone to sleep, on waking up) revert to him without any mistake being committed. It never happens that a tailor may have slept and on waking up, he may have found himself a cobbler. Such happening is impossible. A person wakes up in the very same profession in which he was when he went to sleep. You can, therefore, conceive that the same thing will heppen in the next world also. This is not impossible. It is happening thus in this world too. Therefore, he who will worship will reach the bottom of the act (of supplication and obeisance). He will know in this world everythig that will happen to him in the next and he will see them here and all secrets will be revealed to him. He will know that there is room for everything in God's creation. He will witness many rotten bones in a tomb, but the bones are comfortably lying there and asleep. They alone know the joy that they are experiencing. This is not an exaggeration as it is stated by some people, "Souls rest in peace in the tomb." If, there had been no rest possible in the grave, why do people confer blessing in the following strain:

May that Beloved live for centuries!

May that shaft of his love remain entrenched in my heart!

My heart gladly gave away its life on his threshold.

O My Lord! who was it, who prayed thus that in
his grave may he rest in peace?

In this world this is seen illustrated thus. Just as, two persons are lying in the same bed and are dreaming. One dreams that he is loitering in a well-laid beautiful garden with green lawns, whilst the other finds himself transported into hell and is encircled by snakes, scorpions and is surrounded by flames of fire. But, if you seek the truth, neither of the conditions exists. How strange, then, it is that whilst many dead persons should experience comfort, solace and joy in grave, others should experience misery and pain! By an illustration, you have been able to follow a difficult thing, although the example bears no semblance with the reality. The enlightened man styles ecstasy, joy and blooming of heart as spring whilst the agony and suffocation of heart is styled as autumn by him. One may well say, 'After all, what is the resemblance between joy and spring and sorrow and autumn?' But, this is only an illustration and the intellect cannot comprehend its meaning or imagine it. The Lord Himself says that darkness and light are not the same nor shade and sunshine. Faith is styled light and heresy is stated as darkness. Often, has faith been compared to cool shade and heresy to hot sun which warms up the head, and can give no peace. But, how can light of faith and bliss be compared with light of the world or heresy be compared with darkness of the world?

Whilst I am discoursing, some doze off. This sleep is not due to unmindfulness but because of fearlessness. It can be illustrated thus. A caravan is travelling in a dark and fearful road. It is going at a great speed so that the enemy may not cause trouble to them. But as soon as the persons (in the caravan) hear the barking of the dogs and the crowing of the cocks and ultimately, reach the village, they are bereft of all anxiety and lie down comfortably to sleep. Although when they are in the middle of the path, there is no sound or disturbance, yet due to fear, they get no sleep. But, they find peace in the village in spite of the barking of dogs and worries, they comfortably lie down to sleep. Our discourse has its source in the abode of peace and like a place well-inhabited with people. These discourses are the conversation that passed betwixt the Prophet and the saints. When the words of friends reach the ears, the listeners get satisfaction and are settled in fearlessness because these words carry in them the fragrance of hope and faith. Just as, some one accompanying a caravan is full of fear, and anxiety, thinking there are some thieves mixed up with the caravan-passengers and desires that he may hear the words of friends and get thereby comfort and consolation. "O Muhammad! Tell the people to read (the Qurān), say this because you are very pure by nature and the vision of the people does not reach so high (as yours). But, when you say anything, they discover that you are acquainted with Me, and their souls get peace.

> If I do not talk to you, you will never be able to see Me,
>
> Because my body is so lean and thin (a mere phantom),
>
> Just sufficient to be called a man.

Sometimes, in the fields, a tiny beast which cannot be seen till it shrieks is found. But when it does so, you can see it. So, the people of the world cannot see you because you are very subtle by nature. Therefore, you must talk so that people may see you and recognise you.

If you intend to go somewhere, your heart reaches there in advance and reaching there, it acquaints itself with that place and then, this heart drags the body after it to that place. Now, all these people are like the bodies in the above illustration, compared to the Prophets and the saints, who are like the hearts (of the above illustration). At the outset (in eternity), the Prophets and the saints witnessed the next world, then, leaving the mortal frame here, they went back to see that world more carefully. Then they learnt to walk in this world. After their return to this world, they invited the people to that world to go and see it because this world is a drear desert and a perishable home. They say that they have experienced joy at another place (the next world) and they give us the news of that other world. It follows that the heart of the

Prophets is ever with the Beloved. It has neither to cover the stages nor has fear of robbers and has no anxiety of the camel and the rest house. All these things are for the sake of the poor body which is entangled in the meshes of the world.

> I asked my heart, "O ignorant one! Do you not know from whose service you are debarred?"
>
> My heart replied, "You are mistaken. I am always serving, but it is you who are aimlessly wandering here and there."

Wherever and in whatsoever condition you may be, always try to be in Love. When you will be bestowed love's gift, you will ever continue to be with the Beloved, either in heaven or in hell for ages till eternity. If you sow wheat, wheat you shall reap, in the store house too, the same wheat shall be stocked and in the oven, the same wheat shall be baked. Majnun wanted to write a letter to Leila when he took up a pen in his hand, these words came out:

> "In my eyes is thy picture, on my lips is thy name,
> In my heart dwells thy remembrance, what can I
> write even if I intend to write a letter?

When thy thoughts are present in my mind, thy name is on my lips and thy memory is deep rooted in my mind, when thou art dwelling in all these places in me, to what place am I to address my letter to thee?" So saying, he broke the pen and tore away the paper. There are many men whose hearts are filled with such thoughts and can never express themselves in words whatever is in their mind although they desire to do so. One should not be perplexed by it. This is not the meaning of love, rather it is love itself and the real heart itself. Just as, the child is the lover of milk, he derives benefit from it and gains strength from it, but in spite of it all, he can neither praise nor define it, nor he can express it in writing what pleasure he feels in drinking milk and what weakness and pain he endures when he is deprived of it, although his life desires and loves milk. A developed man, in a thousand ways, can make you understand the virtues of milk, the strength it imparts and the delicious taste it possesses.

## CHAPTER 44

What is the name of that gentleman? Saiffuddin (lit sword of faith). He is like the sword in the scabbard, so it is not visible to the eyes. The real sword is that which should fight the crusade in the name of religion and all its efforts should be in the cause of the Lord. It may discriminate between good and evil and place truth higher than falsehood. But first, he should fight with his lower (carnal) self and improve his habits, "Begin ye, first with yourself." First practise yourself whatever precepts of advice you give to others.

You, too, are a human being. You have ears, hands, feet, eyes, mouth and intellect. These saints, similarly, are endowed with hands and feet. They are men like you but they attain to great spiritual eminence and reach the goal. Then, what is the reason that for them, the way is cleared up and the doors are laid open for them but the doubting person rubs his ears day and night and quarrels with himself. After all, what is his sin and why is he not acceptable to the Lord and why is he not styled the sword (crusader) and the spokesman of the Lord? Take an illustration. Suppose, ten persons want to enter a house. Nine get entry into the house but the tenth one is stopped entrance. That person will, surely, lament and think in his mind what is his fault that he is not allowed entry within. Perhaps, he has been somewhere disobedient. It is meet for him that he should admit that he has been disobedient and place the blame on himself and consider himself ill-behaved. Never should he say that God has been cruel to him and what he should do. It is Lord's will. If He wished, he could have got entry within. To make such an assertion is to abuse God and to strike Him with the sword. Therefore, instead of his being a crusader of the Lord with a sword in his hands, he will be striker of Lord with a sword. God is quite unattached to everybody. None is His friend or relation. "Neither He is the progeny of any one nor has He any progeny."

He who attains to the Lord attains through His service

and obedience. God is Self-sufficient and does not want anything from anybody. It is impossible that he who has found the way to God may have got through His favouritism, that he is dear to Him, is related to Him and through that intimate relationship, he has attained to God, for the simple reason that His nearness is attained only through service to Him. He bestows without rhyme or reason on all. He has filled the bottom of the sea with pearls. He has covered the stony rocks with green herbage and has bestowed on a handful of clay (man) the boon of soul and life. In this gift, He has no axe to grind, nor has any one (donee) any right to expect these gifts from Him. Even the minutest atom is the recipient of His grace. When a person hears that a great philanthrope who confers great boons on the suppliants dwells in a certain town, certainly, he goes to him to draw benefit. So, when the Lord is so Munificent and His rewards are so well-known, why should you not beg of Him the garb of honour and rich rewards? After all, why do you sit like a lazy person saying that if He likes, He will bestow on me, but I shall not ask Him. Take example of the dog who is not possessed of intellect. If he feels hungry and does not get food, he comes to you and fawns upon you waving his tail in endearment meaning, thereby "Bestow food on me for you have food with you but I have nothing to eat." Even dog has this much of understanding. Are you, then, even inferior to a dog? The dog never thinks that he should remain lying asleep and if God wills, He will bestow on him, rather he entreats and waves his tail. So, let you also shake your tail and beg the Lord because it is very necessary to beg of such a Bestower. However, if luck is not in your favour, go and ask for better luck of the one rich with it.

God is very close to you. God permeates even your thought. He is in your imagination and the Creator of those thoughts. But being too close to Him, you cannot see Him. But where is the occasion of surprise in it? In whatever you do, your mind or intellect also works with you, but you do not see that intellect. By effect and signs, you feel its existence but its nature (form) does not appear before you and is not visible to you. Take another illustration. When a person goes in a warm bath, he feels the warmth, so does another person also entering there, but he does not see the fire. But when he comes out of the bathroom, the fire is visible to him. Then, he knows that it was this fire that was heating the bath room and he was getting warmth. In man there are various kinds of warmth (heat), that of the intellect, of the ego and of the soul. But it is only when you reach the next world, you will see the exact nature of the mind, the ego and the soul, with your own eyes. Then, you will know that the understanding, that you possess in this world is due to the heat of that intellect and whatever pretexts you make and plans you use to fix are all the effect of the ego, and life itself is the effect of the soul. You will see the nature of everything clearly there. But, so long you are within the both, you cannot see the fire (so long as you are entramelled in the body, you cannot witness the reality of things.) Take an illustration. Suppose, some one has not seen water flowing. People close his eyes and throw him in the water. He feels that there is some thing soft that touches his body, but he does not know what it is. But when the bandage is removed from his eyes he knows that it is water. Previously, he knew it by its attribtes but now, he sees its nature (form), so, if you seek anything, ask it of God, yes, all your needs of Him and I assure you, you will never be a loser on that account because God has Himself said, "You go on always praying to Me and I shall be ever responding to them (prayers)."

We were in Samarkand when Khwārzān Shāh attacked it and a serious fight raged in the city. In that city, there dwelt an extremely beautiful young girl. She was the most charming girl in the town. Every day, the people heard her praying, "How can You like, O God! that I should fall into the hands of the tyrants? I know you shall never tolerate it, I have faith in Thy mercy." When the town was being sacked and all the persons including the slave girls of the lady were taken prisoners but not even a hair of hers suffered. Although she was the most charming girl, none dared cast his eyes on her. You must learn from this incident that he who has surrendered himself to the Lord is shielded against all onslaughts and troubles. None returns empty handed from His presence. The wants of all are fulfilled by Him, and the prayers are answered.

A dervish instructed his child to ask anything he wanted of God when the child asked him for anything. The child started weeping and with tears prayed to the Lord to give him a certain thing, and he used to get it. This continued for several years. One day, the child was left alone in the house. He felt hungry, and as usual was his practice, he prayed to the Lord to supply him with curry. At once, a cup full of curry appeared before him. He ate it to his fill. When the mother returned and asked him what he would eat. He replied her that his stomach was full as he had asked God for curry and he had got it and had eaten it. The father fell on his knees and prayed that God might be praised that that child had attained to such spiritual eminence by His grace. Addressing his child, he said that dependence on God and faith in Him had made deep seated root in his heart.

The mother of Mary prayed to the Lord that she would present her newly born babe to the house of God (church). So when she was born, she brought the child and deposited her in a corner of the church in Jerusalam. The Prophet Zakaria was keen to support the child as also many others. They began to quarrel amongst themselves about the custody of the child. The practice was prevalent in those days that when a dispute like the above arose amongst two contestants, each was asked to drop a tiny piece of wood in water and he whose piece of wood floated on the water, was entitled to the disputed thing. Zakaria won and the child was entrusted to him. Everyday, Hazrat Zakaria used to carry food to her but when he reached the babe, he found that the very same kind of food was placed in her presence. He inquired, "O Mary! I am your caretaker, then who is he that brings this food to you daily? She replied, "When I feel hungry I pray to God to bestow that food on me and I get it from Him. Vast and limitless is the bound of God's mercy and His bestowal. He who depends on Him is never a loser." Seeing this Zakaria prayed to the Lord, "Since Thou satisfies the needs of everybody, pray fulfil one of my wishes. Confer on me a son who may keep

Thee as his friend and without any instructions from me may love Thee and remain constantly in Thy worship and be engaged in remembrance of Thee. God heard the prayers and Hazrat Yahia was born as a son to him, although both Zakaria and his wife were much advanced in age, and she had never born a progeny till then. But in that old age, she became pregnant and gave birth to a child. It follows that on some pretext or other God does His work (of bestowal). The conclusion is reached that it is He Who is in reality everything, the Ruler and Lord.

Who is a believer? He who knows that behind the curtain there is Someone, Who sees even the tiniest act that he performs and is acquainted with all his activities and Who knows him perfectly but he does not see Him. He has full faith in this. This faith is such that if one places a hundred arguments that all these are tales (about God), his faith will not be altered in the least. For, a day shall come when the dissenter will be punished for his heresy and he will lament why he presented false things and why he did not believe and propagate that God alone is and He is Everything but he did not believe in Him.

The purpose of the prayers (Namāz) is not that you should remain standing the whole day long, or remain falling in obeisances all the time. That is not the object. But, the purpose is that the effect of the spiritual state that comes as an experience by prayers should always remain overpowering you, whether you are asleep, awake, talking or reading. In all the states, the remembrance of the Lord may not leave you even for a moment and you become of the company of those about whom it is said, that they are always in prayers.

Conversing, dining, sleeping, getting annoyed and pardoning, all these conditions are like the revolution of a grinding mill which is revolving. But, this revolution of it is not due to the stony slabs but due to its fans (blades) which are attached to the water and which are moved and worked by the flow of water. He has examined it and knows it. If, now, the fan (blade) were to think that it worked by its own accord or the other parts of the mill were to think that they were moving of their own accord, it would be ignorance on their part. This world is very small and is a little introduction of that (spiritual) world. You, therefore, should pray to the Lord to bestow on you knowledge of the next (spiritual) world beside that of this world. "O Lord Thou art the Satisfier of all our wants and Thy mercy and bestowal are in abundance on all creatures." So, you should always mention your needs to the Lord and remember Him at all times because to the bird of the soul, the remembrance of God is like the wings with which it flies. If the goal is not attained, it does not matter for, at least by remembrance of the Lord, the heart is enlightened gradually and detachment from the world too develops by degrees, just as, some bird tries to reach the highest sky but it fails to reach there, at least it has left the earth and is soaring much higher than many of the birds. Take another illustration, fragrant musk is contained in a little bottle with a narrow mouth. It is not possible to take out the musk by reaching your hand near it (as the mouth of the bottle is small). Although the musk does not come out, yet the contact of the finger with the musk at least causes your hand to emit fragrance and your mind begins to enjoy the pleasure thereof. So is the remembrance of God. Even if you do not attain to the Lord, yet the remembrance of the Omnipotent Almightly Being shall be productive of infinite benefit to you.

## CHAPTER 45

Sheikh Ibrāhim is a spiritually advanced Darvesh. When I see him, I am reminded of (spiritual) friends. Shams Uddin used to be very kind to him and used to address him as "our revered Sheikh Ibrāhim" Thus, did he show to others his affection to him. Grace is one thing and achievement through effort is quite another. The Prophet and the saints did not achieve their high place through effort and perseverance. All they got was through the grace of the Lord. But the established (spiritual) rule is that whosoever attains to that high spiritual state attains through assiduous and hard effort, worship and austere life. This is to teach the common people that seeing their nature, they may have greater faith in the Prophets and may depend on them because the people generally look to the externals and are unaware of the internal activities and seeing their externals, they will be inclined to serve them and obtain their blessings whereby the internal spiritual path shall be revealed to them. Pharoah, too, had practised many austerities, and did many charitable acts but as he lacked in the grace of the Lord, all his effort and service came to naught and God did not even make those acts of his manifest before the world. Just as, a prisoner may be in jail located in a fort and there he bestows gifts and he is kind to the dwellers there with a view that he may make them rebel against the king, then, it is sure that all his manifestation of goodness will be worth nothing. Although it cannot be said that he is totally being divorced of the grace of God, yet may be that God is conferring His grace on him veiled (behind the curtain) and his non-acceptance (of the Lord) may have some great purpose behind it because like the king God has both the powers in Him, of being angry or being pleased with any one and conferring robe of honour or condemning anyone. The lovers of God will not say that God is not kind to the prisoner although apparently everyone will say that he is the condemned one. This is the correct way of approach to the matter. To maintain the external order of society, the King hangs a person on the scaffold at a high level so that the people from very far off distance may see him, although it is possible to behead him in a secret place, but the object of the publicity is that people may take lesson from it and the fact of the passing of the order by the king and its enforcement may thereby be proclaimed and known to all. It is not true that he confers only the wooden cross but also the honours. Dignity is also a great cross. If God desires to fetter a person, He makes him a king and confers on him great honour, as in the case of Namrood, Pharoah and similar persons. These are the cases in which God hanged them on very high crosses so that all the people might know and take lesson (from their cases).

God says, "I am a Hidden Treasure, I liked to make Myself known and I created the whole world with that object, sometimes, manifesting Myself as a Tyrant and at other times, the most Humane Being." He is not such a king that a single person may proclaim His kingship and that may be sufficient. Even if, all the particles of the earth were to possess tongues, praise Him and accept His Emperorship, the whole creation would be helpless in singing His omnipotence and majesty. The fact is that creation is day and night manifesting His greatness. Some feel that they are expressing themselves and are acquainted with His greatness, yet there are others who are ignorant of it, but God manifests in them too. Suppose some officer ordered a person to be whipped. That person is crying as he is beaten whilst the other person goes on whipping him. Both are obeying the orders given to both of them by the officer whose subjects they are, one doing by weeping loudly and the other silently by whipping the other. There is one person who upholds the existence of Truth and proves it. Such a person always expresses the Truth while there is another who denies Truth. He, too, proves Truth because the proof of the existence of a thing does not come in imagination without keeping in view its negation without which there is no joy in it. Take the instance of a controversialist who states a problem in an assembly. If there is no body to refute it saying that he does not believe it, what will the controversialist prove and who will enjoy the discussion?

There is pleasure in proving anything in the presence of opposition and denial. This, too, is a place of the manifestation of God. Without there being some one to oppose and the other to convince, there is no pleasure in the assembly. Both of them, one who denies and the other who accepts, express the Truth.

The friends and companions of Amir assembled and then went to the Amir. The Amir was angry why so many persons had gone together to him. The friends said that they had not gone there with the object to cause injury to anybody but to suffer for the person and help him who was tormented amongst them just as when a person was condemned by the court, the people did not assemble to get the order of the court reversed but to console him a little that he might have been relieved from some worry.

All the believers belong to the one class. All the dervishes say that if a limb of the body suffers from any ailment, the other limbs will also feel the agony thereof. The eye will refuse to see, the ear will refuse to hear and the tongue will become silent. All will be engrossed in that suffering and pain (of one limb). The proof of friendship is that a friend should offer himself as a sacrifice to his friend and jump in the trouble for his sake because the attention of all the friends is riveted on the same one direction and all are drowned in one thought. The proof of faith and Islām is that all the Moslems and faithful ones should help one another. The help that is rendered through any limb of the body is nothing compared to the help, offered giving life. Do they say, "Why should we care since we have to return to God?" When the faithful Moslem has sacrificed himself for God, why should he care for the trouble, the danger and the fracture of the hand and foot in the spiritual pursuit? When he is proceeding to the Friend, why should he care for the injury received by the hands and the feet, and what is the need of hands and feet but for the Friend as He has bestowed them on him so that with their help he may proceed towards Him? When thou art going towards the Lord Who is the Creator of thy hands and feet, if thy hand is permanently injured and turns useless and thou becomes one without hands and feet thoroughly maimed, where is the occasion for thee to be sad as the magicians of Pharoah did not feel any pain of this?

> From the hands of the Beautiful beloved, even poison can be swallowed, and His cruel words can be drunk as nectar. Very delicious is the Beloved, very delicious indeed!
>
> Where delicious salt is available, it is worthwhile eating the heart salted by it.

## CHAPTER 46

God intends both evil and good, but He loves goodness, because He has said, "I was a Hidden Treasure, then I desired that I should be revealed and the people may seek and recognise Me." There is, no doubt, that God orders the performance and non-performance of acts. The order is correct if it is given to him who does not like to perform the act ordered. A hungry person will not be ordered to eat sugar and sweets. If he is so commanded, it will not be a command, rather it will be formality and ceremonial. So, if a person is ordered not to perform an act, it must be such an act that he does not like it. None will be ordered to eat stones and thorns. Such an order cannot be interpreted as a prohibition so to order a good thing and to stop an evil one is correct for one whose nature leans towards evil and the intention to develop such a nature is like an intention to correct evil. But, He does not like the evil nor orders the doing of evil acts. It can be illustrated thus: There is a teacher who wants to teach a pupil. He wants that the pupil must be illiterate, otherwise educating him will not be possible. If he is literate, why should he go in for education? So, it is necessary for the purpose of education that one should be illiterate. To intend a thing, it is necessary to intend all things which are its necessary accompaniments. But in reality the teacher does not like the illiteracy of the pupil, for, if he had liked it, he would have never taught the pupil. So a physician wants that patients should come to him, else how can he show to the world his proficiency as a competent doctor? If none fell ill, whom will he treat and how will the people know his ability although he never wishes that the people should be ill. If he had liked that the people should fall ill, he would never have treated them and given them medicine. To earn his living, a baker wants that the people should feel hungry but does not want them to die of hunger. For, if that were his intention, he would never sell bread. The officer of the king desires that some enemy of the king may raise his head and rebel so that he may display his skill, valour and faithfulness to his master. If that is not the case, the king will dismiss him. But the officer is not the friend of the king's enemy, neither he loves nor likes him. For, if he considered him good, why should he fight him? So also, when a person desires that he should be grateful, pious and obedient, he wishes that the causes of evil may appear, because obedience, and piety can be displayed only when there are occasions of displaying disobedience, impiety and ungratefulness. It is apparent that whatever thing is intended, all other things which are incumbent on it must accompany it. But, the person does not like disobedience, impiety and ungratefulness in his heart, rather he wants that these things may never enter his mind and tries to remove their traces from his mind. So, it is necessary that if you intend a thing, you must also intend all its accompanying things. One of the accompaniments of commands and prohibitions is this carnal self which naturally hates virtue and leans towards evil. All the sins and evils found in the world are the accompaniments of this carnal self. If the Lord did not wish to create these evils, He would not create this carnal self too. If He had not intended the appearance of the carnal self, He would not have created these orders and prohibitions. If He had liked these evil things, He would not have intended these prohibitions and commands. It follows that He indirectly intended these sins and evils.

When we say that God intends all good things, one good thing is that evils must go, for good intends disappearance of evil. Faith is possible only if from before heresy is extant. So heresy becomes a necessary requisite for Faith. It is true that to intend evil is bad, but it is bad when it alone is intended. But, if it is for some ulterior motive, it may not be bad. God says, "Instead of blood (murder) for you, there is life in exchange." It is true to revenge for blood and it is bad to destroy the building (body) made by God. But this evil is only partial evil and is intended to save the people from being killed. This intention is good for perfect good, partial evil device is not bad, but it is responsible conversely to leave partial evil for perfect good. Its illustration is thus. A mother does not desire to scold child because she has eye on his little evil that her rebuke will pain him, but the father beats him because he intends perfect (full) good for him (child). This he does so that that little evil if left unchastised will ruin his future life completely by developing many evil tendencies (if this little evil is not nipped in the bud). The eyes of the father are riveted on the ultimate good of the boy. "In reality, the Lord is the Great Pardoner, Great Bestower and Dispenser of hard punishment." He intends that this nature of His may be truly established. Now, test it. God will be the Pardoner and Bestower only if the people sin, So also, we are advised to keep peace amongst ourselves and this spirit of peace cannot manifest itself if quarrels were nonexistent. Take an illustration. The Chief of Islām says that God has ordered us to acquire wealth and follow a profession, because God says, "Spend money in charity in My name." How can you spend if you have no money? It follows, therefore, that God has ordered us to acquire wealth. So, if a man commands another to get up and offer prayers, it follows that he orders him to perform abulations and for that it is presumed that he orders him to seek and fetch water (for abulations) and also collect all the accompaniments thereof.

## CHAPTER 47

Thanks giving is a trap to entangle blessings. The moment, you hear the sound of thanks, you at once begin to serve the person expressing thanks, with great consideration. If God loves His devotee, He puts him to trials. If the devotee is patient in his trials, He elects him and if he is thankful, he is raised to greater height. Some people offer thanks to God for fear of His terrible nature, whilst others are thankful to Him for His grace. Both the kind of people are good. Gratitude or thanksgiving is an antidote that converts anger into kindness. He who shows thankfulness (gratitude) for that which is present as also for that which is absent and for good behaviour is a fully wise person. He is such a person that God has elected him as His own. If some person is intent on entering hell, by raising complaints, he will obtain his goal earlier because the external complaint is always more intense in degree than the inner one. The Prophet said, "I always smile when I kill." It meant that his laughter before the sinner was like killing him. This laughter meant that thanks were offered on such an occasion, rather than complaint was made. There is a story current that close to the house of one of the companions of Muhammad was the house of a Jew. The house of the Jew was very high and he used to live on the upper storey. One of his drains fell into the house of the companion of the Prophet and through it passed the dirt of his house, urine etc. He used to thank the Jew for it and also asked his people in the house to do the same. Eight years passed like that, when that Moslem died, the Jew came to his house to offer condolence and noticed the dirt of his house passing through the house of the Moslem. He imagined how much trouble had been caused to his neighbour all those past years. He felt much ashamed and inquired of the lady of the dead Moslem why all those years they had not complained about the matter to him. Instead, all these years they had expressed thanks to him. The widow and the children of the Moslem replied that the deceased Moslem always advised them to express thanks to God and rebuked them against ingratitude. Hearing this, the Jew developed faith and turned a Moslem.

The recital of the accounts of the good people turns the mind towards goodness, just as the song sung by a good musician elevates the mind and gives pleasure.

For this reason, God has given the accounts of the Prophet and the saints and related incidents of their lives which are inspiring. What is thanks giving? To suck the breasts of God's grace. The breast may be full of milk but unless it is sucked, the milk will not come out. People asked, "What is the reason of ingratitude and what is the thing that stops one from offering thanks?" The Teacher replied, "The insatiable desire does not permit one to offer thanks. He is not satisfied with whatever he gets. He craves for more. This improper demand has made him ungrateful. He is unacquainted with his hidden state. He is unacquainted with the wealth he has got from the invisible source and it is a mystery to him. It follows that a wrong aspiration is like a raw fruit that cannot be eaten or ill-cooked meat or not fully baked loaf. If these things are eaten, they will surely cause ailment and lead to ingratitude. If a person knows that he has eaten something harmful, he should vomit it. God in His mercy has conferred on him ingratitude which is comparable to the process of vomiting, that he may turn out that injurious thing from within himself. That one ailment (vomiting) shall cure him of a hundred ailments.

"I tried them through ailments and by conferring

My gifts so that they turn their faces towards Me." That is, God gave them food from the source from which they never expected it. That direction is the Invisible One. "God turns away their intention from seeking the causes. Those causes are like the thanks giving to God. Just as, Abu Yazid said, "Oh God! I have never joined anyone with Thee." God answered, "O Abu Yazid! Did you follow this precept in the night in which you took milk?" God meant that night in which he took milk which was followed by great pain in his stomach, although, He was the Conferrer of pain and pleasure." Abu Yazid had sought the cause, so God called him a polytheist (attributer of copartner to God), and said, "It was I Who was the Giver of harm before and after taking milk. Although I made milk the giver of harm, this was with a view to warn you as does the teacher." The teacher warned a student not to eat a fruit and if he ate it, he would strike his feet with a cane. Then, it would be incorrect to say that because of eating the fruit, his feet were injured.

In the same way, God protects from polytheistic influences, the soul of a man who does not join anyone else with God. A trifling thing God values very much. The difference between praising God and offering Him thanks is that thanks are offered when gifts are received. We never say that we offered thanks on his valour and his beauty. Eulogy is a common word.

## CHAPTER 48

A person was a patriarch. He said in (Namāz) "The villagers of Arabiā are very stubborn heretics." In the assembly, there was some Arabian villager too. He slapped the patriarch. The Patriarch read the second verse, "In Arabiā, there are some other villagers who believe in God and in the Day of Judgment." The villager shouted, "My slap has set you right." The invisible Hand is slapping us from behind every moment. If we start to do a bad act, we get a slap from behind, if we do not perform it, we start doing another good work.

It is stated that we cannot tolerate being sunk in the earth or being cast away at a distance. Whilst this is also stated, "It is easier to cut asunder the bonds than to separate joined things. To be sunk in the earth means to enter the world and turn thoroughly worldly and to cast away at a distance means to be cast away from the hearts of the Prophets. Just as, if some one takes food and it putrefies on entrance in his stomach, he will vomit it. If the food had not turned sour, he would not have vomited it, rather it would have become the part and parcel of his body. The pupil serves and pleases the teacher that he may get a place in the heart of the teacher. But if some such act may be done by the pupil that the teacher may not like him and cast him out of his heart. This is like vomiting of the above illustration. If the pupil had not made the mistake, in due course, he would have risen to the status of a teacher. A single fault may cast him away from the eyes of the teacher.

> Thy Love has spread the news by beat of drum,
> And thereby has entangled many hearts in trouble,
> And thereafter, has burnt them to ashes,
> And then, with indifference has thrown the ashes aside.

Due to that Carelessness and Self-sufficiency of the Lord, the particles of ashes of the hearts are dancing and crying. If they are not crying, who has brought this news and is renewing every moment his remembrance? In that burning and in turning into ashes, he finds his life and that is why he craves to burn. But do you ever hear praises of those hearts that have been burnt in the desires of the world into ashes?

> I do not talk useless things, but I speak only that which is revealed to me.
> My food must find me out.
> I seek the Lord with all effort and His search tires me out,
> But if I sit down quietly, He comes over to me without trouble.

I have learnt the mystery about the distribution of food. I do not believe in aimlessly running hither and thither. To what avail my enduring trouble for nothing? Whatever may be my needs in respect of food, raiment, wealth and other desires, all these things shall reach me wherever I sit and for them it is not necessary for me to move. If I run after them, I shall endure trouble and disgrace, and shall tire myself. If I sit down at one place, my food shall come to me there as if attracted by irresistible force. First, it will pull me to itself and if I am not attracted to it, it shall come to me by itself, because my food is ever seeking me, and is making me its seeker.

In short, the purport of all what I said is that if you engage yourself in religious work, the world will run after you. To sit down at one place means to be settled in the work of God definitely. In this condition, if you have to move out, that shall be considered as sitting at one place. But, if one is seated in a wordly work, he will be considered to be moving about. The Prophet has said, "He who has sublimated his varied anxieties into one, God removes all his anxieties." If one has ten anxieties, and he surrenders himself to one thought of religion (God), God will, then, remove nine of his anxieties without any effort on his part. As the Prophets had no anxiety for food, fame and name and cared only for pleasing the Lord, they got food, name and fame without effort. So, if a man tries to please the Lord, he will dwell in this world and the next with the Prophets. He shall be the companion and friend of the Prophets, saints and the martyrs. Besides it, they will sit near God. The Lord says, "I am seated by him who remembers Me." If God does not sit by him, never will the yearning for Him be born in him. There would be no perfume if there were no flower. The perfume dwells in the musk and is with it always. There is no limit to this discourse, and if there is a limit, it is unlike other talks.

The night passed, yet our tale remained unfinished.

This is no sin of the night, rather very long was
our tale.

This world's darkness and night shall pass away but the effulgence of our discourse shall ever remain shining, and conferring light. Just as, the night of the life of the Prophets ended but the light of their teachings is still shining and illuminating the world.

The light of the teachings of the Prophets shall ever remain bright in the world.

People said to Majnun, "If you love Leila, there is nothing surprising in it. You both read together in the same school when you were children." Majnun said, "You all are fools. Is there any beautiful woman who should not be loved? A man will of a certainty love a beautiful woman but the charm is when that woman becomes his food and sustenance and the source of all pleasure, like the pleasure he relishes on meeting his parents and children." Majnun has become famous as lover as the names of Umar and Zaid are in history.

If you are taking wine and eating meat with it,

Then consider it as if you were drinking water in dream.

This world is like the dream of a person asleep. This world and its pleasures are like food and drink taken in a dream. So seeking the worldly things is like asking for and receiving things in a dream. But, when he will wake up, he will find that all that was eaten in a dream was all useless and ineffective. If a person asked for anything in a dream and got it, of him it could be said, "He got what he sought."

The Amir said, "I have understood the minutest details in man, his temperament and his habits, whether warmth appeals to him or cold. I am acquainted with every hair of his but I could never know what is eternal in him."

The Maulānā replied, "If this can be known only through discourses, of what avail are all penances? None will court all troubles and undergo great sacrifices. Take an illustration. Suppose, a man approaches the sea. He will notice only fish, crocodiles and salt water. He may, thereupon remark, 'But where are the pearls? May be, there are no pearls.' How is it possible that by merely looking at these, he can obtain pearls? Now, if he takes a million years trying to take out water and dry the sea, even then, he cannot find the pearls. A diver who is to find out the pearls is needed for the purpose, and it is not every diver who can obtain them. He must be very clever and able, then, he can succeed. All the learning of the world and the external activities, arts and knowledge are like taking out the water of the sea by buckets and throwing it outside. The procedure for obtaining the pearls is entirely different. There are many people who are well-decorated with learning of various kinds. They possess wealth, beauty and everything besides, but they have not the reality (meaning) in them whilst there are others who are ugly and have a bad tongue, yet they have in them the reality that is eternal and that is they have "meaning." It is the chief thing, which gains for a man a high status and spiritual greatness and raises him above all creation.

The lion, tiger and other creatures have some virtuous trait in them and certain special quality but that eternal quality is lacking in them. But, as man has attained that meaning (reality), he has attained that high state, otherwise he could gain nothing of that greatness. All this external learning, knowledge and arts are like the pearls studded at the back of the mirror. They can, in no way, improve the reflecting power of the mirror nor benefit the surface (face) of the mirror. Its face bears no mark of the pearls on it. It simply demands clarity. He who does not like the front (face) of the mirror, will never crave for its back because the face of the mirror speaks truth. He who has a beautiful face will like the mirror with his heart and soul as it reflects his fine form and beauty. A friend of Joseph returned from Egypt. Joseph inquired of him what he had brought for him from there. He replied, "You have scarcity of nothing but as none is more beautiful than you, I have brought a mirror for you so that you may always see your face in it." God has scarcity of nothing nor wants anything. Only a shining heart in which His form may be reflected is to be taken before Him. God never looks at your form and action. He always peers into your hearts.

There is a country where I got whatever I wanted.

But there was scarcity of the merciful and bestower.

Suppose, you come across a city in which you can get everything you want. You are delighted with it but though it gives you enjoyment of varied kinds and comforts, yet it does not contain wise persons in it. Will you not wish that the converse should prevail there? Such a city is the existence of man. It contains thousands of virtues in it. But, if it has not the real meaning in it, it is better if that city is destroyed. But if, on the other hand, it has meaning (reality) but is wanting in external beauty, it does not matter. Such an existence as is ever revealing God in every condition and in which the outward acts of the world do not detract man from remembrance of God is praise-worthy. As a child in the womb of a pregnant woman grows and gains strength and feeling all the time in whatever condition she may be, whether sitting idly or working or eating or sleeping, whilst the mother is not at all cognisant of it. Likewise, man is also pregnant with the GREAT SECRET. Really man is very ignorant and foolish but God will not allow him to continue in his error. If we love somebody's features, friendship or love of a hundred kinds springs up between us and him. If the cause of friendship and love is the SECRET that he holds, where is the occasion for surprise? This is his great possesion in life and what he will obtain after death is beyond the ken of everybody's imagination. That secret should always remain existing because that secret is like the root of a tree. The root remains hid (under the earth) whilst the branches manifest its effect outside. Even if a branch is broken, so long as the root remains intact (firm), it does not matter, other new and green branches will sprout forth but if the root suffers or is diseased some way, neither the leaves nor the branches will come out.

God said, "Prophet, on you be peace." It meant that there might be peace on him and on his people of similar nature. If it were not so, he would not have remarked, "On me and on God's fair creatures." If that compliment had been exclusively meant for the Prophet, he would not have made additions to it. That is, the compliment which the Lord has bestowed on him may likewise be conferred on other good devotees who are like unto him. The Prophet whilst performing abulations before prayers said, "Abulation is necessary, because without it, the prayers do not yield profit." If it means that abulation which was particularly performed by the Prophet, the prayers performed by others would not have been valid. But, it means that any prayer performed by any person who does not perform abulations like that, will not be acceptable to the Lord. As some people say that this tray is like that flower. It does not mean that this tray is the flower. It simply means that its colour is like the colour of that flower.

A villager visited a city and was the guest of the dweller of the city. The host entertained him with exquisite sweets. The villager relished them much and remarked, "Since I have tasted these sweets, I have lost all taste for the carrots which I was accustomed to eat with pleasure in my village. Now, it is not possible to get sweets easily in the village but carrots are easily available there. Now, as carrots are disliked by me, tell me what should I do?" The villager, as a result of tasting those sweets, abandoned the village and settled down in the city, because the dweller in the city had won his heart and he was bound to follow the dictates of his heart.

When some people accost you, the fragrance of musk seems to emanate from their greetings, whilst there are others from whose greetings, the smell of smoke comes out. But such a distinction can only be felt by him whose mind has developed the capacity of discriminating between bad smell and fragrance.

It is but meet to test a friend at the outset, so that later, there may arise no occasion to repent. The law of nature is, "Start with testing yourself (first)." If the ego boasts of humility to the Lord, do not accept it till you have tested it. In abulation, first the mouth is washed, then the nose is washed. Merely looking at the water will not do. The object to see the water is to see if it is pure and that is not possible merely by looking at it but by using and tasting it lest it should be emitting foul odour. The water is tested by placing it in the mouth. That which you keep hid in your self will be revealed by God in your external appearance. The water that the root of the tree draws lies hidden in the earth, but manifests itself in freshness of the branches and leaves. "The marks on the forehead betray the obeisances that they have offered to the Lord," The Lord says, "I shall make marks on their noses." If somebody has no knowledge of conscience, of what avail is the colour on thy face (because the face reveals the internal state).

## CHAPTER 49

All things are such that if you seek them, then alone you will find them. But, the Lord is such a Friend that His search starts after you have found Him. A man really seeks a thing which he does not possess and therefore, he seeks it day and night, but it will be most surprising if he continues to seek it which he has already got. It does not strike a person if such a thing is possible. A man cannot conceive of it for he seeks only that which he does not possess. But, the Thing which he possesses and still he seeks, is God, because all things are in the Lord and in His nature and power for He said, "Be ye (world)" and it was created.

Very great is he who has received Him Who has got all things. He is the great gainer. God is the seeker. Not (only that), He is a Dominating Seeker. He means that a person should seek Him as he seeks a non-eternal object. You are receding far off from the goal, but when your search merges in the search for God, God will dominate thy search and then you will be the true seeker.

A person said, "I have no argument to prove who is an enlightened person and who has attained God. Neither I can perform any miracle nor least of any spiritual practice nor repeat the saying of some great saint to prove it. I have no such method by which I can recognise a saint, because it is possible that the person whom I doubt and try to recognise (if he is a realised saint) might have learnt from others miracle mongering etc., which is displayed by genuine dervishes who tell the secrets of a person's heart and perform many miracles. Then, where lies the difference between magic demonstration and the miracles exhibited by the saints? How is to distinguish the apparently similar feats? How can one know that this is the act of a saint or that of a pretender?" Thus were many things said by that person. Maulānā, thereupon, questioned him, "Do you believe in us or in anybody?" "Yes, I am the faithful one and lover too." The Maulānā, then, asked, "Did you begin to love and have faith in that person on the basis of some argument or finding some particular signs in him or by merely casting your glance at him?" The man answered, "How is it possible that I should have accepted him without argument and signs?" Maulānā, thereupon, remonstrated, "Why do you, then, say that faith has no reason behind it (to support it) and do you talk a jargon?"

Another of the audience said, "Ever a saint or a devotee pretends that he is nearer to God than any one else." Maulānā asked him, "Is it, what you repeat, said by a saint or some one else?" For, if it is stated by a saint, whose it is personal experience and who has witnessed it, there is none to say anything against it, for, every Prophet thinks about himself in the same strain. Then, he cannot be said to be a particular recipient of Lord's grace and mercy. But if these are the words of him who is not a saint, he is a genuine and favourite devotee of God because this secret was hid by God from every Prophet but not from him." Take an illustration. A king had ten slave girls who conferred amongst themselves to know who amongst themselves was the most beloved of the king. Then, they asked the king. The king showed them a ring and said, that she in whose house that ring would be found the next day was the most beloved of him. The next day, having prepared ten similar rings, he sent one ring to every one of the slave girls. The Maulānā said that the question still remained unanswered for the answer of the king was no answer to the question. The Maulānā further asked him to tell him then if that story had been told by any one of those ten girls or by some stranger. If any one of those ten girls had said that, it followed that she had known that the ring was not particularly made for her because every one of the girls had it so there was no speciality about her and she was not the most beloved of the king. But, if that information was spread by any one besides those ten girls, that one amongst the slaves of the king was surely the dearest to the king.

A person said that the lover should live as a discarded person and unknown to every body. The Maulānā said, "A lover should be such that he should obey the beloved's mandates. If the beloved does not want that the lover should be humble and remain unknown, even then if he tries to be humble and unknown, he does not obey his beloved and is obedient to his will and is no lover. If he follows the command of the beloved who does not want him to be humble and unknown, how can he be disgraced and remain unknown? It follows that you can never know the condition of the lover until you know what kind of nature his beloved wants him to develop.

Christ said, "I am surprised how one animal eats another". Apparently, the people remark that man eats the meat of animals and both are creatures (animals). This is a mistake. Why? It is true, that man eats meat but it does not possess life. It is lifeless because after it is killed, the animal ceases to have life. Christ means that the teacher swallows the disciple and it remains a secret. Why does he so? I am surprised at this occurrence.

A person said, "Prophet Ibrāhim said to the king Namrood 'My God can revive the dead, and kill the living.'" He replied, "I also can dismiss a person from a high office. It is tantamount to my killing him. I can also appoint a person who has no appointment and it is like reviving a dead person." Ibrāhim after a moment's silence, said, "My God makes the sun rise in the east and set in the west. Now, do the same, O NAMROOD (Nero)." Apparently, it seems that Ibrāhim offered a second argument. But this is not so. The argument is the same, only a second example of the first argument was given, for, it is not possible that Ibrāhim may be defeated by Namrood in his arguments. Ibrāhim gave a third example, "God brings out the babe at birth from the womb of his mother just as the sun rises in the east and buries it in a tomb on its death. If thou claimest God head, turn the order, O NAMROOD! that henceforward the child may take birth in a tomb and be entombed on death in the womb of a woman." You will say that Ibrāhim's argument was throughout one and the same. God creates man anew every moment and within his heart is sending new ideas every moment, but man does not distinguish that all of them are different, because he has forgotten himself and does not recognise himself.

For Sultān Mahmud, a beautiful horse was brought. On the great festival Id day, he rode on it. The People were watching him from their house-tops. But a man who was drunk remained seated in the house. The people dragged him to see the procession. He said that he did not want to see the horse as he was enjoying his intoxicated state. But they took him to the house top. As the king on horse back passed below his house, he remarked, "Ah! If one could sing a beautiful song to me at this moment, I would offer this horse to him for, what worth does this horse have before that song?" Sultān heard this and ordered him to be shut up in the prison. On the seventh day, he petitioned to the king to tell him, after all what was his crime for which he was imprisoned. The king ordered him to be brought in his presence and told him, "O toper! Why did you speak those insulting words?" He said, "Your majesty, I never said those words. It was a foolish drunkard who said those words and went away. I am not that person I am now a wise person." The Sultān was pleased with his reply, gave him a robe of honour and bade him good bye.

He who is connected with us and is drunk with the wine that we cater, will be really with us, be like us and be one with us wherever he goes and in whatever company he sits. Thc company of others is like a mirror of our association, and on meeting others, excellence of our association, is disclosed because the glory of a thing appears on seeing its opposite. Abu Bakr Sayid styled thanks-giving as wine, an extremely sweet thing. Many other sweet fruits say to sugar, "We have endured much more trouble than you, then we have attained to this state of sweetness which has easily come to you. What do you know of sweetness and its pleasure?"

## CHAPTER 50

They asked the Maulānā the meaning of the couplet:

"When love reaches its climax,

The friendship turneth into enmity."

The Maulānā remarked that the world of enmity is far smaller in ambit than that of friendship. This is because the people run away from the world of enmity that they may reach the world of friendship. The world of friendship, too, is smaller than the world from which have issued both the worlds of friendship and enmity. Friendship and enmity, and faith and heresy are both from duality because for the non-believer, there must be some one who is the object of his belief. This means that heresy and belief are both causes of duality and that world is beyond the ken of friendship and enmity. There is a world where there is no duality. There is only unity and pure love there. When you reach there, you are separated from duality. It means that the world of duality is much inferior to the world of unity and love. The dweller of the world of unity will never like this world of duality but consider it bad.

Just as, in Mansūr when Love of God reached maturity, he turned his own enemy and killed himself. He said, "I am God." By this, he meant "I have effaced myself. God alone exists." This is the highest form of humility and the greatest degree of supplication. It is saying whatever is seen is God. If, however, you were to say, "God and I, His devotee exist," this would be an assertion of vanity for you have, thereby, proved your separate existence and duality thus steps in. Even when you say, "Thou art God," "This statement also smacks of duality, for, as long as there is no "me" in existence, nobody can be styled as "Thou". It follows that it was God Who said "I am God," because there was none else in Mansūr besides God and Mansūr (his ego) was dead. It was a statement by God Himself. Much vaster than the world of imagination and feeling is the world of thought because all the things that are imagined are first born in thought and the world in which thought is born is even vaster than the world of thought. Only this much can be understood through words, otherwise the real import cannot be expressed by description or through conversation. Somebody said, "Then what is the use of discourses and writings?" The Maulānā answered, "The purport of these discourses is to infuse yearning for God and develop enthusiasm in you, and lead you to make effort in the quest. It is not correct to think that by conversation and discourse, the Ideal will be attained. If it were so, all austerities and attempts to annihilate the carnal self would be of no use. Discourse is as if you are seeing from a distance a thing that is shaking and you go on running towards it till you reach it. The discourse, urges you to seek the meaning (reality) which you really do not see.

I learnt so many arts and acquired so much knowledge and probed into so many mysteries but till now I could not know what is that which is eternal in man.

The Maulānā said, "If this thing could be witnessed merely by discourses, where was the necessity to annihilate existence (ego) and endure so many troubles? Why should you make so many efforts and persevere so much that you may annihilate your self completely and that you may know the thing that is eternal?"

A man said, "Kābā exists and I try to see it but I can not see it. Let me climb up housetop and try to see Kābā." He climbs the house-top and even then Kāba is not visible. Then, he says that Kābā does not exist. By this mere talk you cannot see Kābā. If you want to see Kābā from your place, you will never be able to see Kābā. In winter, you earnestly desire to have warm clothing but when summer sets in, you throw off those warm garments and hate them. You want the warm clothing so that you may get warmth because cold outside does not permit your body to get warm in winter. To warm it, it is necessary to have warm clothing. Now, as the winter has gone, you throw these warm garments away. When the sky was rent asunder, the earth suffered from a terrible earthquake,"—these verses mean that you have enjoyed the pleasure due to collection of the elements but a day will come when you will see disintegration of these elements and particles of the body (their total decomposition). You will see the vastness and expanse of the next world and shall be released from this tiny house. Suppose, someone is imprisoned behind bars, he thinks that it is a comfortable place and has forgotten the joy of freedom. But when he will be released from this imprisonment, he will know the joy of freedom and also felt what a place of anguish it was where he was imprisoned. Just as, the children find joy when they are laid in a swing. The hands of the children are tied in the cradle, even then, they find comfort there but if a young man is laid bound in the cradle, how much pain will he not experience? For him, it will become a positive torture. Some people like that the flowers may bloom and many like the petals of the flowers may be torn into pieces and they may be destroyed completely and return to their source. Some people want that heresy, faith, love and friendship all may be destroyed so that they may return to their source because all these are walls that veil the Reality, and are the cause of duality and the next world of unity (consciousness) is vaster. After all, this is a mere statement. Neither it is a very great thing nor full of vitality. How could it be otherwise since it is after all, words and words are cause of weakness. God alone produces effect and also urge. This is hidden in words. How can the joining of two or three letters be the cause of life and fervour? Suppose, a man comes to you, you welcome him and treat him well. He is pleased and this statement becomes the cause of affection. Whilst you abuse a person, the few words excite anger and he is annoyed. Now, consider what relation has this joining of two or three letters or their arrangement with developing anger or creating love and friendship? But, God has created them as veils and causes, so that all may not see His greatness and beauty. For the weak-sighted, very light are the veils and lights. From behind the veils, He commands and creates causes. Just as, food is not the cause of sustenance of life rather God has made it the cause for giving life and strength. Food is lifeless because it does not contain life in it, then, how can it give strength to such life? If it had had life, it would have been alive itself.

## CHAPTER 51

The people asked the meaning of this couplet:

"Man, thou art a thought (belief),
Besides it all is bone and flesh."

Maulānā said, "By thought here is meant a special class of thought. I used the word thought to give an elaborate meaning. Really, it is not a thought and not like the thought as people understand generally by that term. If one desires that instead of it, another word should be used so that common people may follow it, we shall say human being is a rational (endowed with speech) being. Rationality (speech) causes anxiety whether it is open or secret and the man is nothing besides it. So, it is correct to say that man is a mystery. Besides it, all is merely bones and flesh. Discourse is like the sun. All men gain life from the sun. The sun is ever extant and all get warmth from it. But the sun cannot be seen. If through words and writing, thanks are offered or complaints are made, the sun will appear before the eyes. So also, the sun in the sky is always shining but it cannot be seen till its rays fall on the wall. So also if there is no venue of letters and sound, the rays of the sun of discourse will not be visible, although it is always extant. The sun is very subtle and the air is also very subtle. There should be some grossness whereby it may come before the sight.

Someone said, "that God did not disclose to him any internal secret. So, he was helpless and ignorant. But when the people said, "God orders thus." God has said thus, It is a command, then there arises some warmth that he has seen something. Although the subtlety of God was present and was letting fall its effect on him yet he was unable to see it. Not so. So long as, he did not hear the commands and prohibitions qua nature and creatures, he could not see it. There are some people of weak constitution. They cannot eat honey but when they are given it mixed up with rice or other sweets, thereafter they can take it. So, we learn that rationality is like an ever-shining and subtle sun but you need a gross medium that you may be able to see the rays of that sun and enjoy it. When you have gained such strength that you can see that ray without any gross medium, you will see varied enjoyable things and shall have pleasant experience on witnessing the ray in its naked state. That rationality is ever present within you whether you speak or not. If there is no thought in your mind at the time, even then we shall say that rationality is extant in you and shall be always there as it is said that a man is a rational animal. That animality (carnality) is always present in him so long as he is alive. Likewise, rationality is always extant within him. Just as, sleep here may be an animal quality but it is never the cause of animality and we shall not call one who sleeps as animal. So also rationality is there whether you speak or not.

There are three states of man. The first is the state in which he does not approach God although he accepts slavery of everybody. He serves his wife, children, wealth, stones (buildings) but does not serve God. But when some discrimination arises in him and understanding develops, he serves nothing and nobody besides God. If he desires to advance further, he becomes silent. Neither he says that he will serve nor says that he will not serve, nor does he say that he will serve God. He rises above those two states. No one talks of such people in this world.

God is neither present nor absent. He is the Creator of past and present, hidden and visible. So He must be some thing besides these two. For, if He is present, He cannot be said to be Hidden. In God's nature, there is nothing hidden or present nor can it be said that these two are opposites in the eyes of the Lord. Again, how is it possible that two opposite things may be born of One Source. If absent thing is created by Him, the present one cannot be created by Him, for the present one is opposed to the absent one. Besides, it is not possible that God may create one like Himself because God says that there is no compeer of His, none is His co-partner. How can one similar thing be born of the other. Now, you have reached the state when you should become silent because intellect becomes helpless at that point.

All the arts, knowledge and professions are the offspring of speech (rationality). If speech is absent, all professions will be futile and will give no pleasure. Men do not know the real meaning nor is it precedent condition or necessary to know it. Just as a person married a rich lady who had herds of sheep, horses and goats. That person takes care of these animals and also looks after the gardens. Although he does all these kinds of service but real joy comes to him only from the woman's person. If the woman dies, he will find no joy in any of these activities, and will turn cold. So also all the professions and learning are pleasant because they are reflections of the mystic in them and it makes them full of life. If his fervour is lacking in them, all will turn dead, and unenjoyable.

## Chapter 52

Formerly, I used to compose poems. I had a great desire which led me to do that. I had much experience also at that time. That desire has now become feeble and my end is also near but still it is effective. It is the law of the Lord that when a work is started by Him, He nourishes it and many kinds of experience are exhibited by these things, and when the time of their annihilation is reached, even then the same nourishing power works. He is the Lord of the East and the West. It means that He fulfils all desires when they are rising and when they are coming to an end. It is a parenthetical clause—The slave of the Lord creates his works himself. "This means that whatever work is done by the slave of the Lord is his own creation. But this should not be the case, because whatever act a man does is done at the prompting of some desire and with the instrumentality of other, that is, he acts with intellect, strength, soul, body etc., or even he may act without any such instrumentality. It cannot, therefore, be said that he is the creator of his acts, because he creates through these instruments which are not subordinate to him, and without them, he cannot do them. It follows that God is the Creator of all acts and not man. Whatever a person does—good or bad works, he does so by some prompting and motive. But he does not get from them the benefit that he had thought, he would secure. The result of this is that the slave of God does an act but what effective result will follow from it is known in full only to God. He alone knows what fruits the man will reap. Take an illustration, you say prayer with the motive that you will reap benefits (spiritual) from it and will be saved from many troubles and will earn a good name. This alone is not the benefit of prayers. Besides these, it shall confer on thee inconceivable other benefits. These cannot enter your mind. They are known only to God, Who is taking that service from His slave. Man is like a bow in the hand of God. God uses him for all purposes. The real actor is God and not the bow. The bow is merely an instrument and a means. It does not know itself nor it is aware of the bow-man who holds it. How fortunate is that bow which knows the Hand that holds it ! All this is to keep the world going on. How magnificent is that bow which knows that it is God Who is holding it.

What should I say about this world which is sustained through ignorance ? Do you not see when man is instructed and made aware of it, how much does he begin to detest this world and feel unable to live in it? He does not care to cast a look at it and ultimately renounces it. This growth of man from a child to manhood is also based on ignorance and is its product. Then, follow up on him troubles and efforts when he attains youth (which is also due to ignorance) and he has to endure them whether he does so happily or with unpleasantness. These troubles are cast on him to wake him up from the sleep and laziness and make him alert and start persevering. Then, he becomes conscious of the next world. The existence of man is like a mound of rubbish, the store of cow-dung. The heap of cow-dung is liked because it is stored by order of the king. The existence of man is like that bag of wheat about which the king remarks "Where are you carrying it?" In it is his my treasure (scale). But the carrier is so much steeped in thoughts of wheat that he does not care to know about the measure hid in it. If he became cognisant of the measure (of the king), he would turn careless about the wheat.

Now that thought which draws your attention to the next world, makes you careless of this world and makes it distasteful for you. It is the reflection of that measure. It shines and man is drawn to that next world. On the other hand, if man is foolishly drawn towards this mean world, it will follow that that measure has been concealed.

## Chapter 53

Somebody told Maulānā that Qazi Aziz Uddin sent greetings to him and was always eulogising him. Maulana thereupon, replied:

> May God always give name, fame and honour in this world to him who remembers us with feelings of love.

If some one speaks well of any body, the fruit of those good words and feelings revert to the sayer thereof. In reality, he is, thereby, elevating himself, and in reality, he is praising himself. This can be illustrated thus. Suppose some body keeps a nice garden about his house. When he looks around, flowers will come in his view and he will find himself in the garden. If a man develops the habit of speaking well of others, they whom he speaks well will become his friends, and they will remember him with good feelings, and remembrance by a friend is no less fragrant than the flowers in the flower garden. It gives nice odour and comforts the heart. Likewise, if a man thinks evil of another, he falls in the estimation of the other. Whenever he will remember the other, he will feel as if he is bit by a snake or scorpion or accumulated heap of dirt is cast on him. If, then, you can see flowers and heavenly gardens evading them, why should you be wandering recklessly seeking the holes of the snakes and prickly shrubs? You should love all that you may constantly be roaming in the flower gardens. If you constantly think of others in inimical terms, you will feel you are in the midst of snakes and scorpions.

The saints who love others and think well of others do not do so for the sake of others but for their own sake so that no evil or bad thought should ever linger in their mind. Man and his mind are so related that it is difficult to keep the one and reject the other thought. So the saints ever try to remember their dear and good ones, so that evil thoughts may never enter their mind. They always remember that if evil thoughts cross their mind, they shall redound on them. Watch what the Lord is saying, "When a man performed a good act, he did it for himself, likewise, if he did an evil act, he performed it for himself." Again, it is said, "Whosoever will do a particle of good deed will see its good result and he who will do the least evil act, shall reap its evil effect."

God says, "I shall appoint a representative of Mine on the earth". The angels observed, "Why should You give birth to such a one on the earth, as will raise quarrel there and make flow rivers of blood, whilst we are always engaged in praising Thee". Man (Adam) was not yet born, how could the angels, then, accuse man of the nature of quarrel and bloodshed?"

The Maulana said, "Two causes have been assigned to it. The first is the traditional view and the other the intellectual. The traditional view is that the angels read the scroll of fate, that some people who will have that nature will be born. Therefore, they said that. The intellectual view is that by a course of argument the angels inferred since man is born of earth, so he must possess these traits common to brutes for brute is a synonym for quarrel also. May be, these men may possess some humane traits also since they are rational beings, but since animality is in them, then, of a necessity, they will go wrong and shed blood. This is a trait of man.

Some people, however, interpret it differently. They say that the angels are constituted of intellect from head to foot and are the effigy of goodness and are subservient to the (will of God) having no freedom of action. Just as, you act in the dream with no power of control over that act. If you do an evil act in a dream, you are not punishable (for that act of the dream). Whatever is the state of the men in a dream is the state of angels in wakefulness. Men are, however, free and are avaricious also and have many desires and they are ready to kill another for a thing which they want. They desire to Lord everything. These are the traits of animals. The case of angels is quite opposite to it. So, it was natural, if they said these words before

God. Their meaning can be explained thus: If two persons speak against each other and also state their condition, this will be like what is stated by a poet:

"An old tank said that it had grown old". The tank does not talk. Then the meaning of the statement would be that had the tank a tongue, it would have at that time spoken thus about its condition. Every angel in himself has a tablet (recording the transaction of mankind to occur till eternity, written by God) on which are recorded the future events which he can read according to his capacity and status. When he reads it and later finds all events happening in future as they are recorded there, his faith in God grows in strength, and great love and fervour finds expression in him. He is surprised at the foreknowledge of the Lord and in his heart of hearts without visibly expressing it in words or through sound, he praises Him (mutely), Just as, if a mason estimates that the house which is going to be built will require so much material and so much will be the expense on it and the pupil finds that when the house gets ready, the expenses came to what his mason (teacher) had told him in advance, his faith strengthens in him. So is the case with the angels.

Somebody said to his teacher, the greatness of the prophet is such that the Lord says about him, "If you were not born, I would not create heaven". This was what God said about the Prophet and the latter replied, "Alack! Would that, God of Muhammad had not created me!" Now, what is the meaning of this.

The teacher replied that that would be understood by an illustration. He said, "I shall narrate a story to you. In a village a person fell passionately in love with a woman. Both lived in huts located close to each other, and they were very happy and comfortable. In each other's company, they got great satisfaction. They lived in the sight of each other as the fish lives in the water. For years, they lived like that. God very soon bestowed great flocks of sheep and horses on them. Their wealth and servants multiplied. Therefore, they shifted to the city. There they lived in palatial buildings on either bank of the river. Their houses were separated by a long distance. The joy of their close contact was lost although they were growing in riches. They wept in secret and their hearts were tortured. They were troubled with pangs of separation. Formality of the new residence did not permit them to meet freely and express their feelings audibly. They prayed to the Lord that they could not endure separation from each other any more. The Lord heard their prayers and their wealth diminished and soon they were again reduced to poverty. They returned to their village and passed their life in poverty but with joy in each other's company as of yore. When they remembered the pain of separation, they uttered the same traditional phrase," Would that, O God of Muhammad! Thou hadst not given birth to Muhammad." When being unattached to affection of the world, the soul of the Prophet dwelt in the Divinity's Love in union with the Lord, it swam like the fish in the river. Although he enjoyed the unique privilege of leadership and of being the guide of the people, wielded great, power and was honoured greatly, yet when he remembered his past life, he said, "Would that I had not been a prophet and not come from that world of pure union, to this world! All this power and grandeur is a veritable burden on me, and a source of positive trouble.

In this world, all this learning, austerity, obeisance and honour which we perform for the world, are (worth nothing compared to the gifts that the Lord confers on us) like a person serving us for long and then disappearing (without taking anything in return). If one were to cover the whole earth, with obeisances, even then they would not count as one obeisance to the Lord. So great are His gifts to us.

The Lord's gifts and kindness are from eternity, from the time prior to your birth, from where He brought you and then gave birth to you and then prepared you for his obeisances. He conferred so many blessings on you and you are proud that you worship Him. What are these obeisances and worship of your like ? They are like your presenting God with a few dolls made of wood or cotton or felt, and then saying, Be pleased with them as I have made them. Now, it is for Thee to impregnate them with life, for if You enliven them, they will be equipped with all knowledge. If it does not please Thee, let them lie as such (dead or inanimate). Ibrāhim said that God is He Who gives life and takes away life (kills). Namrood answered, 'I also kill and revive'. God had bestowed a kingdom on him and he was puffed up with power. It was not told him by God but he himself at his own initiative said that he could also kill and revive. By kingdom is meant knowledge. God bestows on man cleverness and strength but man thinks that they are all his own works and says with this knowledge that he will perform that particular act and will take pleasure in it. So he does not say that He (God) kills and revives.

Hazrat Ibrāhim told Namrood that his God punishes and burns. He replied, 'I also do this all the moment'. Ibrāhim then said, "My God makes the sun rise in the east and set in the west. If you can reverse the process, I shall admit your Godhead". By giving the second example Ibrahim did not admit defeat of his argument but illustrated his point. This example meant that God made his features in the mother's womb when he was nothing but a mere drop. His birth place was the mother's womb and he rose from there and sank in the hole of the tomb. This is another way of saying the same thing that God kills and revives. Ibrāhim said to Namrood, "Now, O King, if you have power, reverse the process and make it a rule that henceforward a child will be born in a tomb and buried in the mother's womb". The other meaning is that the enlightened saint by obeisances, austerities and other methods and practices, earns and enjoys light, fervour, comfort and pleasure, and is happy and if he cannot perform them, all joys of life are lost to him. So these two conditions of offering worship and not performing worship are like the east and the west of above illustration. "If you have, Ibrāhim further said to Namrood, "the power of reviving, dispel this state of sinking (of the sun of above illustration) which are evil habits like sinning etc. and convert them into virtue and effulgence which are like light, yearning and obeisances and joy of the above illustration. This is not in the power of a creature. It is in the power of the Creator alone. The slave of God cannot do it. It is in the power of God to make the sun rise from the east and set in the west because, He has the power to kill and revive."

The heretic and the believer both praise the greatness and piety of the Lord. God has said, "He who treads the path of righteousness, the right and true path, follows the scriptures and pursues the path shown by the prophets and the saints, light, happiness and life shall fall to his lot and he who will act quite opposite to it shall fall in the well of infamy and trouble shall pursue him". When the heretic and the believer tread this path, whatever has been promised by God shall manifest itself fully. So, both will be proclaiming the majesty of God, the heretic in one language and the believer in another. But there is vast difference between their proclaiming the majesty of God. Take an example. Suppose a thief committed theft. He was hanged. He, too, proclaimed to the Moslems that if they committed theft, they would be hanged. On another, the king conferred the robe of honour for his honesty and good behaviour. He, too, proclaimed to the moslems that by following righteous behaviour, they would earn honour and happiness. But the instruction given by either was in different language, the thief in one set of words and the righteous man in another. Try to discover what is the difference between the two.

## Chapter 54

Maulānā inquired, "How is your good heart?" Heart is a beloved thing like unto a net. If the net is fit and entire, the fish will be easily entangled. If, on the other hand, the heart will be unhappy like a torn net, it will serve no purpose. So, it is not proper to be extremely friendly with anybody or to be extremely inimical to anybody, because thereby the net is torn. So the middle course of friendship with the people is the best. The extreme kind of friendship is good with God alone, and with no one else. Howsoever much friendship you contract with the Lord, it can never be beyond limit. The more it is, the better it is because the friendship with the creatures is trifling and ephemeral. The sky is always revolving and all created things in the world are subject to it. So the state of the creatures is changing with it. When you contract friendship with anybody you want that it should grow more and more. But eternity is not found in creation. Then, how can friendship go on growing always (constantly) and if progress is not made, the heart sinks and remains gloomy. So also, when enmity arises, the desire is aroused in the heart that enmity may grow from day to day and the enemy may be destroyed completely. The revolution of the sky sometimes makes a poor man rich. Sometimes one is in affluence and at another moment, in penury. It is never the case that one man should for ever endure penury. So, one day, even the person who nourishes enmity will be converted.

The love of God is given to all, heretics and believers. How is it possible that men should not love Him Who has given him birth? Friendship is hidden in everything. But the obstruction keeps it hid. If that obstruction is removed, love manifests itself. Not to speak of the kings that are created, even the things non-existent and yet unborn, desire that they may be born. Just as, if four men go to the king seeking an appointment and stand before him in a row. All of them want that the king may engage them and each of them is shy of the other because each is harbouring a desire opposed to the other. So also the non-existent things desire to be born, and every non-existent thing desires to be born first. When this is the desire, of the non-existent things, how keen must be the desire of those extant things? There is nothing that does not praise the holiness of God. Where is surprise in it? Rather it would be a matter of surprise, if it was otherwise.

Heresy and Faith are both running in Thy way,

They say He is alone and has no co-partner.

This house of the world is constituted of ignorance. This world and all the bodies in it are formed of ignorance. This body, too, has grown through ignorance and ignorance is ever heresy. Faith cannot be discovered without heresy because faith means abandonment of heresy. It is necessary that there must be something—heresy—which has to be abandoned. When this is the situation that the two cannot be found alone without the other, so they are one and are not separate from each other and their Creator is also

One. If the Creator had not been One and the Same, they would have been separate from each other. So every Creator creates one of the other thing both separate from each other. If the Creator is One, He must be alone and shall have no co-partner.

People said, "Syed Burhā Uddin discourses well but quotes often from Poet Sanāi". Maulānā remarked, "It is like praising the sun because it gives light and light confers comfort. The poetry of Sanāi is revealed when the poems are read, just as things are revealed in the light of the sun. So, it is the sun that reveals. The object of the light of the sun is that the things may become visible, and of the things revealed by its light, there are many things which are useless. So, that which will reveal the useful things will be the real sun. This sun which we see is the gross pattern of that subtle sun. You should also interest yourself with that sun and seek the light of learning from it. You too, want those things which are not felt and which may be revealed by that sun, so that your knowledge may grow. From every friend and pupil, you expect that he may learn something or discover something. It follows that besides this visible sun there is another sun which reveals the internal inherent mystery and experience. This little learning that you acquire in this world, takes shelter of it and your are happy with it which is merely a reflection and branch of that learning. This little knowledge invites you to that great knowledge. "These people hear the Qurān with such attention as one tries to hear a distant sound."

That knowledge is attracting you to itself and as if it is saying that it cannot be contained within you in this world and you will reach there after a long time. You cannot hold it here and there you cannot reach yet. It is not possible that an impossible thing may become possible but it is possible for a difficult thing to be reached. So, although it is difficult, you should go on pursuing it with perseverance so that you may attain THAT GREAT KNOWLEDGE. Do not fear that you will lose yourself. That is impossible. So also, the rich in love of goods and wealth are collecting them so that they may know the nature of wealth and this is born of the richness of God. But the reflection of that richness says, "I want to recite to you the account of that richness and call you to it. Why do you want to drag me here? I cannot be contained here. Come to that richness which is the root and climax of all the wealth of this world. It is a proverb "All is well that ends well" that is, may the end be good. The best end is that the root of a tree may be in that World (spiritual) and its branches and fruits may be spread elsewhere and the fruits may be dropping from the tree. After all, those fruits will be taken to the garden where the tree stands because its root is there and if the state is the converse, inspite of external (spiritual) acts, as the root is in this world, its fruit will also come in this world. But luckily, if the fruits and branches of this tree remain in that garden, how great a thing will be?

## Chapter 55

Akmal Uddin said, "I am the lover of Maulānā and ever crave to see him. I have no thought even of my end. I never engage myself in any (spiritual) thought besides. The mental picture of Maulānā enlivens me, supports me and gives me comfort. Whether he is present bodily or mentally, I am equally satisfied." Maulānā said, that if the thought of God and the other world did not come in his mind, all these things were hid in that friend. Take an example. A master dancer was dancing before the Caliph and was manifesting her skill with four whirls. The Caliph enquired of her if it was the art of her hands. She answered that it was the art of her feet too. It meant that the joy that he witnessed in her hands was also pervading her feet. So, if a disciple does not remember the last day of judgment in its amplifications, but gains joy by the face of his teacher and fears his separation, all the amplifications are hid in himself. Just, as a person loves his brother and son and is kind to them, So also he loves his other relations considering them too as his brothers and sons—in the hope that they will also confer favour on him. But those hopes are not manifest, rather they remain hidden and when he affectionately treats them, these things do not appear visibly although they are present in his subconscious self just as the fire exists in the wood but remains latent. If it were not so, there would be no effect of the fire on the wood. The wood that is embedded in the earth will not float on water. The fire burns and grows by the help of air and without the air, it is extinguished.

So, while you are conversing, for it, the tongue, the lips, the intellect, and the mind—all are required, so also the sky, the elements, and million other things with which this world exist, are necessary. All these ingredients, then, take you from the world of attributes to the world of unity (truth). Even then, during the conversation, none of these hidden things make themselves manifest but all of these remain hid in the discourse.

A man suffers failure five or six times a day and he has no power over it and he never likes that it should happen like that. But, as this happens not from his side but from elsewhere, from the Lord who rules man, watches his deeds and controls them. It is He who makes the tyrant do an evil act and gives him pain. If there was no one to take work from him, why should he endure trouble and why should his hopes be not fulfilled? In spite of his unsuccess, he is not prepared to accept that there is someone who rules him. "God created man as His replica". There is in man an attribute which is opposed to humility and obeisance.

This has been put in his nature. Although he is so often slapped for it, yet this unruly attribute does not leave him, and he forgets all failures that are consequent on it. But when the thing kept in trust will be returned to him, he will forsake all evil traits, and will not have to endure any punishment.

## Chapter 56

A saint said that he had gone to the shop of purchaser of grains, so that some of his worries might leave him. The saints often visited that place with the same object. When he reached there, he found that the disciple of that purchaser of grains was working there. The purchaser of grains was ordering him to do many things and he was promptly obeying his orders. His obedience and activity pleased the purchaser of grains. He told him if he worked like that, he would make him his successor. On hearing that, the saint smiled and his heart was opened. He learnt that all the rich men of the world dealt with their servants in the same way.

## Chapter 57

Maulānā said, "An astrologer said to me, I can see nothing but this sky and the earth in this sphere: You Sufis claim that there is something besides and beyond it and that I cannot see. Make true your claim and show me that and tell me where He is."

Maulānā said, "From the outset, this question is wrong. You say, 'Show me where He is. That world is invisible (He has no abode)'. May I, therefore, ask you, 'Please show me the location where dwells this objection of yours.' Is it in the tongue or in the mouth or in the chest? If you pound these limbs into pieces, will you be able to locate that objection any where? Has thought any form? It follows that your thought's location cannot be discovered. When you cannot locate the place of the thought, how can you locate the place of the Creator and the Source of that thought? Many thoughts arise in you and many experiences you undergo but you have no control over them. Had it been in your power, you could have improved them. Besides, there is Some One who brings thoughts in you but you do not know from where they come and where they go away and what will come the next. When you cannot know your thoughts, how is it possible to know your Creator?"

A characterless woman says that God is not in heaven I ask her, "How did you know He is not there? Have you searched every nook and corner of the sky, and after wandering everywhere have you now come and said that? You do not know the bad character woman who dwells in your house, how can you know the condition of heaven and the sky?"

You have heard the names of the sky, stars and heaven. Do you have knowledge or everything that is on the sky. Have you ascended to the sky that you talk with so much confidence? Yours is a foolish and presumptive idle talk.

When you say that God is not on the sky, I interpret it that God cannot be circumscribed by the sky, rather He encircles the sky. True, He is related to the sky but that relationship is of different kind. Just as, he is related to you also but it is difficult to describe that nature of relationship. All things are in His subordination. All are His manifestation, and are in His service. Then, why should He not be Superior to and above all the sky and creatures? He cannot be within these things but He encircles and embodies all of them.

A person asked, "Tell me where was God when there was no earth, sky or the higher heaven and the lower terrestrial regions".

The Maulānā said, "This question is more trivial than the earlier one even. God is He Who cannot be assigned a definite location. You ask where was God before all these created things. You cannot locate the position of the things that are within you viz., intellect, soul etc., then how can you discover the location of God, Who has no abode? You can form no idea of the personality of your thought and fancy. How can you locate the abode of Him Who is the Creator and Lord of our thoughts when He is so subtle? just as, a mason who builds house is far more subtle than the house he builds because he can, in a moment, perform many such deeds and devices, and can build them. So, he is much subtler than them. But that subtlety of his is not manifest. They become visible when he manifests those fancies of his in the construction that he makes in the world, that is, when he practically demonstrates them. In the winter, you can see some form of the breath but not in the summer. It is not that the breath has stopped in the summer. The fact is that the summer season is very subtle, and the breath also becomes subtle. So, it is visible in the winter and not in the summer which is opposite to it. So, all the virtues and arts which are within you cannot become known until they manifest themselves in external activities of yours. Suppose, you possess the attribute of extending pardon. This can be known when you visibly pardon a sinner. When you will pardon a person, it shall become clear that you possess the attribute of mercy in you. So, you can conceive of other attributes. God is extremely subtle and therefore, cannot be visible to the eyes. He created the sky and the earth so that His art, excellence and majesty may become manifest. So He says, "Do you not look to the sky and see how majestic. I have made it?"

I am besides myself in my discourse. I have no control over it. So, I suffer pain. I try to instruct and make the audience understand but I find the words get out of my control. Yet, I feel happy that my words transcend me (in greatness) and I am their inferior. God's words, whatever He says, and wherever they reach confer life and produce many sublime effects. "When you shot the arrow, it was not you who shot it but it was God Who did it and took the aim." The arrow which comes out of the bow of the Lord cannot be warded off by any shield. So I am happy that whatever I say is from God. If there had been only wisdom in man and no ignorance, man would have been reduced to ashes; so the necessity arose that ignorance should also be implanted in him, for, man can subsist (and not become extinct) because of it. Wisdom is also necessary in him so that the power of discrimination to recognise God may remain in him. So ignorance and wisdom are helpers of each other, and are companions. All the opposites of things may be understood thus. Although night is opposite to day but is its helper. Day and night perform the same work. If there had been only night, no work could be performed and if there had been only day, all the limbs of the body of man, his eyes, his mind and others would have become tired, weak and useless. So rest is taken in the night that all the tools, namely, senses of sight, hearing, the mind etc. may all gain strength and that power may be spent later in various activities.

All the opposites seen in the world appear as converses of one another and militate with one another but if you think about them in relation to God—the Supreme Dispenser, you will find all of them performing only one work, and are not opposed to one another. Is there any person who is called bad and who has no virtue hid in him and is there any good person who has no evil trait in him? Take an instance. Some one decided to kill another, but he got engaged in a carnal vocation and thus desisted from the murder. So, looked from one point of view, carnality was a pernicious trait but looked at from a different stand point it was good because it stopped a person from committing murder. It means evil and good are one thing and not separate from each other. So I argue with the Zorastrians. They say that there are two Gods, one Creator of good and the other Creator of evil. I tell them, "There is no evil that is not accompanied with good. Show us that there are two Gods, One Creator of good and the Other Creator of evil and we shall accept your version. This is impossible because goodness cannot be separated from evil. When they are not two separate things, how can there be two Creators? I do not insist that you accept my argument. I simply desire that a thought may arise in you that what I say is correct. When you have no perfect faith that it is so, how can you have perfect faith that it is not so? God says, "O fool of a heretic! Do these people not fancy that on the Day of Judgment, the dead shall arise?" The fancy is apparent from this. The purport is that it may not be thought that our promises are without foundation. The heretic will be questioned about these things, viz. Why did you not also conceive of these things? Why did you not observe caution and seek Me?

## Chapter 57

, Abu Bakra's greatness is not due to many fasts, prayers and obeisances that he performed but because of one thing that he had got a firm hold of his mind. God had mercy on him, but what was that mercy like? It was that he loved God. On the Day of Judgment, fasts, prayers and offerings shall all be weighed in scales, but Love of God shall defy being weighed because the scales shall be unable to contain it. It follows that the real thing is love. If you love someone, one, try to develop it. If you have some wealth, try to enlarge it with greater yearning, for, if you do not enlarge it, it will be finished. Are you even lower than the earth? It is ploughed and the seed is sown, then its condition is changed and the vegetables make their appearance. If it were left without ploughing, it would become hard. If any quest arises in you, start to persevere in it. Never raise the question what benefit will accrue from this effort. You go ahead, the benefit will make itself manifest in due course. Why does a man visit a shop? Because he has a purpose. In that purpose is hid the gain. God gives food. If you idly sit at home, that is rank carelessness. The food will not come down from the sky. When the child weeps, the mother feeds him with milk. If the child were to think that his weeping was futile, how could it get him milk? It is apparent to us that it was the child's weeping that had secured milk for him.

Likewise suppose a man thinks to what avail saying prayers. Why does he, then, bow before the rich and the nobles and why does he flatter them? He flatters them because then do the rich show their kindness to him and confer a loaf on him. In the rich person, the quality that arouses in him the feeling of mercy is not his (flesh and blood), for during sleep or when he is senseless, the flesh and blood is present in him and even on his death, these things are there, but he does not know the worth of it (the trait or mercy in him).

It follows that the quality of mercy that is in the rich person is not visible to the naked eyes. Then how is it that we serve that which is hidden behind the flesh and blood but do not see it outside the flesh and blood (body). If this thing (mercy) were not hidden in the body, Abu Jonal and the Prophet would have appeared similar, and it would have been difficult to distinguish one from the other. This flesh (skin) apparently hears and is deaf simultaneously. But, in fact, that thing which hears is hidden within him, and is not visible.

So the real thing is to have favour of somebody. Suppose you are a rich man and you have two slaves. One of them may have served you with great perseverence whilst the other may be lazy. Then, it will be apparent that you will love the servant who serves you faithfully more than him who is lazy, although you will not neglect the other slave totally.

You cannot order that favour should be shown to you. The right and left eyes look similar but the right eye is generally dearer. The surprise is, after all, what good act is done by it that it is preferred to the left eye. So also, Friday is a dearer day in the week than other days. God says, "In the tablet of the heart are written all the things and the food that man will get. There are also other things of food which should be asked for on Friday". What special service has been rendered by Friday that it has got preference over other days of the week? But, God has shown favour to it, so it is honoured. A blind man says, "I am born blind. What should I, do? I am helpless". Will his saying this cure him of his blindness or will he be able to see the light of the day and the faces of the people? So, the saying of the blind and the lame that they are helpless will not remove their trouble.

The heretics pursue heresy. This ugly trait of theirs is also the grace of God, for when they get comfort they forget God and when they will be in trouble, they will remember God. Hell is the temple of worship of the heretics. They will remember God there, just as the prisoners in trouble in jail cry Allah! Allah! The veil of ignorance is removed when trouble falls. At that time, the slave of God accepts God and cries to God to have mercy on him but the moment he again gets healthy, the curtains of ignorance fall on him and he says that God is not visible to him and he cannot find Him and asks where, then, he is to seek Him. When he sees Him in trouble, it means that He in His kindness has bestowed trouble on him so that he may remember Him. The dweller in hell never remembered God and had forgotten His name when he was in the world but now in hell he always repeats, Allah! Allah! God has created the sinners and the men of piety for that purpose so that they may remember Him and worship Him. The heretics do not remember when they are in comfortable circumstances and the object of creating them is that they should remember Him; so they are sent to hell so that they may remember Him.

But for the believers creation of trouble is unnecessary. They do not forget Him even in comfort and the memory of trouble remains in their eye. Just as, if a wise child is once reprimanded, he never forgets it. But the dullard forgets it, and is, therefore, always punished. So also, a clever horse is whipped only once and no necessity arises to strike him again. But a dull horse is ever subjected to whipping and, therefore, he is not used as a carrier for men but the dirt heaps are carried on it.

## Chapter 58

Hearing a thing repeatedly produces the same effect as seeing it with eyes, and man can say as if he has seen it with eyes. Just as, you are born of your father and mother but you have not seen your birth with your own eyes. You have heard about your parentage from people repeatedly and you have become convinced of its veracity. If now someone tells you that it is wrong, you will never accept it. So also you have heard from people that Mecca is a town and so is Baghdad. If now people swear that it is incorrect and they are not cities, you will never accept it. We, therefore, infer that hearing repeatedly with the ears has the effect of seeing with eyes. Here is a man who is equal to a million people. Whatever he says has the same effect as if a million people have testified to that thing. There is no surprise in it. Do you not see that a king in this world is considered like a million of his subjects? Although he is one person, yet if he is considered to be a million people, it is correct.

When such is the matter in this physical world, it shall be much more in the spiritual world. You have travelled round the world but not for Lord's sake. You must, now, go on a second travel. God said, "O Prophet! Tell them to goround the world." Their travel was not for My sake but was prompted by another motive. It was for the sake of eatables like onion. That motive had turned a veil for them and they could not see Me. Just as, suppose you try assiduously to search anybody in the crowd but you are unable to discover him for wherever you look for him, you are confronted with the crowd, but the beloved sought for you do not see. Or again, suppose, you are seeking some problem in a book. In your ears and eyes the same problem is whirling round. Wherever you will seek it in the book, you will find only that and nothing besides. But when your object will be different, whatever spot you will reach, you will find everything filled with the same object and you will not see anything besides.

In the days of Hazrat Umar, there lived an exceedingly old and infirm person. He was so old that his daughter fed him on her own milk like her child. Hazrat Umar remarked that in those days, one could not find a progeny who might serve one's parents like that, realising that it was one's duty. Her father felt that he should also recognise her rights. The girl replied that he was right, but there was difference in her outlook and that of her father. Although she served him fully as her father used to look after her in childhood and was always anxious lest she should suffer the least trouble. But, although she served her father, yet she was constantly praying that he might die so that she might be relieved of that trouble. Although she served her father, yet she asked wherefrom she could bring for him that affection which he had for her in her childhood. On hearing this, Umar remarked, Greater is your understanding, little girl, than mine. I made a remark looking at the externals but you went into the depth of the matter. He who goes into the core of the matter and recognises truth is a person of understanding. It does not mean that Umar was not acquainted with reality of things but it was the way of the companions of the Prophet to express themselves in terms of humility while praising others.

There are numerous people who cannot endure to come before you. They remain happy if they remain away from you. The sun is shining the whole day long but if some one remains looking at it the whole day long, he will become unfit to do anything as his vision will be impaired. For him, it is better to keep himself engaged in some other work and keep away from the sun. It follows that if you take the name of dainty foods before a person who is ill, his appetite grows but if you place them before him, his health will suffer. In quest of love, the fear of affection is absolutely necessary. He who does not possess such fear of love, it is incumbent on him to serve those who have some fear of Him. You have seen that fruits do not grow on the trunk of a tree because it does not shake (out of fear). The branches shudder so the trunk gives them strength. As the fruits come on the branches, so no one cuts them. But the trunk of a tree also shudders, when the axe is applied to it. So, it is profitable if it does not shudder and its remaining steady is beneficial because thereby, it shall be supporting the branches.

He is Muin Uddin, not Ainuddin. The letter (Ain) has been preceded by (Mim).

The addition is the cause of harm to him. The excess of perfection turns often to be the cause of its fall. In the hand, five fingers are the right number. If one has six fingers in one's hand, that is bad. Ahad احد is perfection O Ahmad has not reached perfection till the letter (Mim) is removed from it. When it is removed, it becomes Ahad, perfection. It means God is circumscribing all things. He is the Highest of all. If you try to make any addition in Him, it will be harmful for Him. The digit one (1) is with all the numbers. Without it there can be no number.

Syed Burham Uddin was given some useful instructions. A fool seated there remarked, "We want to hear some exemplary unsurpassable words." He remarked, "If you want to hear such words, first become yourself unsurpassable, and then you will hear them. After all, you, too are an example. What you are is not your body. This feature and body of yours is merely a shadow. When a person dies, the people say such and such a one is dead. If he is this form or body, where has he gone? (He is here)." It follows that your exterior is an example of your interior but your exterior shows what is in your interior. Anything that is visible is due to its grossness.

It is incumbent on the Prophet to display the power of Truth and invite the people to God and wake them up. But, it is not his duty to confer talents and proficiency on them. That is the work of God. There are two attributes of God, His frown and His mercy. The Prophets are the place where these attributes manifest themselves. A believer is an object of manifestation of God's mercy whilst the heretic is the place of manifestation of God's anger. They who believe in God find themselves in the council of the prophets, hear their voice (direction) in themselves and find their fragrance in themselves and thereby turn fragrant themselves. One does not deny one's existence oneself. This is the reason why the Prophets tell their followers, "We are what you are and you are what we are." A person says that it is his hand. None seeks the proof of this from him because it is a part of his body. But, if some body says that such a one is his son, he will have to prove it through witnesses because he is apart from his body and distinct from him.

## Chapter 59

Love is the motive for service and not only that but the beloved demands service. If the beloved wants that he should be served, the lover shall serve him in all cases. If, however, the beloved does not want his service, his non-service will not affect his love for the beloved. Although the lover is not externally serving, yet within himself, he is constantly in the service of the beloved. The real thing is love and service is a branch of it. If the sleeves move, it means that the hand is also moving. Suppose, a person is putting on a huge gown. If he covers his whole body with it and lies down, it is possible that the gown may not make any motion but if it moves, it means that the man is moving. Some understand that the gown is the person. They think the sleeves as the hands and the trousers as the feet.

These sleeves, and socks are other hands and feet. People say that such a person is under such a person's hands, or some person's hand reached so far. The hand does not mean this physical hand.

The Amir came and we assembled and he went away. Just as, the flies collect the honey and wax and go away themselves. What does this connote? Their coming was necessary first and then their going away was not necessary. Our parents are like those bees who join a lover with the beloved and the seeker with the sought, and they themselves disappear. God has created them to collect honey and wax. Honey and wax are left and they disappear. But they (bees) do not get out of the garden, for this is not such a garden that they may leave it. But they pass away from one corner of the garden to another. Our body is like a big jug in which the Love of God is like honey and wax, our parents are like the bees. Although they are, no doubt, means but it is the garden which nourishes them and that jug (honey-comb) is also constructed by the gardener. God has conferred on them another feature also when they were working, they had a dress and form suited to the work. When they passed to the other world, they were putting on another garment. It was changed because they had to perform another duty, but their personality remained the same.

Just as, a person went to the fighting line. He put on the soldier's uniform and took up arms and put on the helmet on his head because it was the occasion of war. When he returned from there and went in an entertainment, he changed his dress because there he had to do another act. But, the personality remained the same. But, when you think of him, you will think of him in the dress in which you saw him. Howsoever many a dress he may change, he will be the subject of your contemplation in that form. A man lost his ring somewhere. People took it away to some other place. But, the person who had lost his ring was seeking it at the place where he had lost it, like the relatives of the deceased person continue to circumabulate the tomb of their dead like mad men, and kiss the earth of the place. It means that they have lost the ring there, but how long will they be tolerated there?

God created so many crafts to manifest His majesty and made this soul guest of the body for a couple of days. If a man whilst alive may be made to sit for a few minutes in a tomb, he will go mad. When you get out of the skeleton of this body and form, how will you dwell in that tomb? So, God has created death to make man fear and this fear may ever remain fresh in him. For this, He has created a sign (tomb) so that men may fear darkness and leneliness of the tomb. Just as, they heap some stones at the place where some caravan is previously looted, so that fear may arise in the minds of the people passing that way that this is a dangerous place. So, this tomb is like that and it teaches them that this is a horrible place. This fear does create a salutary effect but it is not necessary that it should actually be practised. Suppose, some one says that a person quarrels with you very much, then instead of his fear being inculcated in you, you will grow a little kind towards him. But if you are told that such a man insults you, anger will be aroused in your heart for him.

This running away is the result of fear. In this world, every one is running according to his capacity and speed. Man runs in one way, vegetables in another and the soul in a third way.

The running away of soul is without feet and leaves no mark. See how much the grapes (fruit) had to run, then it ripened and turned black in colour. The moment it was sweetened, it attained the great status and was styled grapes but its running is not visible and neither it has any apparent feeling. But, when it reaches the goal, it appears it has traversed a long course. Just as, man is travelling inside the water. His movement is not visible, but when he suddenly raises his head, the people notice that he has covered such a long distance and while moving all the time, he has now reached this place.

## CHAPTER 60

In the hearts of the friends, there are many ailments which cannot be cured by devices, neither through sleep, nor though walks nor by eating nor by the visits of friends because the sight of friend is the healthy medicine of the lover, this visit (interview) is so very effective that if a heretic sits in the company of the believer for a period, he, too, shall become a believer. God says, "When they (heretics) meet the faithful ones they say that they, too, are believers." Then, consider what would be the effect if a believer sits in the company of another believer. When association affects the heretic so much, how much will not the faithful be affected by the association of the believer? Wool in the hands of a clever person turns into a beautiful carpet and clay in the hands of a potter is transformed into the beautiful pot. When the inanimate things are thus improved through association, what must not be the effect of association of the faithful with the man of faith? When the inanimate things by associating with a man possessed of a little knowledge and skill rise to such a high status as the consequence of a little intellect of man, consider what mighty intellect it must be of God Who has created heaven, the vast earth and the sky!

Everything found in this world is the shadow of the perfect intellect. The little shadow of the intellect is in accordance with the capacity of the intellect of the person. The whole creation which is the shadow of that perfect intellect is in accordance with it. The lovers of the Lord have seen many such heavens (skies and spheres) in comparison to which our sky is nothing. They have crossed those spheres treading carelessly over them. Where is surprise in it, if one person amongst many may get this greatness that he may cross all those spheres? See, were we not mere clay? God conferred on us a power whereby we progressed further than our genus and He made us lord over that thing (earth). We can do anyting we like with that earth. We may spread it under foot or place it over head. Sometimes, we make of it houses and sometimes make pots out of it. It is up to us to shorten or lengthen them. They are all in our possession. Although previously, we were it and of its genus, yet God conferred on us honour. Therefore, if amongst us who all are of the same genus, God confers dignity on some one before whom we may be like earth or a piece of clay or a stone and he may take any work at his pleasure and we may be ignorant of it whilst he may be fully conscious of it. When we say unaware, it does not mean merely unaware because in that state of unawareness, a thing is often conscious of other things. Earth is a lifeless thing. But in that inanimate state, it is aware of the fact that God has bestowed gifts on it. If it were quite unaware, how could it seek water and how could it nourish every seed like a nurse? A man with great perseverence is doing a work with great care, at that time his attention is withdrawn from everything besides, but this inattention is not perfect unawareness. People wanted to entrap a cat. They could not, however, catch it any way. One day that cat was engaged in hunting a bird and was so engrossed in that, she became unaware of herself. People entrapped her in that state. So, you should not engross yourself totally in worldly activities.

You should select the simpler activities and get a little engaged in them according to your need. Never think that the world will get annoyed if you do that; rather this must be instilled in your mind that God, Who is the Treasure of the world, may not get displeased with us. If the things of the world get displeased with me, what does it matter, for, God can confer them on us again but if God gets angry, who is there to reconcile Him?

Suppose, you have goods of all kinds with you, and your ship is sinking, then, you will be thinking which thing to take out of it. Although you need everything but under the special circumstances, you will elect that which is the costliest and most useful. You will take that up, because if one such ruby or diamond is taken, it will fetch a hundred things. A tree gives sweet fruits. Those fruits are a small part of that tree. God liked that small part and gave it honour. That is, He conferred on it sweetness which is not found in any other part of the tree. So, that small part excelled every other part of the tree in sweetness, and became the goal of the tree. God says that the heretics wonder that one amongst them has come as a Prophet to inculcate fear in them.

A person said that he was, sometimes, in such high spiritual state that even the Prophet and the angels could not dare dwell with him. The Maulānā said, "I am not surprised that you should attain to that high state, even for a moment, that even Muhammad cannot dwell in your company, but the surprise is that never an occasion arose in Muhammad's life that a dirty fellow like you could dwell in his company.... Just imagine the foolery of yours that you say that you sometimes attain to that high state where even Muhammad cannot dwell with you then, it will be a matter of great surprise that Muhammad should not attain to that high state that a mean person like you may not be able to sit in his company. Look at your pride, you have got a little experience and you are boasting of it. This is, after, all the fruit of Lord's blessing and grace. First, all these gifts are bestowed by Him on them (Prophets) and by them they are bestowed on others. This is the rule followed by the Lord. When God said, "O Prophet! May My blessings and mercy be on you," It means that all good things and eulogies God has offered to Muhammad. Muhammad then said, "And on the devotees of yours also, O Lord!" The path leading to the Lord was very frightful and was covered with snow. It was the Prophet riding on horse back that cleared that path and opened it (for others) and he did it at the cost of his life. Now, he who will tread that path will do so with his kindness because it is he who has made that road, and fixed the sign posts, so that the followers may tread only that path. If they do not tread that path, they will be destroyed like the Aad clan. And if you tread this path, you will get salvation.

The whole Qurān is full of the mysteries disclosed openly therein. "The object of fixing poles as marks on the road is that if anybody treading that path tries to remove these sticks, the faithful ones will beat him because he who means to destroy the path will be considered a robber. So, the secret is kept with Muhammad and he is the foremost of all. Until he gets the thing (secret), we shall not get it. Just as, when you intend to go anywhere, your intellect will first be your guide that you should go there as there is good in it and the eye will show you the path and your hands and feet will move to take you there. These will be the many stages through which you will have to pass, then you will be able to proceed. Although the hands and feet do not know what the eye did, nor the eye knows what the intellect did. Man is ignorant but others are not so.

So, do not hold fast to the worldly activities, because if you start persevering hard in worldly activities, you may forget the real duty you have to perform (worship of God). Seek the pleasure of God and not of the people of the world. For, the worldly pleasure is short-lived and that, too, is conferment of the Lord on the worldly people. If God wishes he may withdraw all satisfaction that follows from blessings and make all comforts the cause of trouble. All the causes are like a pen in the hands of the power of the Lord. The mover or writer of the pen is the Lord. So long, He will not desire, the pen will not move. On seeing the pen, you say that there must be some hand to hold it. On seeing the pen, you are reminded of the hand. Ponder on what you say and see. But the Prophets always see the hand, and on seeing the hand, they say it must have a pen too. The truth is, that being captivated by the beauty of the hand of the Lord, they do not care for the pen, but believe that such a hand cannot be without a pen. Just as, the sight of the pen so captivates you that you do not care to see the hand holding it, so the Prophets are so enamoured of the sight of the hand that they do not care for the pen. You enjoy the bread prepared of barley, so you do not remember wheat. But these Prophets possess the loaves of wheat, why should they care for the barley loaves. Lord has Himself given such pleasure to the earth that the people do not care for the pleasure of heavens, although it is the heavens that are the real abode of pleasure. If there is no heaven, how can the earth subsist? Now, you can know yourself why the dwellers of heaven do not care to remember the earth? Do not think that causes are responsible for the pleasures. You must always keep in mind that there is a meaning hid in these causes and it is He Who is the Dispenser of profit and loss. When the gain or loss is from Him, why do you think of other causes?

Much talk compared to a single good talk is not worth it. That verse says "God is Unity (One)." This is a simple statement and very brief. But it transcends even the Sura Baqra. It is so full of meaning. Hazrat Noah invited the people to God for a thousand years but only forty people accepted Him. Muhammad preached for a much shorter period but several countries came in his fold, and many saints were created by his teachings. So never think that since the words are so brief, how can they be effective? The main matter is to produce a salutary effect. For some a brief talk is more effective than a discursive one. Just as, if an oven becomes full of great fire, you can derive no benefit from it and you will not be able to go near it. But, from the light of a small candle, you can draw great benefit. The object is to draw benefit. Some people are such that they need no instruction in words, but mere seeing them is enough for them. Such a person may suffer loss if he is made to hear much. A saint of India went out to meet another saint. When he reached the cave in which the saint dwelt, a voice was heard from within, "Return. Your purpose is served. It is enough profit for you that you have reached my door. If you see me with your eyes, you will suffer loss." A brief but useful talk is like a lighted candle which just kisses a dead candle and it is revived. This kiss is enough for the dead candle. His hope is fulfilled. The Prophets are not the body you see, but they are pure God's Love which is eternal, just as the camel of Prophet Saleh was a camel to external appearance but in reality he was a miracle.

A person asked, "When the preachers ascend the pulpit and eulogise God, why do they add the name of Muhammad also with Him?" The Maulānā said, "To praise Muhammad is to praise God. Suppose a person prayed, "O God! Prolong the life of the king and also of him who took me to the king, and told me the name of the king." Then, the praise of that person is really the praise of the king. The prophet does not say, "Give me something. I am in need. Give me your gown or wealth." What will he do with your wealth and gown? He simply wants to lighten your clothing, so that you may feel the warmth of the sun. For, it is said, "Give loan to God in plenty." He does not seek wealth and gown from you. He wants sacrifice from you. He has given you many things, If you have no wealth, it does not matter. He has given you knowledge and the power to think, intellect and memory. He simply wants that some of that intellect and power of remembrance, you should spend on Him. From these things you have earned wealth. So spend a little of it on Him. Not from man alone but also from the birds and the animals He demands sacrifice. If you can remain naked before the sun, it is a very good thing. That sun will not turn you black but will make you handsome. If you cannot be naked, at least wear light clothing, so that you may enjoy the warmth of the sun. For long, you have enjoyed saltish savoury food, taste some times sweets too.

## CHAPTER 61

In the house of Amir Parwānā, Maulānā was giving a discourse. Amir said, "Maulānā! The real thing is following advice of some one." Maulānā said, "That is no practice, but that is understood by that name." The word following someone may be illustrated thus: There is a king who is very enlightened, generous, just and possesses many other such virtues and has his army and treasure. He may proceed to another well-populated country and his heir-apparent sits on his throne. "The men of learning are the heirs-apparent of the Prophets." He should follow all those good traits and practices that were found in the previous king, then he is really following him. It is not following if some faquir stands up and the other standing up says, "I am following him."

## CHAPTER 62

"I am nothing and absolutely worthless." Such a statement is full of humility, but the difficulty is that the people do not follow the import of it. It means that a person should carry on worship for the pleasure of God. He should not intervene. He surely intervens if he thinks that he is serving God. That is, he is conscious of himself as also of God. Such a person cannot be said to be submerged in God. He who makes no movement in water is drowned although the water may take him anywhere or turn him in any direction. A lion pursued a deer. The deer continued to run. So long as he was running, there were two existences the lion and the deer. But when the lion caught the deer in his claws and he fell senseless before the lion, there remained only one existence of the lion, the deer became non-existent. Drowning means this state. Just as, the people fear the lion and the tiger, so the Prophets fear God. They are made to understand that fear, peace, comfort or joy everything emanates from God.

## CHAPTER 63

Sirājuddin said, "I stated a problem which caused me pain." The Maulānā said, "The pain is like a sentinel which stops you from uttering a word. You do not perceive that sentinel till you feel that something is stopping you from some enjoyment and thereby you feel pain. Suppose, you are journeying on a river. You are feeling the perfume of the flowers but when you get down on the banks, the thorns prick your feet. You at once feel that on that side there are brambles and thorny bushes, and there is a beautiful garden on this bank. Although you do not actually see these things with eyes, yet through feeling you note that. This is said to be intuitive. This is a truer experience than seeing through eyes. Just as, hunger, thirst, anger and joy are not visible to the naked eyes but they are felt more vividly than things seen through eyes. If you try to see with the eye cold and warmth, sweetness and discomfort, they are all vividly experienced but they are not actually visible (to the eyes). Look to your body. After all, what is your relationship with it? You exist without this body also. When you go to sleep in the night, you have no care of the body. In the day, when you get busy in varied activities, you forget this body and are careless about it. Then, why do you fear this body which is not always with you? You are somewhere and your body is elsewhere.

What is your relation with this body after all? The magicians of Pharoah were acquainted a little with this. They sacrificed their body and saw that they could live even without the body and the body was not related to them. So also Ibrāhim and other Prophets were acquainted with this secret, so they had no anxiety whether this body survived or not. A person took opium and when he was intoxicated, he lay his head on the threshold and began to cry, "Do not touch my head or it will fall down." He was experiencing that his head was separate from the body and was connected with the threshold. The other people and I are like that intoxicated person. It is mere belief of ours that there is a relationship subsisting between us and the body and we are extant because of the body.

## CHAPTER 64

"God created man in His likeness." All the people desire that they find something that should manifest their good qualities. Many women live behind the curtain (veiled). But open their face to test their lover as you test a razor. The lover complains to the beloved that he fasted in her absence and did not sleep and has turned so lean. The fact is that you desire a place where you can be manifested. God says, "I am the place where thou art manifested that the lover and the beloved may manifest themselves." So also all the men of learning and artists desire to display their art. "I was a hidden treasure. I desired to make myself known and be recognised."

God says, "I manifested Adam in My likeness." It means, "I created him in accordance with My commandments." The commandments of God are apparent in every one because everything is the shadow of God and a shadow resembles the original. If you open your fist, the fingers are also opened. If a man bows so does his shadow. If he lies down, the shadow also lies down. All the people desire to become beloveds that all may love them and serve them and that they may love their dear ones and be inimical to those who are their enemies. Those are all the virtues and traits of the Lord and His commandments, which are manifest in His shadow. It means, in short, that this shadow of ours takes no care of us but we are conscious and that consciousness of ours is fragmentary as compared to the knowledge of God and is tantamount to no consciousness, because the shadow does not reveal everything that is in the original. Only a few qualities are visible. So, all the qualities of God are not manifest in us, His shadow. God says that a very little knowledge is bestowed on us.

## CHAPTER 65

The knowledge that is gained by effort in this world relates to the body and the knowledge acquired after death is spiritual knowledge. To acquire knowledge of "I am God" is knowledge of body and to turn "I am God" is the knowledge of spirit. He who learnt what is "I am God" witnessed the glory of 'I am God'. His knowledge is knowledge of body. He who turned 'I am God', has spiritual knowledge. The perfect and infallible knowledge is seeing and all knowledge besides it is merely mental and intellectual learning. Suppose an engineer imagined a school and drew a mental map of it. His imagination is correct but is no more than a thought. The reality will appear when he will construct the house and it will be ready. There is difference between thoughts too. The Prophet had many companions but the thoughts and experience of Abu Bakar and Usman and Ali were higher than those of other companions, just as a person makes a plan in his mind to build a house and an engineer also makes a similar plan but there will be great difference between the two plans, because the imagination of the engineer touches the reality.

So also, there is great difference between the seeing of the spiritual world by different persons. It is stated that there are seven hundred veils of darkness and there are seven hundred states of light. It means that the mental world is like darkness and the world of a reality is like light. But, the veils in themselves are alike in form and there is apparently nothing to differentiate them, because very subtle is the domain of imagination and thought so, they are not visible to the naked eye. So also the states of spiritual experience are very subtle and it is difficult to see their difference.

## CHAPTER 66

The dwellers in hell remain happier in hell than in the world, because in hell they remember the Lord but do not do so when they live in the world. There is nothing sweeter than the remembrance of God. Even there, they desire to go to the world that there they may do some act that may confer joy on them. It is not that hell is better than the world. The heretic was given a dwelling in the lowest region of hell because when faith approached him, (and faith was stronger than heresy) he took to heresy and did not go in for faith, so he was given a harder punishment, so that he might remember God. But the condition of the heretic was such that faith had no effect on him. His heresy was too strong to get the little punishment. By severe punishment at once the remembrance of God was aroused in him, just as cotton wrapper is easily cleaned by one person, but a woollen blanket requires frour men to clean it. So the dwellers say in hell, "Please give us some maintenance out of what is given to you." It is not that they ask for eatables but they ask for the remembrance of God which is available in immense quantity in heaven.

The Qurān is like a bride wrapped in a muslin wrapper and seated as a shy maid. Unless you pull the wrapper with force, it will not disclose its face to you. If you study it but do not enjoy it, the reason is that though you have drawn the wrapper, yet it does not allow itself to be fully revealed and tells you on pretext that it is ugly faced beloved. It is within the power of the Qurān to reveal the kind of form good or otherwise as it likes but if you pull the wrapper with ease and with its permission and serve it in many ways and persevere in the matter as it commands, without your pulling the wrapper, it shall reveal its face to you. "Seek ye, therefore, My devotees" for therein is stated, "Enter the company of My devotees and then enter ye My heaven." (The Qurān).

God does not talk to every body as the king in the world does not converse with every commoner. The king appoints ministers and officers so that he may be approached through them. So God has also elected some of His slaves so that people may attain to Him through them. The Prophets have come to lead the people to Him and they are the guides and besides them there is none who can lead.

## CHAPTER 67

They asked Christ, "O soul of God! Which is the most difficult and biggest thing in this world and the next?" He said, "The anger of God." "What is that which protects one from His wrath?" then they asked. He replied, Drink your anger and destroy your displeasure. The method to do it is this. When the carnal self in you complains, you should act contrary to it and offer thanks to God and should be so grateful that His love may find a place in you, for even offering showy thanks is also seeking love of God.

Maulānā says that to complain about people is to complain about God. Anger and enmity lie hid in you in such a way that they are not visible to you. It is like unto the fire. The moment, a scintilla appears, at once extinguish it so that it may be totally destroyed and return to the source from which it has proceeded. But, if instead of that, you pour oil or sulphur on it, it will grow into a wild conflagration and then, although from non-existence, it had appeared, yet it will be difficult for it to return to non-existence. "With careful means try to remove it so that you may gain victory over the enemy." For two reasons, first, because it is not the skin and flesh of the enemy that is inimical, the real enemy is his thought. When you praise and eulogise the enemy very much, his inimical thought will disappear, and enmity with his body will also disappear. One reason is that all are slaves to Lord's kindness. Secondly, when they do not see any gain on any side, they do not direct their attention anyway, just as, children in a joke call a person their slave. If that person gets annoyed and abuses them, the children enjoy it and they pursue him thinking that the person is irritated and has become an object of their joke. But, if they see that the person shows no sign of anger and their joke has fallen flat on him, they do not give any thought to him. The second reason is that when within you, the quality of pardon is aroused, you will know yourself that the enemy's enmity is due to the fact that he has not understood you really and his opinion of you is based on a misconception. He will, then, know that it is he who is bad and nct you. The best way to put an enemy to shame is to disclose his falsity. So, when by praising him, you will, in fact, give him sugar-coated poison, it will mean that he has disclosed your faults whilst you have conferred your kindness on him. That is, you have told him that you are dear to God, because God says, "Those who pardon others are liked by Me more than those who perform good acts and are friends to them." The one dear to God can never be a bad person. Praise the enemy as much as he is praised by his friends. He will then begin to doubt if you are his friend or enemy.

> Although they are mighty proud, yet you should
> be very humble to them so that pride may dwindle.
> Although the core of their collar bone is very hard
> yet through your endurance, you should break it.
> May God help you.

## CHAPTER 68

Between God and man there are two veils, first is health and the second is wealth. Besides these, whatever other veils exist are the offsprings of these two. He who is strong and healthy questions the very existence of God and says that he does not See Him. But no sooner does he fall ill than he begins to remember God and weeping converses with God. It follows that health was like a veil unto him and God was hid behind the ailment. A person owns or assembles goods, furniture and other articles so that they may satisfy his desires. He is entangled in enumerating and thinking of them for the whole day and night and never remembers God. But no sooner does he face poverty than his ego softens and weakens and he begins to call God. When he is in that condition, God says:

"Thy poverty and ecstasy bring thee nearer to Me.
I am lover of this ecstasy and poverty in thee."

God bestowed the life of four hundred years on Pharoah and a kingship to boot and besides that many comforts and dignity. All these were like veils to keep him off from the presence of God. All those days he did not even suffer from headache even for a day lest he should remember God in agony. Only he was commanded to remain merry and not remember God.

Solomon got tired and felt worried at a kingdom.
But Ayub felt no worry even in the face of trouble and misery.

## CHAPTER 69

Thus goes the saying that there is within the ego of man an evil which is not found even in the animals. This is stated not to lower man in the scale of creation than the carnivorous animals but is said to bring out the fact that these evil traits veil his fine qualities of human nature which is hid in him. These evil traits become a veil unto his human nature as is well known, the more priceless is a thing, the more it is kept under veils. The evil traits and bad habits in a man hide his fine traits from his eyes and these veils cannot be removed without performing great austerity. These penances are of various kinds. One, for instance, requires us to associate with those friends whose eyes are turned towards God and who have turned their back to the world. There is no greater austerity than to sit in the company of good friends. It is also very difficult because at their very sight, the ego melts and dies away. This is the reason why the saying goes that if a serpent does not see a human face for forty years, it turns into a dragon. That is, he knows of none who can destroy his evil habits and mischievous nature and it is this fact which makes him fat and huge. If you see a big lock put on anything, know that it contains a valuable thing. It means that the thicker is the veil, the more valuable is the thing that it hides. Therefore, like the snake who sits coiled up on a treasure, do not cast your eyes on the veils (snake) rather direct your attention to the treasure.

God's Omnipotence demands that people may direct their attention to it and the natural leaning of man is always towards greatness and never towards lowness. The Omnipotence of God is greatness of all creation. To permit it to suffer is also an index of His Omnipotence. This contributes to the good of the world and is the proof of its transcience. You contemplate on pleasures and desire to know their climax. In this state, all your pleasures will turn sour. If, therefore, you perform your duty and contemplate on God simultaneously, you will experience joy from that contemplation on God. It means that you should remain the seeker of God and His lover and leave aside all intellectual disquisition, finding causes of limitation, attributes and evanescent traits. Leave them all and you shall find God. This is the thing which will lead you to greatness. This pain which you are feeling in hands and feet, should be treated as a froth which is coming out of the vessel on account of the warmth of love. God says, "So long as you do not forget yourself, you shall not know Me." Likewise, should you deal with every trait of the Lord so that whatever comment you make on rules of syntax or on problem of life, or on wisdom or seek knowledge of Arabic or search anything, let your quest be such that you may attain to the core and reality of the problem. Let you remain engaged in the study, in the comment and in the experience of that thing day and night and for years and let no thought go towards worldly activities, then fragrance of that act will spread in the world like musk and the people will recognise your greatness, and you shall also in that one word enjoy the pleasure of quest of God. Such will be the pleasure in it that in whatever activity you may be at that time or you may be thinking of any problem, remembrance of God shall never leave you.

Such smartness will arise in you at that moment that all the words will appear as one word (profession of Fatih) and all the colours as the colour of the soul. If in that word (Muhammadan confession of Faith KALMA) you do not find pleasure and nearness to God, all knowledge and learning will turn tasteless to you. Fervour and love of God and honour is that you should transmute your existence into His colour, and that trait which may attract other souls by its glory and effulgence may develop in you and it may turn those souls restless to meet God and throw them in ecstasy, and no remembrance of this world and of the next may be left and you may forget all the things that cause anxiety and in this effulgence all things may be so hidden as stars and candle light remain hid in the day time. When you shine like that and get enlightened so much, your light of a necessity shall be visible to others and they will compliment your wisdom and goodness. Now do not hurry but spend this little life in few WORDS (Kalma, the profession of faith). All your books and your perseverence will turn into wisdom for you. If you do not come, it is possible that your not coming may cast aspersion on God. If you come, it will be to your benefit.

In the Name of God, the Compassionate and Great Bestower, God says, "O Prophet! I have bestowed on you open victory." Enumerating the acts of kindness done to the Prophet by God and the bestowals He made and the promises He made, God says, "I opened the door which you knocked because I accepted your prayers. Secondly, I pardon you." To Pardon is a trait indispensable of friendship. The sin of him whom you love will not appear to you as a sin, and his faults will not appear to you as faults. This is the secret of pardon. Thirdly, The Lord will perfect His bestowals. To perfect the gifts is His particular nature. It means that many people do not get perfect gifts. Compared to them, these are very great bestowals and have received special instructions, have attained to reality of God and are well-established in truth. Fourthly, "God shall bestow on you great victory." This is index of kingship and great dignity. What is this great dignity? To see that everything comes from God. Just as, Ibrāhim entered fire, Moses entered the river, Solomon ruled the sun, and Noah was the master of the storm and David softened the iron and made the mountains start music and Christ ruled the souls of human beings and likewise Muhammad ascended heaven, and even excelled them and performed such innumerable acts. Since these people considered all things as slaves of the Lord and said that the real order was the order of God, therefore all things became their slaves and they became the slaves of God.

God says, "I pardon all thy past and future sins." About this, Ibn Ata says, that when Muhammad on the occasion of his ascension to heaven reached Sadar Ul Muntana, which is on heaven and is the abode of angel Jabriel, God ordered him to proceed further but Jabriel stood at the step and did not proceed further. Muhammad said, "Brother Jabriel, why have you left me alone to proceed in this dreadful place?" God showed His displeasure to Muhammad and said that walking a few steps with him had developed such love in him for the Lord. When God says that He pardons the sins of others, He means the sin which consists in loving other than God. He means that He has cast aside that affection too from thy heart and made thee fully careless of every thing non-God.

Ibn Ata says that God involved the saints and the prophets in sin and when they laid complaint before God and prayed for pardon, He pardoned them. But the prophet was given this honour that this state never came on him that he should pray for pardoning any person for his sins. But He exonerated him from all his past and future sins and did not even enumerate any of his sins. This shows the degree and height of Lord's Love for him and it did not fall to the lot of others. Ibn Ata says, that God says, 'I have pardoned the first sin of Adam and later sins of his followers for your sake because your followers look to you for intercession and you are their guide.' This means that the people who preceded you or those who are to follow you cannot reach God without you. Your intercession is necessary.

Some state that the pardon was sought by Muhammad when he was in perfect conscious state and related to the ecstatic state, whilst others say that he sought it in the ecstatic state and related to the period when he was fully conscious and in perfect understanding. A third class says that the pardon was sought for both the states because his eyes were ever riveted on God and he was always witnessing God. These ecstatic and normal conscious states relate to ordinary people whose states are always changing. But for the Prophet, there are no such changes, neither ecstasy nor conscious normal state of understanding. He was constantly seeing God, so he was pardoned qua both the states. You have fallen in a riddle which the Divine tablet nor pen can elucidate. But that tablet which is the attribute of God, is called Tablet but it is an extraordinary and limitless attribute.

> Under this vast sky, there are many things to see
> but the eyes are sore (what is to be done?)

If God wills, all troubles can be eliminated and made easy. If all these things which we know now had been described to us in childhood, we could not have followed them.

> We are content with what God has given in our share.
>
> We have entrusted all our work to God.
>
> Whatever is past God did well.

So, what remains undone shall also be done by Him well. Relating to the good people, of the thousands of signs which Lord has disclosed to us, we offer our gratitude for them because "offering gratitude paves the way to getting more." If God wills, He will bestow His gifts on you." To perfect the gifts is the domain of Love. First you were gifted with power to seek love, then, from the stage of lover, you rose to the status of the beloved. You were the successor of other Prophets and became an officer and ruler. You were poor but reached heaven. You were relieved from black and white. You have become king of black and white. You used to remember God, now the people ascend the minarets and take your name and draw your form.

God says, "I shall show you the right path," That is the way that will lead you to God. God shall bestow on you the great victory. You will be made the master of many undesirable thoughts and desires that arise in you and gain total victory over the devils amongst men who are the heretics. Your victory is such that it shall never know defeat. God further says, "Tranquillity was bestowed on you." Tranquillity is that which manifests the light of the heart. Tranquillity is that in which he has reason for depending greatly on God. Some say that tranquillity means that in which you differentiate the internals just as you differentiate the externals of a thing. God says, "Those people may progress in faith." It means that the light of faith of the Dervishes may be clear every day, just as the light of the moon. The armies of heaven are the armies of God. The armies of heaven are the angels and they always fight against the armies of carnal self. Others say that the heavenly armies are the hearts and the earthly armies are the bodies. Some say the devil is also of the army of God and he tries to conquer man and if God wills He makes devil predominate.

The Lord says, "I have sent you as a witness." It means by your action, by your words and by your state, you may testify to the (truth of the) revelations, to the existence of Divinity, Lord's Unity and to His being the Dispenser of Bliss. It means the messenger of glad tidings of forgiveness and chastiser of those who preach against the dictates of faith (religion) giving new rules and exciter of fear in them who adopt a wrong course. He reprimands and praises by God's decree and does not do so on his own initiative. God says, "Let people believe in Me," It means that they know the speaker of truth as the true one, and respect him whom I have given honour. You should also respect him by your deeds and service and praise him by words. Again God says, "Those who believe (in Me) holding thy hand believe holding My hand. It means that in thee a thing is held in trust and man must consider that he should seek that real thing, which is "the hand of God" and which is ever on their hands. It means when he accepts us as followers and we accept his as the teacher, in fact we accept the Lord and He bestows His gifts on us. Others say that many of the followers draw their strength from God and are subordinate to Him and if He does not take any work from them, they become useless. All the strength in man is from God. Independent of Him, man possesses no strength.

God says, "Had there been no believers..." Suhel says that the true believer is he who is not ignorant of his (carnal) self and his heart and who ever sits as a sentinel watching all acts performed by him at all times. If he sees some error, he at once begins to cry and seeks pardon as when the sun and the moon go in eclipse earthquakes come, rain falls in torrents, darkness prevails and insects destroy crops. Then, the dwellers in the world know that it is the consequence of their sins and this has come on them as punishment and then, they begin to raise cries of lament, so also does the believer when the light of faith diminishes in him, the tears begin to dry and heart sickens and much of his time is wasted, he begins to weep. Although the above mentioned troubles and catastrophes that come on the world are not the signs of separation of God, yet the troubles that come on the heart are the signs of separation of God. So the faithful one should see in his worldly loss, his spiritual gain and in his worldly gain, see his spiritual loss, just as the worldly people conversely fear loss of worldly goods. The faithful one should fear in excess of worldly goods, that disbelief in worship may never come in his heart even for a moment and he may never think the worship as useless for, even such unworthy thoughts will destroy worship of a long period.

God says, "When the heretics showed favouritism...," It means that the heretics obeyed their carnal self, troubled the faithful ones and in this they saw their good and made the life of the faithful ones unpleasant. They themselves enjoyed and asked the faithful ones to fear the end (Day of Judgment). The faithful ones must know that the heretics do not make their life unpleasant but want that by joining their life with the life of the faithful ones, they may make their life eternal for an example, a man snatches away wheat forcibly from another person who is ignorant and illiterate and sows it for him in his field that he may have plenty of grains to serve him as food but the fool from whom the wheat is snatched is crying that great tyranny is being practised on him.

A seal of iron that was engraved with the name of the king began to boast before an unengraved ring of gold that the latter had not such engraving as it had. The gold ring confessed that it had no such engraving. The iron ring said, 'Then I am much superior to thee.' The gold ring called it by its name. It said 'But you are iron ring' Then, the iron ring remarked that engraving on it had divested it of the name of iron. The gold ring said that it was not so. The gold ring further said, "Then, have I, for not keeping engraving on me, been deprived of my name—gold?" The iron seal said, that it was not so. The gold seal said, "Go and ponder who is the gainer?" God alone knows the real thing. "We have to return to Him."

**This is also from the sayings of the Maulānā:**

> I make this testament, "Fear God both externally and internally." I further advise you, "Sleep less, converse less, avoid sins and evil conversation and ever be renouncing your desires and continue to endure troubles offered to you by others. Always keep fasts, and worship night long and seek the company of the good and respectable people and avoid association with the mean and ignorant people. O my brethern! remember this will of mine and never aspire for name, fame and wealth but remain constantly praying so that God may open your hearts."